## DATE DUE

| | | | |
|---|---|---|---|
| | | | |
| | | | |
| | | | |
| | | | |
| | | | |
| | | | |
| | | | |
| | | | |
| | | | |
| | | | |
| | | | |
| | | | |
| | | | |
| | | | |
| | | | |
| | | | |
| | | | |
| | | | |

GAYLORD                    PRINTED IN U.S.A.

Creative Financing for Energy Conservation
and Cogeneration ————————————————

# Creative Financing for Energy Conservation and Cogeneration

by *F. William Payne*

THE FAIRMONT PRESS, INC. • P.O. Box 14227 • Atlanta, Georgia 30324

Printed in the United States of America

Library of Congress Catalog Card No. 83-80094
Library of Congress Cataloging in Publication Data
Payne, F. William, 1924–
    Creative financing for energy conservation and cogeneration.
    Includes index.
    1. Electric power-plants—Energy conservation—Economic aspects—United States. 2. Public utilities—Energy conservation—Economic aspects—United States. 3. Buildings—Energy conservation—Economic aspects—United States. 4. Energy conservation—United States—Equipment and supplies—Finance. 5. Cogeneration of electric power and heat—United States—Equipment and supplies—Finance. 6. Industrial development bonds—United States.
    I. Title.

HD9685.U5P39   1984              338.4'362119              83-80094
ISBN 0--915586-69-X

Distributed in Europe, Japan, India, Middle East, Southeast Asia, West Indies and Africa by E & F. N. Spon, 11 New Fetter Lane, London EC4P4EE.

# Preface ─────────────────────────────

The chapters in this volume review a comparatively new phenomenon: the development of innovative financing mechanisms that can put energy systems in place which otherwise might not go beyond the planning state (no matter how practical the process nor urgent the need).

Technological capability is not a key factor, as engineers and even major consulting firms have learned. Their abilities to assess, plan, develop and monitor systems for energy conservation or cogeneration are taken for granted.

Engineers in the early days of the "energy crisis" tended to be exuberant: they understood the problem, had (or could develop) the answers, and stepped forward with proposals that could not only relieve the threat, but save money in the process.

They thought—and it seems logical—that in a technological society, their plans would be accepted enthusiastically and implemented promptly. But only the industrial sector, with its basically technological orientation, responded in this way.

Several countries pride themselves on being "high tech" societies. This is a misnomer. Technology is one of many societal components. Engineers must understand, and work with, other forces which are increasingly influential.

One of these forces is finance, accompanied by legal and accounting services. Today, it is innovative financing which propels the development of advanced energy systems.

The process can be complex. Often, it must synthesize contradictory needs of system owners and financing agencies, and resolve federal and state regulatory and tax questions. In the case of major financing projects, a tremendous volume of innovative supporting documentation is needed. It took two years to arrange the financing package for a major new $35.2 million cogeneration facility for Trenton, New Jersey; almost 4,000 pages of documents were prepared, nearly all of them drafted from scratch.

Fortunately, most of the financing structures required to set up energy-conserving systems are nowhere near this intricate. Several of the chapters in this reference describe simpler financing methods to meet the needs of small to medium-sized firms and institutions.

Shared-savings techniques are explored in considerable detail as well as financing for cogeneration projects.

Every contributor of this book is actively engaged in the creation or implementation of financing arrangements. Appreciation is given to each author for making their experiences available. Special appreciation is given to John Yewell, Energy Coordinator for the Maryland State Department of Education, for his enthusiastic support and advice.

F. William Payne
*Editor*

# Acknowledgment ────────

A wide variety of authorities in their field have contributed material to this reference. Special appreciation is given to the following individuals and their companies.

James W. Benefiel
Peat, Marwick, Mitchell & Co.

Sandra K. Brown, *Vice President/ Communications,*
Time Energy Systems, Inc.

Jack W. Caloz, *Vice President— Project Development*
Flack & Kurtz Energy Management Corp.

Anthony M. Carey, P.A.,
*Attorney at Law*

Robert N. Danziger, Esq., *President*
Roger R. DeVito, Esq., *Vice President*
Sunlaw Energy Corporation

Robert T. DePree, *President*
Lease Management Corporation

Robert G. C. Dunn, *General Manager*
Steuart/STM Associates

Richard M. Esteves, *Manager of Conservation Communications*
General Public Utilities Corporation

George M. Greider, *Vice President*
Hospital Efficiency Corporation

Alan Hills, *Vice President, Municipal Finance,* Prudential-Bache Securities, Inc.

Philip M. Huyck, *Vice President*
The First Boston Corporation

Martin Klepper
Joseph Sherman
Megan Carroll
Lane and Edson, P.C.

John C. MacLean, *Financing Consultant,* Higher Education Energy Task Force

David Seader, AICP, *Vice President*
Parsons Brinckerhoff Development Group, Inc.

Barry Sedlik, *Director, Industrial Energy Planning,* Dames & Moore

Project Finance Group
Dean Witter Reynolds, Inc.

# Contents ————————————

# Chapter 1

# The "Chauffagiste" Energy System Concept: Energy Efficiency with Guaranteed Savings

Robert G. C. Dunn

One of the unexpected effects of the oil crisis of 1973 is the success of energy efficiency around the world, especially in the United States, which—being the world's most wasteful energy consumer—certainly had the longest way to go. Today energy efficiency is having a substantial effect, reducing demand for energy below what was anticipated even three or four years ago. With today's changing fuel supply and pricing situation a question needs to be raised. Can energy efficiency habits and attitudes be kept up during a period of complacency engendered by the so-called oil "glut"?

The answer is yes—provided that energy efficiency measures can be developed that affect the consumer's bottom line in the shortest period of time. Human nature is such that large expenditures for energy efficiency are difficult to make when the immediate shortage has subsided. But energy efficiency measures that can bring about substantial savings without large capital outlays will be attractive, no matter what the energy supply situation may be.

*1*

In the best of all possible worlds the consumer is looking for a system of energy management that will immediately improve his bottom line with no cash outlay on his part.

Too good to be true? Quite the contrary. Various concepts to achieve this are presently in operation in the U.S. One unique system—quite different from the "shared savings" approach—applies principles developed by energy-conscious firms overseas.

## Chauffagiste—A System with European Origins

This system was imported from Europe about five years ago. The term "chauffagiste" is derived from the French word for heat, *chauffage*. The concept is one of several thermal management systems that have been prevalent in Europe for many years. In France, alone, 140 "chauffagiste" companies serve over three million apartments. Europeans originally devised the chauffagiste approach because Europe has long felt the pinch of high energy prices.

Among the most prominent companies in thermal management in Europe are members of the Royal Dutch/Shell Group of Companies. So it was only natural, when energy efficiency became as important in the U.S. as it had long been in Europe, that a member of the Royal Dutch/Shell Group of Companies would be the company to introduce the concept in this country.

Through a subsidiary, Scallop Corporation, a company called Scallop Thermal Management (STM) was set up to pioneer the selling of energy services in the U.S. Established initially in the New York area, the company quickly expanded to the Washington/Baltimore area by forming a partnership with Steuart Petroleum Company, one of the leading independent petroleum marketers in the Mid-Atlantic states. The resulting entity was called Steuart/STM Associates.

## The Concept

What was this new "chauffagiste" energy services concept and what made it unique?

The idea—like most good ideas—couldn't be simpler. Technical expertise, combined with financing, evolves to something called "complete energy services contracting."

On the technical side this means that the contracting company provides the customer with the delivery and maintenance of heating/cooling comfort and electrical needs on a contract basis. The package includes taking over payment of energy bills, upgrading the existing heating, cooling and electrical systems and training personnel to operate the systems at peak efficiency.

On the financing side the contract price is set at a figure below the current cost of lighting, heating and cooling the building. The price includes payment by Steuart/STM of capital improvements and central plant maintenance costs. The price quoted is adjusted to give building owners the benefits of less severe winters and cooler summers. Adjustments for changes in the cost of energy are made according to a mutually-agreed-upon index.

What this arrangement really means is that the energy services company only makes money if it can exceed the agreed-upon savings, which—and this is all important—are *guaranteed*. In other words, all the risk is with the contracting company. The customer receives the guaranteed savings whether or not the contractor achieves the contractual target figures. Steuart/STM's profit comes out of the savings which can be achieved over and above the target. However, those savings are increasingly shared with the customer as they rise above the guaranteed amount.

What is really happening here is that building owners and managers of large institutions are, for the first time, buying what they really want—comfort. In effect what is being sold is not fuel, kilowatts or Btu's, but degrees of warmth in winter, a comfortable temperature in summer and a well-lighted work place.

Nobody wants oil, or gas, or coal as such. These fuels have absolutely zero value to the consumer. The consumer is buying 72 degrees, or 68 degrees, or whatever temperature provides the desired comfort level for the occupants of his building. The less fuel burned to achieve that level the better he likes it. The chauffagiste technique is the first one to be aligned with the consumer's attitudes.

This approach to energy consumption represents the only really effective way to use energy efficiently—i.e. efficiency based on an economic incentive. It is a far cry from the "sacrifice" approach contained in former President Carter's MEOW (moral equivalent of war) speech of unlamented memory.

This concept of selling thermal comfort, rather than fuel, is central to the chauffagiste approach. It is thoroughly grounded in energy theory and follows principles long advocated by leading energy economists. An aging Thomas Edison, for one, was appalled when he found that the utilities had translated his electric light into current— i.e. kilowatts. Edison insisted that people don't buy kilowatts. They buy light and should be billed for light. The old man, unfortunately, was overruled.

Edison's lament in 1898 was prophetic: "The reason I did not want to sell current was that from my experiments, I knew that the incandescent lamp was only the beginning and that there were great possibilities of enormously increasing its economy . . . But for some reason the selling of current was introduced, thus destroying all chances of the company's gaining any benefits from lamp improvements. In fact, such improvements were a disadvantage; which in my mind is a poor business policy for the company and for the public."

Steuart/STM has taken Edison's words as its credo. Where once the cost of fuel units was so small that no one cared about the terms in which they were sold, today the rising costs of fuel requires that energy companies recognize and respond to the public's demand to understand—and get—exactly what it is paying for.

This fundamental principle is underlined by Roger Sant, one of today's foremost energy economists and a former federal energy official. In a significant article for the *Harvard Business Review* Sant pointed out that "the opportunity for traditional energy industries to broaden their business is immense. In addition to selling oil, gas or electricity, they could provide customers with the best available competitive products and technologies, thereby assuring customers of energy services at the lowest possible costs." Sant refers to this approach as the "least-cost strategy."

The concept stated by Sant illuminates an important part of the Steuart/STM approach—providing thermal comfort, with wise use of capital expenditures, to improve efficiency.

Carrying this concept one step further, the firm envisions the day when builders of new buildings will not even budget for a heating plant as part of their capital investment. Instead the entire system will be owned and operated by an energy services company, leaving the building owner to concentrate on and worry about those things that are more compatible with his experience and expertise. This is the same principle under which many companies today lease their truck delivery fleet or farm out other functions which would otherwise consume valuable management time and effort.

## The Concept Applied to Hospitals

The energy services contracting concept as practiced by STM and Steuart/STM is not equally applicable to all situations. It is most effective in large buildings and building complexes (over 500,000 square feet) and in buildings that are five years old or older.

This latter criterion is an extraordinarily broad-based one in this country where the average heating plant is 22 years old. This means that almost all plants are inefficient by definition. Steuart/STM's engineers seldom encounter a situation where they fail to discover ways to save 10% to 20%.

Since the potential market for this particular kind of energy services contracting is so large—estimates are that it could reach $5 billion to $7 billion in billings by the end of the decade—Steuart/STM has decided to concentrate initially on large institutional situations, especially hospitals.

Hospitals are prime candidates from two points of view. First, since hospitals, like educational and nonprofit institutions in general, are always strapped for capital, they find that one of the few ways they can upgrade their HVAC plants is by taking advantage of the financial aspects of the Steuart/STM package.

Secondly, hospitals are, in the words of the Institute for Health Planning, "the most energy intensive commercial buildings in the United States." They consume approximately two-thirds more energy per unit of floor area than the average of all buildings in the commercial sector.

The reasons for this intensity of energy use are readily apparent: Hospitals are continually occupied; their heating systems must maintain varying levels of temperature and humidity; they have high ventilation and air treatment requirements; and they typically contain an extensive and complex array of facilities to provide auxiliary medical and support services. The rapidly increasing use of energy-consuming biomedical equipment continues to add to this consumption level.

Nationwide estimates for the United States suggest that in 1980, hospitals and other health care facilities accounted for approximately 12 percent of primary energy usage in the commercial sector. Table 1-1 illustrates the distribution of energy usage in a typical hospital.

Table 1-1.  Components of End-Use Energy in Hospitals

| General Category | Function | % of Total End-Use Energy | Typical Fuels |
|---|---|---|---|
| 1. Climate Control | | 40–65 | |
| | Space Heating | | Nat. gas, oil, elec., coal, LPG |
| | Space Cooling | | Elec., nat. gas |
| | Ventilation & Purification | | Electricity |
| 2. Lighting | Illumination | 10–20 | Electricity |
| 3. Water Heating | | 8–15 | Nat. gas, oil, elec., coal, LPG |
| | General Water Usage Laundry | | |
| 4. Food Service & Cooking | | 5–10 | Nat. gas, elec., LPG |
| 5. Medical Equipment | | 3–5 | Electricity |
| 6. Sterilization & Incineration | | 2 | Nat. gas, oil, elec., LPG |

Figure 1-1 illustrates one of the major problems faced by every hospital administrator today: Energy costs constitute one of the fastest growing components of hospital expenditures. Nationwide, they are now on the order of 2 percent of total hospital costs.

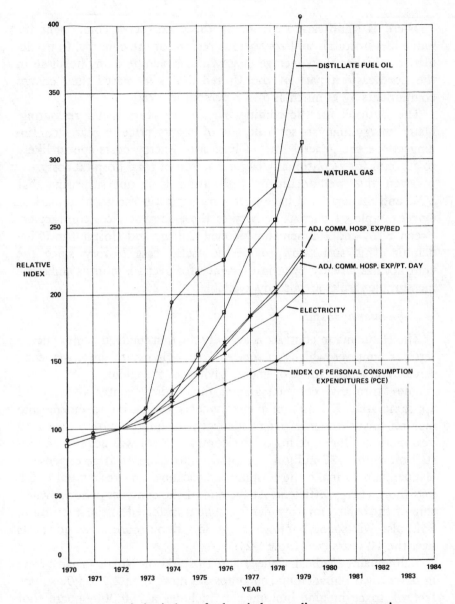

Figure 1-1.  Relative indexes for hospital expenditures, energy prices,
and personal consumption expenditures (1972 = 100)

Source: *American Hospital Association Guide,* Table 1: *Wisconsin energy statistics,* p. 67;
and *State BTU unit price data base,* Table 3.

There is significant variation in the energy cost component for individual hospitals and for various regions of the country. In particular, the higher than average energy prices paid by many hospitals in the northeastern part of the United States increased their energy components by as much as 5 to 8 percent in 1980.

The outlook for the coming five to ten years is not reassuring. Many energy analysts see a decade of energy price increases continuing above the general rate of inflation. Energy costs appear likely to account for a continually larger fraction of total hospital costs.

Given this well-documented situation it is not surprising that STM and Steuart/STM have been very active in the hospital market. One example of current activity is the energy services contract between STM and Hahnemann Medical College and Hospital in Philadelphia. This situation provides a useful case history since the contract has already been in existence for over six months and some measurable results are already available.

### Hahnemann Hospital

The Hahnemann contract is actually the first medical center energy services contract which *"guarantees"* specific capital improvements, service and a percentage of energy savings to the client.

The "turnkey" contract assures the medical center a savings of approximately $13 million in energy costs, capital improvements and maintenance through efficient management and operation over a 10 year period. Under terms of the contract, STM will acquire and install more than $2 million in capital improvements at no expense to Hahnemann to make the hospital, educational and residential buildings more energy efficient. At the end of the contract period, ownership of the capital improvements can be transferred to the institution. STM also will spend approximately $2 million more in service costs over the 10 years (see Table 1-2).

Hahnemann Medical College and Hospital on North Broad Street in downtown Philadelphia, encompasses more than 2,200,000 square feet of space in nine buildings. It includes a 700,000 square foot university center with medical college and graduate school of health science; a 700,000 square foot teaching hospital with 600 patient beds, and 800,000 square feet of residence halls.

**Table 1-2. Energy Budget and Savings Over the Contract Period**

| Year | Total Energy Budget (electrical-steam-oil) | Contract Energy Savings $ | Contract Energy Savings % | Capital & Service Cost Saved |
|---|---|---|---|---|
| 1981/82 | $ 5,516,672 | $ 165,500 | 3 | $2,272,696 |
| 1982/83 | 6,176,734 | 247,069 | 4 | 183,856 |
| 1983/84 | 6,915,848 | 345,792 | 5 | 219,480 |
| 1984/85 | 7,743,490 | 464,609 | 6 | 152,945 |
| 1985/86 | 8,670,266 | 616,918 | 7 | 168,239 |
| 1986/87 | 9,708,062 | 873,725 | 9 | 185,005 |
| 1987/88 | 10,870,180 | 1,141,369 | 10.5 | 203,620 |
| 1988/89 | 12,171,526 | 1,338,868 | 11 | 224,075 |
| 1989/90 | 13,628,787 | 1,635,454 | 12 | 246,367 |
| 1990/91 | 15,260,655 | 1,983,885 | 13 | 270,958 |
| | $96,662,220 | $8,813,189 | 9.1% | $4,137,241 |

*NOTE:* These figures are based upon a 12 percent a year energy unit cost escalation, in dollars of the day. Additional price adjustments will be made to give the institution the benefits of less severe winters and summers.

At the time the contract was signed, Dr. William Likoff, president and chief executive officer of Hahnemann Medical College and Hospital, pointed out that a major goal in the plan for renewing and revitalizing the medical college and hospitals is "to reduce costs to a realistic minimum without eroding Hahnemann's primary institutional purpose, as well as to rehabilitate the older campus facilities and replace aging equipment."

Energy changes to the Hahnemann complex under the project are as dramatic as use of a helicopter to transport a large chiller unit to one of the Hahnemann buildings—and as unobtrusive as changing a light bulb.

Keystone of the capital improvements will be the installation of the latest load sequenced control automation system for adjusting temperatures in buildings throughout the medical center campus. The computer system will monitor temperatures through 200 electronic and 350 pneumatic temperature sensing locations to provide a distributed control system for building-by-building and zone-by-zone feedback of room temperatures. The information simultaneously will be fed into the local controls and the central console, which together will automatically fine tune the heating, ventilation and air conditioning to maintain desired temperatures while cutting down on wasted energy.

This will reduce equipment replacement costs and lost productivity created by uncomfortable space temperatures.

The computer system spots potential efficiency improvement opportunities, as well as any improper operations, much sooner than even the most competent building engineering staff. The operations and maintenance staff of the hospital and college will be more productive, there will be far less need to visually check so many locations. The computer system also will give an early warning of potential equipment failures and the need for control adjustments.

The building automation system also will program schedules for preventive maintenance and replacements, set energy delivery rates and track other service requirements. It will maintain energy consumption records and retrieve information for periodic checks and summaries of performance levels, so that areas of wasted energy may be identified and desired temperature controls maintained.

Other steps in the STM program for greater energy efficiency include improved use of outside air for the heating and cooling systems, testing and repairing of all main heating and cooling systems and more than 1800 reheat coil controls, upgrading of all lighting systems and installation of a more efficient electrical drive refrigerator machine in a residence building.

The contract calls for STM to provide preventive maintenance, repairs and replacement to the main control systems, providing an additional saving to the institution, which previously had to call in outside suppliers.

As part of the arrangement, STM will undertake a training program for the operating staff in the utilization of the new computer control systems. There will be ongoing reviews and improvements of preventive maintenance programs in all the buildings throughout the life of the contract.

The contract not only contains a binding commitment to save a percentage of Hahnemann's heating, cooling, hot water and electrical costs, but includes handling all sources of energy supply, supervision of plant operations, reliable service, and implementation of preventive maintenance programs to reduce repairs and prolong equipment life.

Most importantly, the medical college and hospital is assured a greater saving in energy costs than they could possibly achieve by themselves. This frees $2 million of capital expenses they would have had to invest themselves and another $200,000 per year in operating expenses. (See Figures 1-2 and 1-3.)

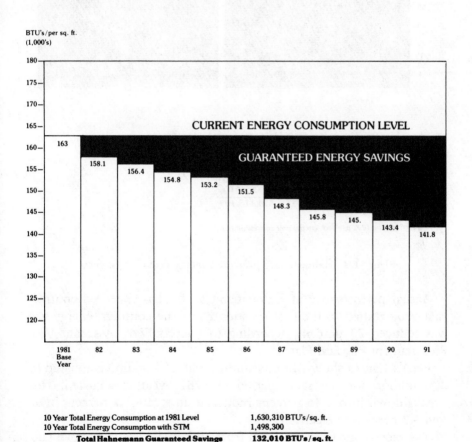

| 10 Year Total Energy Consumption at 1981 Level | 1,630,310 BTU's/sq. ft. |
| 10 Year Total Energy Consumption with STM | 1,498,300 |
| **Total Hahnemann Guaranteed Savings** | **132,010 BTU's/sq. ft.** |

Figure 1-2. Hahnemann's guaranteed energy savings over 10 year period

(millions)

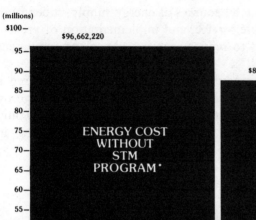
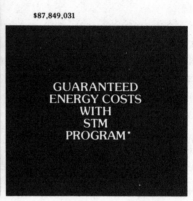

Contract Savings:

| | |
|---|---|
| Energy Costs over 10 Years | $ 8,813,189 |
| Service Costs over 10 Years | 2,000,000 |
| Capital Improvements, First Year | 2,300,000 |
| **Total Savings** | **$13,113,189** |

*Based upon a 12% per year energy unit cost escalation*

Figure 1-3. Hahnemann's projected energy costs for 10 years

Actual performance at Hahnemann so far has exceeded contractual projections. In the first six months of the contract, energy use
was reduced 23 percent, according to Everett Ferri, Assistant Vice
President for Physical Plant.

Ferri's figures show Btu consumption at 154 million compared to
200 million for the same period in 1981, weather adjusted. This
breaks down into a 36 percent reduction in steam, 18 percent in oil
and 4.3 percent in electricity.

The electricity figure is down from an initial 12 percent saving because the computer controls have not yet been installed on new refrigeration components. By summer 1983 the electrical savings will

return to the 12 to 15 percent range. At the same time steam savings are expected to reach 40 percent.

At this pace STM is well ahead of the first year savings goal of 25 percent, with 23 percent already accounted for. This has all been achieved even though the fine-tuning process has not yet begun.

Savings at Hahnemann are consistent or better than Steuart/STM Associates' historical track record covering a number of years and a multiplicity of customers. Performance has regularly exceeded targets. (See Table 1-3.)

## Implications for Government

So far, entry into the biggest institutional market of all—local, state and federal governments—has been an elusive will-o'-the-wisp as far as energy services are concerned. The need is certainly there and it is unquestioned. The GAO recently published a report entitled "Millions Can be Saved through Better Energy Management in Federal Hospitals" (GAO/HRD–82–77, Sept. 1, 1982). The report, which only surveyed a few Navy, Veterans Administration and Indian Health Service hospitals estimated that these agencies alone could "save between $16 million and $55 million each year if additional energy-saving measures were adopted."

The government has frequently been criticized by Congress and others for its lackadaisical efforts to save energy in its own buildings. At a 1981 Oversight Committee hearing Congressman Dingell (D. Mich.) asserted that "unless progress is achieved in reducing energy consumption, the government's energy bill is projected to escalate from $8.9 billion in fiscal 1980 to $20.3 billion in fiscal 1985." As it is energy costs represent 1.7 percent of the federal budget.

Yet in spite of these and other equally dramatic findings, because of antiquated procurement policies the government is unable to take advantage of such programs as those offered by Steuart/STM. Primarily the problem is two-fold: (1) The inability of the government to enter into multi-year energy services contracts, and (2) the difficulties perceived to be associated with the fact that during the life of the contract title to capital improvements located on government premises would reside in the energy services company.

Table 1-3.  Percentage Savings Record/Customer (as at 12/81)

| Year Signed | Sq Ft in Thousands | HVAC* Plants | $ Historical | Target Savings % | Actual Savings % |
|---|---|---|---|---|---|
| 1978 | 521 | 1 | $ 410,000 | 9.0 | 17.4 |
| | 752 | 4 | 435,000 | 7.9 | 11.2 |
| | 60 | 1 | 70,000 | 27.0 | 38.4 |
| 1979 | 327 | 1 | 466,000 | 11.0 | 12.0 |
| | 381 | 1 | 565,000 | 11.0 | 14.0 |
| | 138 | 1 | 155,000 | 14.0 | 17.0 |
| | 369 | 1 | 178,000 | 11.0 | 12.0 |
| 1980 | 82 | 1 | 50,000 | 21.0 | 35.0 |
| | 122 | 1 | 87,000 | 25.0 | 31.0 |
| | 46 | 1 | 65,000 | 18.0 | 21.0 |
| | 997 | 20 | 973,200 | 15.0 | 32.0 |
| | 556 | 1 | 184,000 | 10.0 | 11.0 |
| | 322 | 2 | 185,900 | 12.4 | 16.0 |
| | 800 | 1 | 363,130 | 8.0 | 11.0 |
| | 632 | 5 | 511,750 | 8.4 | 12.0 |
| | 112 | 1 | 134,033 | 10.0 | 17.0 |
| | 240 | 1 | 166,021 | 10.0 | 10.0 |
| | 916 | 4 | 792,816 | 9.5 | 10.0 |
| | 310 | 1 | 117,179 | 10.0 | 12.0 |
| | 242 | 1 | 117,042 | 8.0 | 17.0 |
| | 540 | 3 | 340,000 | 10.0 | 20.7 |
| | 425 | 1 | 238,396 | 10.0 | 18.0 |
| 1981 | 300 | 1 | 290,000 | 22.0 | 29.0 |
| | 3,000 | 10 | 3,000,000 | 15.0 | – |
| | 2,200 | | 6,500,000 | 25.0 | – |
| Totals | 14,390 | 65 | $16,394,467 | | |

*HVAC = Heating, Ventilation and Air Conditioning

We have had many conversations and meetings with government officials at all levels and have found that officials almost without exception can clearly see the advantage of a long-term energy savings contract, but are universally stymied by the inertia represented by monolithic and immovable contracting procedures. Oftentimes we have been told that it would take legislative action to change these procedures. There is no need to dwell on the difficulties, pitfalls and man-hours involved in going down that road.

Nevertheless, we remain optimistic over the long run and are continually probing for a precedent-setting breakthrough that could help put the government on a truly innovative energy savings track. All taxpayers would benefit thereby.

## Summary

Overall there is certainly a very bright future for energy services programs which combine service and capital investment with a guaranteed saving. As such programs become recognized as something very different from the conventional "shared savings" proposal, they will become increasingly in demand.

Little by little consumers will believe that "guaranteed savings with no money up front" is *not* too good to be true.

# Chapter 2 —————————————————

# Energy Services Companies: The Value for Public and Non-Profit Energy Users

George M. Greider

## Energy Services Companies

One of the ways in which European businesses adapted to expensive energy was by contracting for comprehensive energy management services. In France, nearly 140 such companies are currently in business; approximately 70% of the buildings in France are managed by a "chauffagiste" or heat manager.

In the last several years, this concept has been introduced to the United States by a variety of existing, new and immigrating companies.

An energy services company (ESC) will design and install new equipment; repair or replace existing systems; and assist the operation and maintenance of the facilities. They may do this for an annual or monthly fee, guaranteed to be less than savings. The company may ask that the client split the savings with them on some percentage basis. Or, the ESC may purchase all fuel and utilities for the building and then bill the client an amount guaranteed to be less than the costs would have been without their services and improvements. The essential appeal of these organizations is that they offer to stabilize or reduce energy use costs; make capital improvements in the facilities; and maintain and assist the operation of the plant—at a cost less than current energy bills.

The appeal is obvious:

    a. capital improvements;
    b. no capital investment; and
    c. guaranteed cost savings.

For organizations with limited capital, limited access to capital, or a reluctance to borrow at today's lending rates, an ESC may be the only available method of conserving energy. With oil and electricity prices up and tax revenues and business receipts down, the United States (especially the Northeast) is a particularly active market for energy services companies.

According to research done by *Energy User News* (EUN) in 1981, there were approximately 20 energy services companies or energy conservation companies in the U.S. *EUN* did not attempt to list only those companies that were functioning along the lines of the European heat managers. The list contains companies which provide several distinctly different types of energy services, as well as one (EBASCO Services Incorporated) which is no longer in business.

In general the types of services available are some combination of:

    a. engineering;
    b. financing; and
    c. building or system management.

To be effective, an energy services company (ESC) should provide all three.

    a. *The company must have skilled building and energy use systems expertise—mechanicals, light, envelope, etc.—virtually everything associated with a building affects its energy use.* Many of the companies are outgrowths of established engineering firms. Some are totally new ventures. Energy services units are currently being developed by a Fortune 100 company and by an interstate utility. The heritage or affiliation of an energy services company will greatly affect the type and quality of services available. For example, a ten year guarantee or contract offered by a totally new venture is much less bankable than one backed by United Technology Corporation or Royal Dutch/Shell.

There are companies which provide financing assistance for the installation of only one type of product—i.e., the one they manufacture. Installation of this single product may result in energy and cost savings, but it will ignore a large number of other improvements that could also be made and perhaps should be made first. In order for an energy user—especially a large energy user with multiple or complex systems—to maximize energy conservation and cost savings, a comprehensive program of retrofits and operating and maintenance procedures is necessary. The effective ESC cannot be tied to one product line or technique or only have experience with a single type of building or system.

b. *The company is responsible for the financing of the necessary improvements.* Without financing, most clients cannot do the project; indeed, it is the pairing of project financing with engineering services that make ESC's a unique new market entry in the U.S. Individual ESC's may differ significantly on the financial structure they provide. As stated before, some ESC's will offer to split the savings on some percentage basis—usually 50/50.

This means that the client writes the ESC a check for 50% of the client's savings. Others will merely specify engineered improvements to energy use systems with specified paybacks bonded by the company; thus guaranteeing that the ESC will make up the money difference between predicted and actual performance.

In other words, if the improvements are guaranteed to save 1000 gallons of oil a month but only save 950, the client gets a check from the ESC for 50 gallons times the current price per gallon. This guarantee is bankable to the extent that the ESC has adequate assets and cash flow. However, the ultimate source of security for the financing will be the client company which will have to persuade a lender of its ability to repay the loan based on future cost avoidance.

The simplest arrangements have the Energy Service Company arrange for financing from whatever sources it chooses and charge the client a fixed rate.

c. *The company must assist the operation and maintenance (O/M) of the building and systems.* Some will take over total building management; others act as advisers or consultants to existing staff. Again, the companies will differ on what they provide.

This last component is critical but too frequently overlooked. The most sophisticated energy controls can be thwarted by poor upkeep; the most efficient burners and boilers can turn into guzzlers and the tightest distribution system into a sieve if not properly maintained. Client building personnel must be taught how to operate and maintain new equipment. The cheapest sources of energy savings and cost avoidance are the "brains and screwdrivers" work which if ignored can undercut any savings program. The effective energy services company must be able to identify and install new equipment *and* tuneup existing equipment *and* be able to operate and maintain the whole building's energy use system or help the client do so effectively.

An energy services company makes money by doing a better job of improving and managing a client's building than the client can do alone. The money comes from the client who is guaranteed to be paying less in this arrangement than otherwise. However, unless inflation is zero and energy prices don't rise, the payment for energy services and energy will tend to increase. In other words, it is important to keep in mind that these avoided costs may not offset price rises. An ESC does not guarantee that a client's costs will go down, only that they won't go up as much or as fast.

### ESC's and Public/Non-Profit Clients

State, county and municipal governments; schools, churches, public housing projects; and other non-profit institutional energy users are well-suited to take advantage of an energy services company.

They tend to be large energy users; their access to capital is limited; and they are not typically organized to manage energy conservation. The last point may not be obvious, and should not be taken as an indictment of management quality outside the private sector. Rather, what is at issue is the difficulty of developing new operating and maintenance techniques; of justifying the repair or purchase of equipment; and of altering employee and client behavior.

Private businesses, being profit motivated, are organized to respond to changing economic conditions. Their employees are incentivized to make these changes rapidly and efficiently. Typically, the ultimate concern of business is profitability and the business organization will make whatever changes are necessary to ensure profits; employees will advance or not on the basis of their contributions.

Government and other non-profit organizations have a great many other concerns besides their cost of operation. Many, such as quality of service provided, are not quantifiable; and some, such as employee job security, may impede rapid changes. Because their revenues are from outside sources—donations, third-party payments or taxes—which they do not directly control, their fiscal management interests are different. It is typically easier to pay steadily increasing bills than to get money for capital improvements.

Public and non-profit institutions are, finally, not well suited to undertake risky or apparently risky projects. A technical risk that a business could justify as promising increased profitability, would tend to be viewed as an unacceptable political risk by a public administrator. In the language of investments, the business manager works to maximize "upside" rewards; the administrator, to minimize "downside" consequences and costs.

*Example*

The following figures are based on a proposal developed by an energy services company for a multifamily residential complex. The company's technical proposal specified the installation of new boilers, burners, and control systems and the upgrading and repair of the distribution (pipe and duct) network.

Table 2-1 presents annualized figures for the ten year contract period. In the base year (1982–1983) the client's energy costs are $1,190,000. In addition, subcontractors would normally be paid $10,000 for maintenance and small repairs. Thus, the client's base year energy and service budget is $1,200,000. This figure was escalated at 10% per annum to generate Column 1: "Energy & Service Budget." This column represents the basis upon which avoided costs or savings will be computed. For any given contract, the escalation assumption would change based upon best current estimates of energy price and supply futures and the prevailing rate of inflation.

The second column stipulates the savings that the ESC guarantees to the customer. The company actually expects to save more than

Table 2-1.  Ten Year ESC Contract Analysis

| Year | 1<br><br>Energy &<br>Service<br>Budget* | 2<br>Guaranteed<br>Customer<br>Energy<br>Savings % | 3<br><br>ESC<br>Contract<br>Amount | 4<br><br>Energy<br>Dollars<br>Saved |
|---|---|---|---|---|
| 1982/83 | $ 1,200,000 | 3 | $ 1,164,000 | $  36,000 |
| 1983/84 | 1,320,000 | 4 | 1,267,200 | 52,800 |
| 1984/85 | 1,452,000 | 6 | 1,364,880 | 87,120 |
| 1985/86 | 1,597,200 | 8 | 1,469,424 | 127,776 |
| 1986/87 | 1,756,920 | 10 | 1,581,228 | 175,692 |
| 1987/88 | 1,932,612 | 15 | 1,642,720 | 289,892 |
| 1988/89 | 2,125,873 | 18 | 1,743,216 | 382,657 |
| 1989/90 | 2,338,460 | 18 | 1,917,537 | 420,923 |
| 1990/91 | 2,572,306 | 20 | 2,057,849 | 514,461 |
| 1991/92 | 2,829,537 | 20 | 2,263,630 | 565,907 |
|  | $19,124,908 |  | $16,471,680 | $2,653,228 |

Ten Year Forecasted Savings  =  $3,810,228

*Includes $10,000/Year for subcontracted maintenance costs

that guarantee and the rate of the realization of those total savings will not actually follow the course of the savings passed to the customer.

In other words, the ESC anticipates total savings in the 26% range by the second year of the contract while customer savings remain in single figures. In general, an energy services company wants to retain the bulk of the early years' benefits to offset their up-front costs and flow more of the benefits through to the customer in the later years.

The third column is the amount the customer will pay the ESC each year. Comparing Column 3, "Contract Amount," with Column 1, "Energy & Service Budget," produces the data in Column 4: "Energy Dollars Saved." These figures represent the costs avoided under the contract presuming the energy and service costs escalation occurs as projected.

In this case, the client would probably have to spend $19,124,908 for energy and maintenance over this 10 year period. By contracting with the ESC, the expenditures will be limited to $16,471,680. Thus, the client is guaranteed a savings of $2,653,228 in avoided costs.

In addition the client gets the capital improvement, avoids interest charges on the money spent on the improvements, and gets the benefit of improved operations and maintenance service.

Table 2-2 presents a financial summary of the data from Table 2-1. The ESC plans to save a total of 25.5% of the client's energy and service costs. The company will make $520,000 in capital improvements on the premises and will not charge the customer any interest for the use of this capital. The company will provide an additional $637,000 worth of operating and maintenance service. (This figure is calculated on a $40,000 base year figure composed of the $10,000 the client was already spending for equipment maintenance and repair plus $30,000 the ESC will spend on energy program management client personnel training, and operating assistance and advice. The base year figure is escalated at 10% per annum for 10 years for a total of $637,000.)

These two benefits to the customer total $1,157,000 or 6.0%. That figure added to the $2,653,228 in projected energy dollars saved yields the total customer benefits of $3,810,228 or 19.9% of the project energy and service budget. The customer's benefits subtracted from the total projected energy and service cost savings ($4,884,759) equals the energy service company's revenues; in this case $1,074,531 or approximately one fifth of the total savings.

In other arrangements, the energy services company might have stipulated that the client pay all fuel and utility bills and, in addition, pay the ESC a fee equal to one-half of the savings.

At this point it becomes obvious that the energy and service cost projections must be adjusted for real conditions. If the client closes down a building; if the weather is more temperate; or if the cost of fuel stays the same or declines, the projected data would be an unfair index of the ESC performance. The result would be disproportionate windfall profits to the energy services company. Likewise, increased operating demands, temperature extremes and rapid price rises would be a hardship for the ESC. Therefore, contracts should estab-

Table 2-2.  Financial Summary

| | | |
|---|---|---|
| Energy Budget | $19,124,908 | |
| Forecasted Total Energy Saved | 4,884,759 | (25.5%)* |
| Benefits: | | |
| Guaranteed Energy Saved | $ 2,653,228 | (13.9%) |
| Capital Improvement Saved | 520,000 | (2.7%) |
| Maintenance Cost Saved | 637,000 | (3.3%) |
| | $ 3,810,228 | (19.9%) |
| ESC Revenue | $ 1,074,531 | (5.6%) |

*This savings target assumes a savings of 17.5% in year 1 and 26% in all years thereafter. Since these targets are presumed to have a ±15% accuracy, the Energy Service Company will split all savings above 20.125% in year 1 and 29.9% in years thereafter.

lish methods for monitoring facility use, renegotiating terms when use changes, and adjusting by formula for temperature and energy price changes.

## Factors and Issues in Energy Service Contracting

The relationship between energy services companies and their clients are unique for each set of services provided, facilities and systems involved, and institutional hurdles which must be overcome. Any given contract will be unique and will likely take some time to develop. Both parties need to be committed, patient, and flexible. Organizations—whether businesses, non-profit institutions, or government agencies—should consider the following factors about energy services contracting:

1. Technical expertise of the ESC;
2. Corporate stability and security;
3. Type of guarantee;
4. Effect on collective bargaining agreements;
5. Effect on bulk purchase arrangements;
6. Contract term and buyout options;

7. Competitive bidding process;
8. Equipment ownership;
9. Incentive participation; and
10. Lines of authority and management.

1. *Technical expertise.* The first and most important consideration is whether the company has the technical ability to do the whole job and do it well. The company should be skilled in comprehensive energy management and not be simply a marketing device for selling a single system or product. The efficient operation of equipment is as important as the products installed, so a competent ESC must be skilled in operations as well as design engineering. The company must be demonstrably able to accommodate the unique needs of the type of institution or building; whether it be a low income housing project, a multi-purpose community center, a hospital, an incinerator, a skating rink, an airport or whatever.

Units of general purpose government which may be seeking energy services for all of the above must take special care to select a firm with truly catholic energy generalist credentials.

2. *Corporate stability.* Since this is a new market, there are many new organizations emerging. It will be important for potential ESC clients to consider how stable the various companies are and how likely it is that they will remain in business. A guarantee from a defunct organization is obviously valueless. Even worse, is a contract for the installation and maintenance of equipment upon which the installer has defaulted on the loan. The lender would ultimately be able to remove and resell equipment that the hapless ESC client was counting on to keep the building warm.

The type of security offered by an ESC will vary, but the client should be assured that whatever is promised can be and will be delivered by the company *and*, if it is not, that there are some major "deep-pockets" resources behind the company from whom the client can seek damages.

3. *Type of guarantee.* As noted above, there are many different arrangements by which businesses claim to provide energy services. Potential clients of ESC's should evaluate the utility of the various guarantees to their own particular situation. Shared savings arrange-

ments provide more client incentive, less in the way of benefits and less certainty on prices than guaranteed, fixed price contracts. Fixed price contracts typically will have some type of adjustment formula for factors outside either party's control. If not, both parties face uncomfortable risks due to unpredictable fluctuations in weather and fuel prices.

The essential element for a client to consider here is the manner in which the ESC guarantees the level of heat, light, water, cooling, etc. in the building. If there may be changes in the use patterns of the building, there must be a provision for renegotiating the contract.

Related to the question of performance guarantees is the matter of emergency repairs. If an ESC installs a new piece of equipment, how responsive will they be when it breaks down at 2:00 in the morning and nobody on site knows how to fix it?

Whatever form the savings/payment arrangement takes, the client must be certain of an explicit guarantee of system performance in terms of: comfort; useable energy supply; requisite air changes; adequate illumination levels, and so forth.

The guarantee offered by the ESC should also address questions of liability for faulty installation, system performance, and consequential damage. In line with this, the client should be guaranteed that subcontractors employed by the ESC—whether for installation or maintenance—are bonded or insured for their performance for the life of the contract.

4. *Collective bargaining.* If the client organization has an organized work force under contract, a new arrangement with an ESC will likely affect that contract. For that reason, labor should be represented from the beginning in the negotiating process. Two possible issues are: job displacement and position upgrading. Union representatives will be concerned that a contract with an ESC not be used to supplant or replace existing employees or to interpose a new line of authority in existing management/labor relations. Management should consider the impact of an energy service company's training workers to do a better or more efficient job or teaching workers how to operate new and more sophisticated equipment. This may be deemed by labor to be grounds for a raise.

5. *Bulk purchasing.* Most large institutions have standardized methods for obtaining fuel through bulk purchase agreements with suppliers. A true energy services company will typically want to make these purchases itself, perhaps in conjunction with other purchases to be used for other clients. To the extent that a given client's current supplier is the cheapest source, there is no problem. However, there is the likelihood that the ESC will find a cheaper source and disrupt what may have been a long-standing relationship between a client and supplier. This may be a problem for a local government which has a commitment to supporting local businesses.

This question should be addressed in the contract development process. The ESC should be willing to use a designated supplier if the client insists, but the client should be prepared to pay more if the ESC cannot seek the absolute lowest cost supplier.

6. *Contract terms.* The ESC will offer to provide a level of capital improvement and operating assistance for a set period of time at either a set price, an automatically adjusted price, or on the basis of a share of the savings.

The first question a client must address here is whether it is willing or, in some cases, legally able, to enter into such contracts. Some finance officers may be uncomfortable with the shared savings approach. Some government entities may find they are constrained by law from long-term operating or service contracts.

At some point in the contract, there should be an option for the client to buy out the ESC residual interest in the improvements. This buyout figure will represent some significant portion of the ESC's profit for the remaining years. The buyout option should be specified in the original contract document and, like other contract terms, should be prudently negotiated.

In general, the ESC is interested in writing a long-term contract for equipment with relatively shorter term paybacks. The client needs to make an independent analysis of the improvements proposed and the likely paybacks, in order to negotiate the best balance between costs and benefits for both parties.

7. *Competitive bidding.* Public entities are generally required to seek competitive bids and most purchasing officers in businesses

would prefer to have a choice among suppliers. Unfortunately, it may be quite difficult to develop a truly comparable array of competing proposals due to the small number of ESC's currently in existence and the restrictions they operate under. Some will not take on clients with less than $1 million in annual energy bills; others will not contract with government or non-profit agencies. Many have a narrow geographic focus or do not provide the full range of services.

The best course for the manager seeking competitive bids is the development of a draft Request for Proposal (RFP) which is then circulated for review and comment. The draft RFP should be sent to whatever list of *soi-disant* energy services companies is current, with a request that reviewers indicate whether they would be interested in responding to such an RFP, and if not why not. The final RFP should stipulate the issuer's tax status, location of buildings, size and type of building and energy use systems, annual energy bills, services, and guarantees sought, length of contract and type of savings sought, and some specifications of the issuer's preference on the factors and issues discussed in this section.

8. *Equipment ownership.* Some public agencies may find problems in their governing laws or regulations with a private organization owning property installed and used in public facilities. In any case, the question of liability should be considered where one organization (an ESC) is going to own something which is installed on another organization's (the client's) property. Especially difficult is the question of liability for consequential damage in the event of equipment failure.

Some organizations may find limitations in their laws, regulations, charter, articles of incorporation, mortgages, bequests, insurance policies or operating procedures that will preclude or favor certain ownership or lease arrangements. In general, an energy services company as discussed here provides services and installs equipment under an "operating lease." Some government agencies may find that they are limited in lease arrangements to the more common "capital leases." This has not been a widespread general problem, but it can represent a time-consuming hurdle for some institutions.

9. *Incentive participation.* The total amount of energy used in a

building is determined by everyone who works there, and all the systems in use. An energy services company can install more efficient equipment, but the potential savings can be negated by poor maintenance or wasteful operations. It is therefore critical to the success of an energy savings program that everyone from the chief executive to the janitor be committed to the goal.

Simply contracting with an ESC and then ignoring the problem will result in some savings. Indeed, if the energy services company is going to make any money, they will see to it that there are savings. But the greatest savings will be realized by cooperation between the ESC and client personnel. The most effective way to ensure that cooperation is to arrange some way to share the incentives.

At the most basic level, the ESC has the incentive to save energy in order to make money. The effective ESC will have some type of management incentive program for their own personnel on-site. The most effective company will agree to share with the client some of the savings.

The sharing process and its computation will be defined in the contract development process. However, some clients—particularly government agencies—may not be able to participate in these incentive arrangements. There may be no provision under law or an outright prohibition covering payments from a contractor to a public employee.

Yet if an energy savings program is going to work, the people who make it work should be rewarded. If there is going to be more work keeping new equipment running at peak efficiency and making sure that leaks are patched quickly, etc., the people who do this work should get more than they were getting before by doing business as usual.

This may be the most difficult problem for a public agency to solve; it may require new legislation or ordinance. In any case, there should be found some method of rewarding managers for organizational behavior changes without which energy savings would be minimal.

One possible technique would allow the program, facility or building manager to retain, in an account, a share (say 50%) of all savings realized. This money could then be spent at the manager's official discretion for other program services or improvements.

10. *Authority and management.* The effective energy services company must have a continuing relationship with the operating and maintenance staff of the facility. However, as an external contract agency, it cannot actually be integrated into the management structure.

The most appropriate relationship is that of staff adviser to the level of management responsible for operations and maintenance. The ESC's function is to advise the manager. In the ideal situation, this manager stands to profit—either personally or programmatically —for implementing the advice.

In any case, the ESC should be required to see to the operation and maintenance of new equipment; and to train client staff in both the new equipment and improved techniques for operating and maintaining existing equipment and facilities. At the end of the contract, client staff should be able to take over all installed equipment and maintenance should be able to oversee a more efficient operation of the entire facility.

The ESC should also provide on-going consultation on new technical developments or new equipment purchases which become economically attractive as energy prices and other economic factors change.

The client should be assured of access to the ESC books, especially if the ESC is paying all fuel and utility bills. During the contract negotiation process, both client and ESC should satisfy themselves that they have made the best possible deal on a mutual understanding of benefits. That done, there is no reason not to have a completely open book operation.

In the unhappy event that severe problems arise during the contract, there must be agreed upon procedures for the resolution or arbitration of disputes specified in the contract.

These elements and more must be discussed and should be documented in the process of developing a contract. Some present peculiar problems for government bodies and may require changes in regulations, ordinances, or statutes. The process of developing a contract with an energy services company must be intelligently planned and carefully negotiated. It is necessary that both the ESC and the client be committed to working up an agreement. The energy services company will, of course, have a proprietary interest in this work. The client, once an executive decision has been made to work up such a contract, must commit staff time to planning, specifying, and negotiating the final contractual relationship. Clients should review proposed arrangements with their own operations staff, financial or budget officers, legal counsel, insurers, and union representatives.

**Self-Financing Energy Conservation**

Although many municipalities and States do not have the option to finance energy conservation out of public debt or revenues, some do. Most potential clients for energy services are capital starved—locked out of the public bond market by tax or debt limitations, poor market conditions, or other institutional and legal hurdles; or unable to access private capital for an equal number of other reasons.

But the possibility of self-financing energy conservation services is worth considering for the further point it makes about the benefits of an ESC contract.

Consider the same project presented in Tables 2-1 and 2-2 being financed by a municipality for 10 years at 14% with no discount. Table 2-3 presents this project evaluated under three different sets of assumptions:

a.  Assumption A—Table 2-3A—A municipally financed energy conservation project on the same buildings making the same improvements realizing the same level of savings guaranteed by the energy services company;

b.  Assumption B—Table 2-3B—A municipally financed energy conservation project on the same buildings; making the same improvements realizing a greater savings (generally double) of energy dollars than that guaranteed by the ESC, but less than the total savings anticipated by the ESC;

c.  Assumption C—Table 2-3C—A municipally financed energy conservation project on the same buildings; making the same improvements and realizing the total savings anticipated by the ESC.

**Table 2-3A. Municipally Financed Energy Conservation**

| Year | 1<br>Energy &<br>Service<br>Budget | 2<br>Projected<br>Savings | 3<br>Dollars<br>Saved | 4<br>Debt<br>Retirement | 5<br>Mgt &<br>Service<br>Costs | 6<br>Net | 7<br>Cumulative |
|---|---|---|---|---|---|---|---|
| 1982–83 | $ 1,200,000 | 3% | $ 36,000 | $ 99,691 | $ 40,000 | $ (103,691) | $ (103,691) |
| 1983–84 | 1,320,000 | 4% | 52,800 | 99,691 | 44,000 | (90,891) | (194,582) |
| 1984–85 | 1,452,000 | 6% | 87,120 | 99,691 | 48,000 | (60,571) | (255,153) |
| 1985–86 | 1,597,000 | 8% | 127,776 | 99,691 | 53,000 | (24,915) | (280,068) |
| 1986–87 | 1,756,000 | 10% | 175,692 | 99,691 | 59,000 | 17,001 | (263,067) |
| 1987–88 | 1,932,612 | 15% | 289,892 | 99,691 | 64,000 | 126,201 | (136,866) |
| 1988–89 | 2,125,873 | 18% | 382,657 | 99,691 | 71,000 | 211,966 | 75,100 |
| 1989–90 | 2,338,460 | 18% | 420,923 | 99,691 | 78,000 | 243,232 | 318,332 |
| 1990–91 | 2,572,306 | 20% | 514,461 | 99,691 | 86,000 | 328,770 | 647,102 |
| 1991–92 | 2,829,537 | 20% | 565,907 | 99,691 | 94,000 | 372,216 | 1,019,318 |
| | $19,124,908 | | $2,653,228 | $996,910 | $637,000 | $1,019,318 | |

**Table 2-3B. Municipally Financed Energy Conservation**

| Year | 1<br>Energy<br>Service<br>Budget | 2<br>Projected<br>Savings | 3<br>Dollars<br>Saved | 4<br>Debt<br>Retirement | 5<br>Mgt &<br>Service<br>Costs | 6<br>Net | 7<br>Cumulative |
|---|---|---|---|---|---|---|---|
| 1982–83 | $ 1,200,000 | 5% | $ 60,000 | $ 99,691 | $ 40,000 | $ (79,691) | $ (79,691) |
| 1983–84 | 1,320,000 | 10% | 132,000 | 99,691 | 44,000 | (11,691) | (91,382) |
| 1984–85 | 1,452,000 | 10% | 145,200 | 99,691 | 48,000 | (2,491) | (93,873) |
| 1985–86 | 1,597,000 | 10% | 159,700 | 99,691 | 53,000 | 7,009 | (86,864) |
| 1986–87 | 1,756,000 | 10% | 175,600 | 99,961 | 59,000 | 16,909 | (69,995) |
| 1987–88 | 1,932,612 | 10% | 193,261 | 99,691 | 64,000 | 29,570 | (40,385) |
| 1988–89 | 2,125,873 | 10% | 212,587 | 99,961 | 71,000 | 41,896 | 1,511 |
| 1989–90 | 2,338,460 | 10% | 233,846 | 99,961 | 78,000 | 56,155 | 57,666 |
| 1990–91 | 2,572,306 | 10% | 257,231 | 99,961 | 86,000 | 71,540 | 129,206 |
| 1991–92 | 2,829,537 | 10% | 282,954 | 99,961 | 94,000 | 88,263 | 217,469 |
| | $19,124,908 | | $1,852,379 | $996,691 | $637,000 | $217,469 | |

## Table 2-3C.  Municipally Financed Energy Conservation

| Year | 1*<br>Energy &<br>Service<br>Budget | 2**<br>Projected<br>Savings | 3<br>Dollars<br>Saved | 4<br>Debt<br>Retirement | 5<br>Mgt &<br>Service<br>Costs | 6<br>Net | 7<br>Cumulative |
|---|---|---|---|---|---|---|---|
| 1982-83 | $ 1,200,000 | 17.5% | $ 210,000 | $ 99,691 | $ 40,000 | $ 70,309 | $ 70,309 |
| 1983-84 | 1,320,000 | 26% | 343,200 | 99,691 | 44,000 | 199,509 | 269,818 |
| 1984-85 | 1,452,000 | 26% | 377,520 | 99,691 | 48,000 | 229,829 | 499,647 |
| 1985-86 | 1,597,000 | 26% | 415,220 | 99,691 | 53,000 | 262,529 | 762,176 |
| 1986-87 | 1,756,000 | 26% | 456,560 | 99,961 | 59,000 | 297,869 | 1,060,045 |
| 1987-88 | 1,932,612 | 26% | 502,479 | 99,691 | 64,000 | 338,786 | 1,398,831 |
| 1988-89 | 2,125,873 | 26% | 552,727 | 99,691 | 71,000 | 382,036 | 1,780,867 |
| 1989-90 | 2,338,460 | 26% | 608,000 | 99,691 | 78,000 | 430,310 | 2,211,177 |
| 1990-91 | 2,572,306 | 26% | 668,800 | 99,691 | 86,000 | 483,109 | 2,694,286 |
| 1991-92 | 2,829,537 | 26% | 735,680 | 99,961 | 94,000 | 541,989 | 3,236,275 |
| | $19,124,908 | | $4,870,186 | $996,910 | $637,000 | $3,236,275 | |

*Includes $10,000/yr for subcontracted maintenance

**Cf. footnote Table 2-2

The critical variable under the three different assumptions is the extent to which the client believes it possible to achieve the projected savings without the ESC. The client is purchasing a guarantee and capital improvements by giving up a share of its interest in future savings. As a comparison of the three tables shows, the closer the client can come to realizing the same efficiency as the ESC, the less attractive it is for the client to contract for energy services. However, the less certain it is that the client can do no better than twice what the ESC contract guarantees, the less attractive going it alone becomes.

Table 2-4 indicates that to cover debt service plus management and service costs the project would have to realize approximately 12% in the first year declining to approximately 7% by the tenth. In other words, anything less than an 11.6% savings would require a payout; negative cash flow.

Table 2-4.  Energy Conservation Costs as a Percentage of
Energy & Service Costs

| Year | 1<br>*Energy<br>Service<br>Costs* | 2*<br>*Debt Retirement<br>and Mgt/Service<br>Costs* | 2÷1 |
|---|---|---|---|
| 1982–83 | $1,200,000 | $139,691 | 11.6% |
| 1983–84 | 1,320,000 | 143,691 | 10.9% |
| 1984–85 | 1,452,000 | 147,691 | 10.2% |
| 1985–86 | 1,597,000 | 152,691 | 9.6% |
| 1986–87 | 1,756,000 | 158,691 | 9.0% |
| 1987–88 | 1,932,612 | 163,691 | 8.5% |
| 1988–89 | 2,125,873 | 170,691 | 8.0% |
| 1989–90 | 2,338,460 | 177,691 | 7.6% |
| 1990–91 | 2,572,306 | 185,691 | 7.2% |
| 1991–92 | 2,829,537 | 193,691 | 6.8% |

*Combines Columns 4 and 5 on Tables 2-3.

The decision for the potential client hinges upon the question of the client's relative ability to achieve those savings alone. The ESC has the following advantages:

1.  It can guarantee savings;
2.  It provides operating and maintenance assistance;
3.  It provides capital improvements without requiring a capital investment.

If the municipality, county or state is willing and able to take the risk, assume responsibility for improved building energy management, and invest the capital, then it can ignore ESC's. However, if the client is willing to give up some of the potential savings, an ESC will underwrite the risk, assume the responsibility and put up the money.

All three tables are based on the same project, same investment ($520,000); same terms and rates (10 yrs; 14%; no discount); and same service costs.

Column 2 instead of detailing "Guaranteed Customer Energy Savings" estimates "Projected Energy Savings." There is no longer the guarantee, but the customer gets to keep all of the savings. Table 2-3A assumes that the customer can at least realize the savings guaranteed by the ESC; 3B, that the client can do better; and 3C, that the client can do as well as the ESC (working on its own). The third column converts percentages to dollars.

Columns 4 and 5 point out how much this cost of money affects the value of savings. Borrowing money at a fixed rate guarantees one annual cost which is eventually exceeded by the escalating value of energy saved. However, as the cumulative figures indicate, it is not until nearly the end of the period that total savings (in 3A and 3B) offset total expenditures. This means that net increases in the operating budget are necessary for 3 or 4 years and that the project does not break even (provide savings in excess of expenses) until around the seventh year.

In Table 2-3C, note that the realization of these benefits is possible only if the client is able (1) to secure technical design and installation expertise equivalent to the ESC and (2) able to manage and motivate employees to perform as well as those of a profit-oriented firm and (3) able to operate and maintain building systems as well as a proprietary engineering firm. The benefits under the self-financing option are far from guaranteed.

In each table Column 4 lists the annual cost of debt retirement, the annual payments of principal and interest on the bond issued to finance the project. Over the 10 year life of this analysis, the client will pay back $966,910.00 in order to get the use of $520,000.00 in the first year and the benefit every year thereafter.

### ESC's vs. Self-Financing

All other things being equal, an organization with access to long-term tax-exempt debt would be money ahead to finance this project rather than contract with an ESC. However, of course, all other things are never equal. In this case, the inequalities can be seen in the advantages and disadvantages of the two options:

|  | Advantages | Disadvantages |
|---|---|---|
| Energy Services Company Contract | 1. Guaranteed savings<br>2. Capital improvement with no capital investment<br>3. No risk to client<br>4. O/M assistance<br>5. Client capital available for other public purposes | 1. Client gives up some savings<br>2. Time consuming to select and develop ESC contract |
| Self-financed by long-term tax-exempt debt | 1. Keep all savings realized<br>2. Energy conservation leadership by example | Risk factors<br>Equipment<br>  a)  selection<br>  b)  installation<br>  c)  operation<br>O/M<br>  a)  expertise<br>  b)  motivation |

Obviously, an organization which does not have access to the type of money assumed (10 years at 14%), does not have this choice. But for a state or local government which can get approval for an energy conservation issuance, the considerations must be to balance these advantages and disadvantages.

It should be clear that except for those strongly committed to a public leadership role in energy conservation who are also certain of their staff expertise and administrative ability to overcome the risks, the advantages of an energy services contract far outweigh the costs.

Energy services companies are an excellent method of utilizing private expertise and private dollars to do work that public money and public employees might not be able to do as well, thus freeing scarce public resources to do things—like provide police or welfare services for which no private money is available.

## Industrial Development of
## Local Energy Services

There is another theoretically very interesting possibility for a municipality or state concerned with energy conservation. Most States have provision for the issuance either by a State, regional or local authority of so-called Industrial Development Bonds (IDB). These are tax-exempt bonds secured by project revenues the proceeds of which are to be used by a private party in a trade or business. A private party financing with commercial loan money or private bond issues would face even worse cash flows, the higher private interest rate being only slightly offset by tax credits and depreciation. (The accelerated depreciation schedule may also reduce the term of loan repayment to much less than the payback period, thus loading the early years with excessive negative cash flows.)

Presuming that a local company could be found or created which would be willing and capable of developing an energy services business, there are many practical benefits to using IDB's to help create such a local service business.

In order to secure the bond issuance a contract would need to be developed between the local ESC and a client. Public housing authority projects, school campuses, or municipal services complexes would all be potential clients. The term of the contract would be the same as the duration of the bonds. The amount and timing of the contract payments would be calculated to guarantee savings to the client while providing the developing ESC with adequate cash flow for debt service, operations, profit, and future development.

The advantages with the creation of a local ESC are several. Money and jobs do not leave the local economy. The energy and capital savings are available to the public authority not otherwise able to make the improvements. And, a new service business is created in the community, uniquely able to assist local businesses and local institutions use energy more efficiently, save costs, and compete more favorably in the market.

The interest, discount rates and placement difficulties which intermittently plague the bond market must be taken into consideration in developing such an issuance. However, the most critical task is the identification and development of a suitable local corporation to enter this business. Energy Services Companies are new to this country and energy conservation or energy efficiency projects, techniques, and equipment may be new to some engineers. Turning a small engineering or weatherization operation into an effective and bondable energy services company will take planning, organization development, engineering and financing skills and a good deal of commitment from both the public and private sectors.

The costs of developing a new business are very high. Personnel costs including recruitment and training, accounting, legal, space, transportation, etc. must be paid from the first day; while revenues would not be realized for 6 months to a year. The very real prospect of less than optimum performance in the early years would reduce projected revenues substantially and at a critical time. Several pioneers of energy services in the United States estimated start up costs ranging up to $1,000,000.00 annually for one, two, and even three years. Obviously, the sort of captive local company we describe would not have long start-up lags or heavy marketing costs, but start-up costs would be significant. It would certainly not be feasible to justify such a company for a single project the size of the example discussed in this paper.

However, when the project size is such that start-up costs of several hundred thousand can be absorbed and the repayment schedule sufficiently delayed, this option becomes viable. It would probably require energy user bills between $5,000,000.00 and $10,000,000.00 and provision for a period up to one year before contract revenues flow.

At least two New England communities are exploring this option. Although the idea is novel; the risks, great; and the process, complex; the potential rewards are very attractive: for the government agency, guaranteed cost savings, capital improvements without capital investments, and a real improvement in the health of the public budget; for the community, more jobs, more money in the local economy, a new service business able to help everyone cut energy costs, an improved competitive posture for local businesses, and a brighter economic and energy future for all.

## Summary

Energy services companies represent an important resource for capital-limited energy users—particularly government units—to arrange for energy conservation capital improvements with no capital expenditures and receive guaranteed energy savings.

Because these are new market entities and new relationships, the development process must be cautious and thoughtful and will be time consuming. However, the unique benefits to contracting with an ESC, especially in comparison to self-financing, are quite persuasive. The profit-oriented company, provided its guarantees are adequately secured, is a better bet to achieve energy savings than an internal program of energy efficiency improvements.

Finally, a community interested in making a strong move towards a more efficient energy future, should explore the creation of a local ESC financed by Industrial Development Bonds secured by municipal services contracts.

# Chapter 3 ⎯⎯⎯⎯⎯⎯⎯⎯⎯⎯⎯⎯⎯⎯⎯⎯

# An Evaluation of Shared Savings Financing Programs for the Public Sector

Richard M. Esteves

General Public Utilities (GPU) provides electric service to half of Pennsylvania and New Jersey including about 175,000 institutional, commercial and industrial customers. Although this group represents only about 10 percent of our customers, it consumes approximately two-thirds of our electric output. The GPU Companies (Jersey Central Power & Light, Metropolitan Edison and Pennsylvania Electric) have long recognized that some of the most cost-effective conservation opportunities are among such customers.

Over the past several years these companies have performed thousands of energy audits, either free or at nominal cost, for larger customers and have implemented specific conservation improvements, usually of the low-cost variety. Unfortunately, only a relatively tiny percent of their customers have made the significant follow-up investments necessary for the next generation of energy savings to be realized.

To deal with this situation, GPU began examining innovative conservation financing mechanisms, especially those which required no up-front financing and which included a guarantee that savings would exceed project costs. Such financing was found feasible, available and reasonable along with a number of hidden benefits.

Nearly all of these resulted from the guarantee, making the vendor a strong ally of the building operator in undertaking cost effective—and only cost effective—conservation and load management programs. The building operator now had an energy expert with an undeniable vested interest in doing what was best for the building operator.

The two most popular financing mechanisms were leasing arrangements with the payments tied into a monthly savings guarantee and a "shared savings" operation in which the vendor undertook all of the energy improvement at no cost to the operator, but received a "share" of the resultant savings, usually 50 percent or more.

When the total costs were analyzed it was found that there was *no penalty* for the use of leasing or lease-purchase agreements. Shared savings options were usually the number one choice, frequently by a significant margin.

### Shared Savings Best

In virtually every major example, shared savings was the option with the greatest benefits to the customer. The elimination of first year costs and the lack of servicing costs were two of the most important reasons why shared savings showed up at the top. Perhaps most important, the impact that present value has in evaluating these alternatives should never be overlooked or underestimated.

In simplified terms, the present value (or present worth, or discounted value, etc.) equates to the value a particular company or institution places upon having cash this year compared to some future year. This is loosely related to the preferred simple payback. The shorter the payback required, the higher the present value discount rate. For example, a company that requires a simple payback of four years (25% return in year one), would have a present value discount rate of 25%. Those requiring a two year payback would have a discount rate of 50%. A 25% discount rate is used, meaning that a dollar of benefits due us in a year is worth only 80¢ ($1 divided by 1.25 = $.80) to us today. A dollar coming to us after four years is worth 41¢ now ($1 × .80 × .80 × .80 × .80 = $.41).

## Assumptions

For purposes of this comparison, which is summarized in Table 3-1, it is assumed that annual maintenance and servicing costs for the installed conservation equipment are about 10% of the original purchase price. A 10% additional first year cost for such things as engineering, auditing and various "shake down" costs is also assumed. A five year program life is used for the bank loan (at 17%), the straight lease agreement (at 20%), the lease purchase plan (at 22%) and the shared savings program (with a fifty-fifty split of savings).

Because the non-profit building owner is not subject to income taxes, we are not concerned about the availability of a 10% investment tax credit or a 10% energy conservation tax credit (ECTC). Questions of such tax deductions as accelerated depreciation and interest payments are also moot.

Finally, the cost of the equipment plus installation was set at $200,000, with resultant first year energy savings of $100,000. Savings are estimated to increase by 10% annually (as are fuel costs). At the end of five years, the equipment is assumed to retain 15% of its original value ($30,000) and is purchased at that time by the shared savings and leasing programs. The other alternatives already have ownership.

## Evaluation of Financing Programs

Owner/operators of institutional, not-for-profit buildings have the greatest incentive to prefer shared savings plans over the alternatives. We could also include in this group building owners who have a zero tax rate. Since none are subject to income taxes, they must also give up the availability of tax credits and tax deductions frequently available from ownership. (In this instance, we assume that the building owner cannot "sell" the related tax benefits.)

Based solely on the total undiscounted dollar benefits of the five alternatives, the so-called "common sense" alternative of internal funding may appear to be the preferred economic choice. In this case, the benefits total $290,000 over the five years. Very close behind, though, is the shared savings alternative at $275,000. Bunched together in a second tier are lease purchase, straight leasing and the bank loan financing.

## Table 3-1. Annual Benefits of Alternative Financing Plans
### (Thousands of Dollars)

| | Year 1 | Year 2 | Year 3 | Year 4 | Year 5 | Total | Comments |
|---|---|---|---|---|---|---|---|
| Energy Savings | $ 100 | $ 110 | $ 121 | $ 133 | $ 146 | $ 610 | Increases @ 10% annually |
| Shared Savings | | | | | | | |
| Annual Payment | | | | | | | |
| Equipment | $ (50) | $ (55) | $ (61) | $ (67) | $ (73) | $ (305) | 50% of savings each year |
| | — | — | — | — | (30) | (30) | Purchase at end of contract |
| Net | $ 50 | $ 55 | $ 61 | $ 67 | $ 43 | $ 275 | Total Net Savings |
| Present Value | $ 50 | $ 44 | $ 39 | $ 34 | $ 18 | $ 185 | Uses 25% discount rate |
| Internal Funds | | | | | | | |
| Installation | $ (20) | $ — | $ — | $ — | $ — | $ (20) | 10% cost for 1st year costs |
| Equipment | (200) | — | — | — | — | (200) | |
| Servicing | (20) | (20) | (20) | (20) | (20) | (100) | 10% annual servicing |
| Net | $ (140) | $ 90 | $ 101 | $ 113 | $ 126 | $ 290 | |
| Present Value | $ (140) | $ 72 | $ 65 | $ 58 | $ 52 | $ 106 | |
| Loan | | | | | | | |
| Installation | $ (20) | $ — | $ — | $ — | $ — | $ (20) | |
| Servicing | (20) | (20) | (20) | (20) | (20) | (100) | |
| Loan Payment | (62.5) | (62.5) | (62.5) | (62.5) | (62.5) | (313) | |
| Net | $ (2.5) | $ 27.5 | $ 38.5 | $ 50.5 | $ 63.5 | $ 177 | |
| Present Value | $ (2.5) | $ 22.0 | $ 25.0 | $ 26.0 | $ 26.0 | $ 101 | |

| Lease | | | | | | | |
|---|---|---|---|---|---|---|---|
| Installation | $ (20) | $ - | $ - | $ - | $ - | $ (20) | |
| Equipment | - | - | - | - | (30) | (30) | Purchase at contract end |
| Payments | (56) | (56) | (56) | (56) | (56) | (279) | Covers equipment cost plus |
| Servicing | (20) | (20) | (20) | (20) | (20) | (100) | 20% interest |
| Net | $ 4 | $ 34 | $ 45 | $ 57 | $ 40 | $ 181 | |
| Present Value | $ 4 | $ 27 | $ 29 | $ 29 | $ 17 | $ 106 | |
| **Lease Purchase** | | | | | | | |
| Installation | $ (20) | $ - | $ - | $ - | $ - | $ (20) | |
| Payments | (57) | (57) | (57) | (57) | (57) | (286) | Covers equipment cost plus |
| Servicing | (20) | (20) | (20) | (20) | (20) | (100) | 22% interest |
| Net | $ 3 | $ 33 | $ 44 | $ 56 | $ 79 | $ 204 | |
| Present Value | $ 3 | $ 26 | $ 28 | $ 29 | $ 28 | $ 110 | |

*Assumptions:*

| | |
|---|---|
| Annual Servicing Costs | = 10% of Original Cost |
| First Year Installation Cost | = 10% of Equipment |
| Five Year Program Life | |
| Residual Value | = 15% of Original |
| All Payments/Benefits Occur at Mid-Year | |
| Equipment Cost | = $200,000 |
| First Year Savings | = $100,000 |
| Energy Savings Escalator | = 10% Annually |
| Interest | = 17% for Loan |
| | = 20% for Lease |
| | = 22% for Lease-Purchase |
| Shared Savings Split | = 50%–50% |

However, when a reasonable present value discount of 25% annually is used, the relationships change markedly in favor of the shared savings program. At $185,000 in net benefits, shared savings produces about 70% greater benefits than any of the other four alternatives, which are grouped between $100,000 and $110,000 in present value benefits.

## Changes in Assumptions

Table 3-2 summarizes the effect that changes in the various assumptions have on the net benefits resulting from the financing alternatives. Manipulating the reasonable assumptions changes some of the dollar benefits, but does not remove shared savings as the number one preferred economic choice.

a. *Present value discounts.* Even if the present value discount factor was reduced from 25% to a very conservative 15% discount, shared savings would still be the most economically beneficial. At that discount level, its present value benefit of approximately $212,000 is more than 30% greater than the number two choice of internally generated funds. In fact, the discount rate must be less than 5% before that option overtakes the shared savings alternative as the most attractive.

b. *Shared savings splits.* It is true that some shared savings companies will not deal with not-for-profit buildings because of the lack of sufficient tax considerations. Of those who do, some request a greater than 50% split, especially in the first few years. While this affects the shared savings total, it will not change its number one ranking except in the most extreme cases.

A fairly "high" shared savings split was tested; 70%-30% in years one and two, 60%-40% in year three and 50%-50% in the last two years. The effect was to reduce the shared savings present value benefits from $185,000 to $139,000. While this was significant, it was still about 30% better than the four alternatives. Only when we went to the "extreme" case of a 90%-10% split in year one, 75%-25% in year two, 60%-40% in year three and 50%-50% in years four and five, did the shared savings benefits get down close to the other alternatives. Even at that point, it is still the preferred economic choice.

**Table 3-2. Summary of Five Year Benefits**

|  | Shared Savings | Internal Funds | Loan Financing | Lease | Lease Purchase |
|---|---|---|---|---|---|
| A. Present Value as Shown in Table 3-1 | $185K | $106K | $101K | $106K | $110K |
| B. Total Net Savings (No Present Value) | $275K | $290K | $177K | $181K | $204K |
| C. Present Value Discount = 15% | $212K | $161K | $125K | $129K | $140K |
| D. Shared Saving Splits: 30%, 30%, 40%, 50%, 50% | $139K | $106K | $101K | $106K | $110K |
| E. Shared Saving Splits: 10%, 25%, 40%, 50%, 50% | $115K | $106K | $101K | $106K | $110K |
| F. Loan Interest = 8.5% and 0.0% | $185K | $106K | $139K (8.5%) $177K (0.0%) | $106K | $110K |
| G. No Servicing Cost for Leases | $185K | $106K | $101K | $106K | $110K |
| H. Seven Year Benefits (With Seven Year Shared Savings; All Others Stay Same) | $242K | $193K | $188K | $173K | $197K |
| I. Ten Year Benefits (With Ten Year Shared Savings; (All Others Stay Same) | $300K | $292K | $287K | $292K | $296K |

c. *Loan interest rates.* Another scenario examined was one in which the borrowing rate of the building operator was assumed to be much less than the 17% original hypothesis. This might well be the case for most municipal and tax-free borrowings. For this evaluation, we cut the financing rate in half, from 17% to 8½%. Although the percentage figure is significantly below normal interest rates, even for tax-free securities, we use it to demonstrate the impact for interest rates.

Assuming an interest rate of only 8.5% would obviously improve the loan financing option significantly. Its related benefits increase by more than a third to about $139,000. This places loan financing in second place among the alternatives—but still significantly below the $185,000 of benefits available from the shared savings program. In fact, if there were *zero* interest charges, the resultant total loan financing benefits ($177,000) would still be less than that available from shared savings ($185,000).

d. *Maintenance and servicing.* Some leasing plans provide for a maintenance contract at a reduced or even "no charge" basis, sometimes in a trade-off for another benefit less important to the building owner. To conservatively test the impact of reduced cost or even free servicing, we assume that the leasing company makes no other change in any of the economic aspects of the contract. This increases the value of the leasing alternatives by over 60% to about $175,000— but still leaves them slightly behind the shared savings alternative. Any charges or economic trade-offs for the maintenance services would push the leasing plans that much further behind the shared savings approach.

e. *Scheduling of equipment payments.* In this example, it was assumed that all costs and benefits occur at the mid-point of each year. Because purchase, installation and financing costs normally begin long before energy costs savings, this assumption artificially increases, by a great deal, the present value benefits of the internal funding alternative. The leasing and loan financing plans also benefit, but by a smaller amount. For example, if the equipment were purchased, installed and tested before the savings year began, net benefits for internal funding drop by a fourth to about $79,000, making it the least attractive alternative. Because only a small portion of the leasing and loan financing costs occur before savings begin, the benefits of these alternatives are reduced by a much smaller amount. (Because of the great variability of possible assumptions, these figures are not summarized in Table 3-2.)

f. *Years of shared savings contract.* In all of the scenarios, the customer owns the equipment and realizes all savings after five years. Let's examine the results of all options *except* for shared savings, which was assumed is a seven year contract—a fairly common contract length.

The present value benefits of the shared savings alternative increase by about $57,000 over these extra two years while the alternatives increase by $87,000. (The shared savings plan purchases the equipment at the end of seven years and we assume a 20% reduction in value for each year after five.) The shared savings plan is still the top economic choice with 20%–25% greater value.

Even a ten year shared savings plan shows slightly greater benefits than the alternatives do over the same time period. This assumes that the leases and loans are closed out after five years and the only "costs" in the plans other than shared savings are $20,000 annually for maintenance servicing.

## Conclusions

By far the most important conclusion from these evaluations is that each building owner/operator should seek to make a full financial analysis based upon his or her particular circumstances and should not rely upon so-called common sense or "rules of thumb" about the preferred alternatives. It is also important to realize that this is not a job solely for the building superintendent or similar person, but should be done with the active assistance of the financial department or someone who understands the intricacies of financial evaluations and their dependence upon various time factors.

The other major conclusion is that for non-taxpaying building owner/operators, the shared saving option, strictly from a financial/economic standpoint, will very frequently be the top choice, perhaps by a significant amount. The higher the discount rate (i.e., the shorter the effective payback period required), the greater will be the shared savings option benefits, relative to the other options and especially the option of using internally generated funds. Similarly, if interest rates are significantly less than the 17% used in our examples, the loan financing will obviously increase its attractiveness relative to alternatives.

Finally, there may well be special arrangements available for one or more particular methods from individual vendors that will shift the benefits in one direction or another. For example, some vendors may be willing to reimburse the customer for their auditing and engineering and shake down costs, while others may reduce or offset servicing costs.

However, when all is said and done, unless there is a combination of very significant variations from the "standard" situation, the shared savings alternative appears to be the preferred alternative for non-taxpaying buildings.

## Reference

A *Catalog of Innovative Conservation Financing Companies* has been prepared by Mr. Esteves, and is available (see Appendix B).

# Chapter 4

# Energy Service Contracts with Local Agencies: Do They Constitute Debt Obligations?

Anthony M. Carey, P.A.

Almost all states have adopted regulations to guard themselves against overextension of credit. These are accepted by city and county authorities—which then add amendments and qualifications to meet specific local needs.

When multi-year agreements are required, as in the case of energy service company or shared energy savings contracts, these state and local statutes are often restrictive. There is a growing awareness of the need to revise these legal limitations, and progressive states and communities have done so. In many instances, however, the processes of amendment have not yet been undertaken.

Legal guidance is necessary. The analysis which follows refers specifically to the State of Maryland, and is an example of what must be done before a multi-year energy service contract can be considered.

Although private firms supplying comprehensive energy management services are widespread in Europe, the industry is only in its beginning stages in the United States. It is generally expected a large market will develop. Typically, such a company enters into a long-term contract, and, at its own expense, designs, installs, manages, and maintains an energy conservation system for a building or plant. In addition to any tax benefits which accrues to the owner of equipment, the company receives a share of the value of energy saved by the system installed.

This kind of long-term arrangement may be of particular value to local public entities which own and operate a great deal of energy-inefficient building stock such as schools, hospitals, and colleges. These public agencies often lack two of the crucial ingredients energy service companies can provide: expertise and capital.

The public sector, however, is normally cautious about entering into long-term contracts, particularly for services for which there is not widespread precedent among other public agencies. This hesitancy tends to be reinforced when there are institutional or legal barriers, real or perceived.

One of the possible legal objections which can arise to an energy service contract is that because it is multi-year, it is a debt obligation as a matter of municipal law and can be entered into only by complying with various statutory or state constitutional procedures. These procedures are time consuming and burdensome and may be enough in themselves to put off even the hardiest public administrator.

In fact, however, it seems quite certain that at least under Maryland municipal law, a multi-year energy service company contract with a local government agency would not be a debt obligation. The purpose of this paper is to analyze this legal issue and provide support for this conclusion.*

---

*This paper deals only with contracts with local government agencies. Contracts with the major state contracting agencies, the Departments of General Services, Transportation, Budget and Fiscal Planning, and the University of Maryland, are governed by a recently enacted State Procurement Code found in Article 21 of the *Annotated Code of Maryland.* Although that Code does not preclude multi-year service contracts (*see* Article 21, § 3–705), it does require inclusion of a clause that any obligation beyond the current budget year is subject to the appropriation of funds, and if such funds are not appropriated, the contract terminates automatically or in accordance with the termination clause of the contract, if any.

## The Terms of an
## Energy Service Contract

For purposes of the analysis, I have summarized the contract terms and procedures offered by one firm to public sector owners. Under its standard arrangement, this company first performs a no-cost audit. If the savings potential is great enough to meet its investment threshold, it then offers the owner a ten-year contract, under which it agrees to install specified equipment, repair, and upgrade the existing building energy systems, and manage, repair, and maintain the new equipment which it installs over the life of the agreement. The building owner is guaranteed a certain percentage of annual reduction in energy use, which is relatively low at the beginning of the contract but goes up each year.

As a matter of mechanics, under this form of agreement, the owner pays to the energy service company each month an amount equal to the owner's fuel and utility bills for the year prior to the agreement, normalized for a standard temperature year. The monthly payments are further adjusted to reflect changes in fuel and electricity prices, changes in building use, or other factors affecting the price or use of energy over which the service company has no control. The owner deducts and retains from these payments the current value of its guaranteed percentage of reduction in energy use. As agent for the owner, the company pays all fuel and utility bills, retaining the difference, if any, as compensation for its services.

The contract, which has a ten-year term, is without right of termination by the owner for the first two to four years depending on the amount of initial capital investment and assumptions concerning the rate of payback, except for default by or the bankruptcy of the energy service company. Thereafter, the owner may terminate provided it purchases its equipment at residual value. There is no requirement that the owner exercise the purchase option at the end of the term, and if it does not do so, the service company must remove the equipment.

After notice to the owner, the company has the right to place additional equipment in the building, and may remove equipment, provided removed items are replaced by equipment of similar use or design. The risk of loss is on the service company for all the equipment installed; it also agrees to maintain general liability and machinery insurance, as well as workmen's compensation insurance for its own employees.

## Legal Analysis

To protect against overextension of credit, all states impose limits on the extent and manner in which governmental entities may incur long-term debt. In Maryland, these limits are found in a number of constitutional and statutory provisions. For example, Article IX, Section 7 of the Maryland Constitution prohibits Baltimore City from incurring a debt, unless such action is approved by the State legislature and incorporated in an ordinance approved by a majority of the voters in the City. Similar restrictions apply to the counties and through them to their agencies, such as the local boards of education. See, *e.g.*, Article 25A, §5(P) of the *Annotated Code of Maryland* as to chartered counties; Article 31, §3 of the *Code* as to contracts by state or local officers concerning public buildings or works. Unlike some states, New Jersey, for example, Maryland does not have a statute which limits all local government contracts to a period of one year, with certain specified exceptions.*

There are two alternatives for local government in Maryland to comply with the legal limitations on debt: (1) appropriation of the full amount of a multi-year debt obligation at the outset, or (2) inclusion within a multi-year agreement of a so-called fiscal funding out clause, which provides that any obligation beyond the current budget year is contingent upon the appropriation of funds, and if funds are not appropriated, the agreement is terminated without further liability to the public entity.**

---

* The New Jersey statute was recently amended to permit local governments to enter into shared energy savings contracts for periods of up to ten years without inclusion of a fiscal funding out clause.

** Some energy service companies will not enter into multi-year contracts with fiscal funding out clauses.

Certain types of multi-year agreements, however, have been held not to constitute debt. A contract for services, for example, even though multi-year, is considered by most states not to constitute a "debt" for the aggregate amount of the contract when entered into, if payments are to be made periodically as service is rendered. 15 McQuillin, *Municipal Corporations,* §41.38; 2 Antieau, *Municipal Corporation Law,* §15.41.

As stated by the Indiana Court in *Protsman v. Jefferson—Craig Consolidated School District,* 231 Ind. 527, 109 N.E. 2d 889, 891 (1953):

> A municipal corporation may lawfully contract for necessary services over a period of years and agree to pay therefor in periodic installments as the services are furnished. In such cases the aggregate of the amounts to be paid as the services are rendered under such contract are not considered as an indebtedness of such corporation, and such contracts are not rendered invalid by the fact that the aggregate of the installments exceeds the debt limitation.

A good number of these cases involve contracts for the furnishing to municipalities of electricity, water, or gas and the great majority of states hold these contracts do not constitute debt obligations. Although I have found no Maryland case dealing with the furnishing of electricity, water, or gas to a local government, the case of *Wyatt v. State Roads Comm.,* 175 Md. 258 (1938) involved in part the validity of multi-year contracts for the repair and maintenance of roads and makes it clear that Maryland shares the view of the majority of other jurisdictions concerning the non-debt natures of public entity service agreements. The Court there observed:

> . . . [A]n undertaking to pay undetermined, undeterminable, amounts of the cost of maintenance, repair, and operation in the future from day to day, month to month, and year to year, as need arises, if it can be classed as containing an element of debt at all, is not one for which taxes to pay interest and principal, and to pay the principal completely in fifteen years, might be provided in a tax law. . . . However heavy the burden might possibly become the contract to carry it is not such a debt with principal and interest as is dealt with by the Constitution. . . . p. 268.

The multi-year energy service contract outlined in the first section of this paper would appear to fit readily into the category of an agreement for the furnishing of services. The building owner pays to the company each month a proportionate amount of its adjusted baseline energy bill less the value of its guaranteed percentage of reduction in energy use. The monthly amount will vary depending on the season. As agent for the owner, the service company pays most of this amount over to the local suppliers of fuel and electricity and retains the difference, if any, as compensation for the thermal services it has agreed to provide. The exact amount it will receive each month cannot be ascertained at the outset because it will depend on how efficiently the services are provided. But, from a financial accounting point of view, a substantial portion of each monthly payment and possibly all of such payment, constitutes a current expense item for fuel and electricity, and the balance a current expense payment for energy management services, which include repair, maintenance, management, technical advice, and training.

It could be argued that some portion of the service expense payment constitutes rental for the use of the equipment installed in the owner's building. Aside from the lack of any clear measure of how much of the monthly payment should be considered rental, it seems clear, based on the contractual terms, that this equipment is integral to and in support of the thermal services provided and not equipment being separately used by the building owner.

Although the service company agrees to install certain equipment to produce a targeted reduction in energy use, it retains ownership and control and may remove it as long as it replaces it with equipment of like design and purpose. Moreover, the company is responsible for loss or damage, is required to repair and maintain, and retains the risk of loss of economic value since the owner is not compelled to purchase the equipment at the end of the contract term.

A similar question is involved in a line of Internal Revenue Service rulings and cases concerning the applicability of the investment tax credit to equipment, such as telephone gear or copying machines, placed by a private company with a public entity. If the equipment is found to be placed under a lease, it does not qualify for the investment tax credit; if under a service agreement, it does. The reasoning used by the IRS to determine whether an arrangement is a lease or service agreement is stated in Ltr. 7913003 and reinforces the point that the energy service company contract described is a service agreement:

> In determining whether an agreement is a lease or service contract, both Rev. Rul. 71-397 and Rev. Rul. 72-407 focus on whether the owner of the property in question utilizes such property to provide a service to another party or whether the property is provided to another party who utilizes such property to provide services to itself.

And see *Xerox Corporation v. United States,* 81-1, U.S. T.C. ¶ 9579 (Ct. Claims, 1981).

But even if a Maryland court found that some portion of the payment stream constituted rent for equipment, it should not transform the energy service agreement under analysis into a debt obligation. In Maryland, as in other states, rent due beyond the current period under a true lease does not constitute a present debt, and the arrangement described here has all of the hallmarks of a true lease rather than a disguised installment sale. *Hall v. City of Baltimore,* 252 Md. 417 (1969); *Eberhardt v. City of Baltimore,* 291 Md. 92 (1981). (And *see Allstate Leasing Corp. v. Board of County Commissioners,* 450 F.2d 26 (20th Cir. 1970), applying the same principle to leases of tangible personal property).

The energy service company retains the risk of loss for the equipment throughout the term; the owner is never compelled to exercise an option to purchase, and the purchase price under the option is at a fair market residual value. This arrangement contrasts with the usual installment sale, where set payments are made over a term of years and at the end of the term, the owner takes title automatically, or for nominal value or for a bargain value.

Thus, although there is persuasive support that the agreement is a service contract, even if a Court found that it involved a lease of equipment, it should have no effect on the ultimate conclusion that the agreement constitutes a non-debt obligation.

Finally, as a matter of policy, an energy service contract of the type under review should not be considered a debt obligation because it does not diminish the credit of local government, the evil the debt limitations are intended to prevent. To the contrary, the effect of a sound shared savings arrangement is to reduce the current energy bills of public entities, helping to preserve, not impair, their future financial standing.

# Chapter 5

# Creative Financing of Energy Management Systems for Smaller Organizations

Sandra K. Brown

In the economic climate of the 1980's, with its combination of recession and high utility costs, energy management is highly relevant to the corporate bottom line. Why then, when it comes to committing the capital to energy conservation, do these projects receive low priority?

Lack of available capital is one reason. Many smaller companies and institutions such as high schools, public or private, simply don't have the funds to invest in what they consider nonessential projects. Others that do have access to capital prefer to invest in projects that more directly contribute to their basic operations. Payback for energy conservation projects can take several years and is often difficult to calculate, given fluctuating energy prices.

Moreover, many smaller organizations don't understand the technical aspects of energy management. A type of third-party financing called "shared savings," however, is rapidly changing the low priority status of energy conservation projects.

Under a shared savings arrangement, an energy services company agrees to purchase, install, operate and maintain equipment needed for energy efficiency projects in commercial, industrial or institutional facilities in exchange for a predetermined share of the actual savings. The agreement may give the customer as much as 50 percent of the savings over a seven- to ten-year term. What this does for the customer is provide the cost avoidance reduction of its operating expenses without any financial outlay and without risk (i.e., off-balance sheet financing). The customer also enjoys another benefit. Because the energy services company has invested its own funds in the energy management system, and because its return on that investment depends solely on the quality and maintenance of the system, the customer has greater assurance of the best possible system, continuing maintenance and maximum energy savings.

Energy management is a fast-growing billion-dollar industry whose annual growth is predicted at 50 percent over the next decade. According to governmental statistics, there are approximately 1,200,000 buildings in the private sector alone that are between 10,000 and 200,000 square feet. By sharing the savings generated by energy management systems, both the customer and the supplier of the system win. A customer with a monthly fuel bill of $10,000 can expect to save more than $225,000 over a seven-year period, assuming a 20% reduction in energy usage and a 10% annual increase in utility rates.

Projections such as these have brought many new entrants into the energy management field—consultants, engineering firms, manufacturers, vendors—and many of them are experimenting with the shared savings approach. Many, unfortunately, will fail, because the success of shared savings financing for energy management systems depends almost wholly on the technical knowledge and skill of the firm providing the system.

With the entire return on its investment dependent upon the savings generated by its system, it is imperative that appropriate control strategies are used, the installation is expertly done, the system is fine-tuned and properly maintained, and the system performs as expected over the life of the contract. Otherwise, the savings will not meet the projections, and both the customer and the energy management company will lose.

This chapter is based on the shared savings financing case studies projects implemented by Time Energy Systems, Inc. Over 90% of its nearly 400 installed systems (and an additional 800 systems contracted or committed by national chains) are financed by shared savings contracts. Most of these systems serve smaller organizations.

Commercial customers currently make up the majority of the customer base. National chains represent a large percentage of the commercial installations. A prime example is a national chain of retail children's stores, consisting of 71 locations in 13 states. The average size of these stores is approximately 35,000 square feet; the average system price is $22,000. The initial $1.5 million investment was financed under a shared savings arrangement. The average monthly savings projection is $600 per store, or a cost avoidance factor for the entire chain is in excess of $20,000 per month.

Many different kinds of firms are engaged in the energy management business. Some specialize in energy audits, some in system design or manufacturing, others in installations and service/maintenance contracts. An *energy services company*, on the other hand, provides *all* of these services and in addition usually provides the financing in the form of shared savings.

*The energy audit.* The approach to energy management usually begins with an energy audit of the subject facility. A preliminary "walk-through" audit is taken to determine if there is a possibility for energy savings. If there is, a detailed engineering audit is made; the existing heating, air conditioning, lighting, process and other equipment are surveyed, the hours of occupancy or use are recorded, and an energy consumption history is gathered.

These data are then entered into a computer simulation along with the recommended control strategies to project energy usage in a post-energy conservation mode. If such projections appear economically feasible, the customer is provided with a proposal outlining the details of the system and the shared savings plan.

*Custom engineering.* Once a contract is signed, system design begins. Each system installed should be custom-designed. System components are selected from a variety of manufacturers to meet the needs of the specific building and the recommended control strategies.

A total system might include various control strategies for the heating, ventilation and air conditioning system, lighting controls, automatic power factor correction or waste heat recovery. Large industrial or institutional projects may also include the construction and operation of cogeneration or small-scale hydroelectric power facilities.

Control strategies are incorporated into the software of the basic system as required, and the system is then fabricated or assembled. Detailed installation drawings are then made for each system. Actual installation in commercial facilities is handled by authorized contractors.

*The team concept.* Larger industrial or institutional projects require a slightly different engineering approach. For these facilities, the "team concept" for engineering and installation is used. A team is assembled from experts in the subject industry or methodology. For example, if a cogeneration facility is being considered, a team of professionals experienced in the cogeneration field is assembled. If an energy conservation project in a glass factory is being considered, a team with knowledge and experience in glass industry processes is assembled. The team concept is the logical extension of a custom-designed system, since it is, in a sense, "customizing" the staff for a specific project.

*The energy control center.* At the heart of operations is an Energy Control Center which provides day-to-day management of remote energy management systems via telecommunications. Systems in the customer's facilities are connected by standard telephone lines to a central computer. Operators monitor the building's energy usage to collect data and spot potential trouble before it occurs. The customer's system can be programmed or reprogrammed via telecommunications which allows many problems to be corrected remotely.

What types of problems can the Energy Control Center spot? Virtually anything to which the customer wants to be alerted. The customer and engineers decide on certain alarm conditions which, when met, will be communicated automatically to the Energy Control Center.

One alarm condition might be that the system has been manually overridden. The system can be programmed to alert the Energy Control Center if this condition persists past a preset period of time. Other alarm conditions might include a maximum or minimum temperature that should not be exceeded or a certain predetermined demand level. If the temperature in the building rises above or falls below the preset levels, the Energy Control Center is alerted and the operator proceeds to determine the cause and take corrective measures.

If a demand level is exceeded, the operator may alter the demand limiting portion of the system. A system can even be programmed to alert the Energy Control Center when a warehouse door has been left open too long, thus allowing cooled or heated air to escape. The reaction to any alarm condition is to either alert the customer at the remote system to check out and correct the situation or, if required, to handle the corrections by reprogramming the remote unit via telecommunications.

In addition to ongoing management of the remote system, the Energy Control Center generates a variety of management and maintenance reports from data collected throughout the month. These reports are not simple raw data, but an analysis of that data using proprietary analytical software. One such report is an "anomaly report" which detects unusual occurrences in, for example, a dramatic change in the HVAC system performance. Once such an anomaly is detected, it can be traced to its cause and corrected.

A central computer identical to the one in the main Energy Control Center can be installed in a customer's headquarters if the customer desires to monitor his or her own system. With certain software adjustments, full and exclusive control can be given to the customer's computer.

The Energy Control Center, with its detailed monitoring of facilities, is ideal for those smaller firms or national chains that don't have in-house maintenance personnel other than a janitorial staff. In conjunction with several major manufacturers, an energy management system has recently been developed that is much more adaptable to the smaller facility when operated through the Energy Control Center.

The Energy Control Center, combined with the shared savings approach, can produce significant benefits for small to mid-sized buildings. Nearly 100 systems are now on line at the Energy Control

Center (which has the capacity to handle 5,000 systems). All future installations will be offered this communications link.

In a shared savings arrangement, the customer receives the benefits from an energy management system without any initial charge. In return for its investment, the energy services company usually receives any available tax benefits (because it owns the system) and a percentage of the savings for a predetermined time. The first question usually asked by a prospective customer is: How do you arrive at the savings? The answer: Through a mutually established base year.

Simply stated, a base year is a reference point against which future energy savings are measured. The base year consists of monthly energy usage stated in fuel units based on the customer's historical usage. In some cases, a simple monthly average of the past three years is used; in other cases, adjustments may be made for increased or decreased occupancy, unseasonably hot or cold months, or the addition or deletion of energy intensive equipment.

For example, if energy usage increased in, say, November of 1981, it may have occurred because a half-full office building suddenly leased all its space or perhaps an office began a heavy computer operations. Either of these situations would increase energy usage making the simple average of the past three Novembers inaccurate.

Moreover, if the area experienced an unusually hot August or an unseasonably cold January, a simple average would not work either, and adjustments would be made to the base year. In complicated cases involving production facilities formulas using linear regression can be used to determine per unit cost. However the base year is established, it must be agreed upon by both the customer and energy service company.

Once the system is installed, each month's utility bill is compared to the corresponding month of the base year. The fuel units (kilowatt hours or cubic feet of gas) of the same month of the base year are multiplied by the current utility rate; then the dollar figure of the current bill is subtracted from this amount. The result is the dollar savings for the current month. The customer is billed by the company for that portion of the savings as stated in the shared savings contract.

This billing procedure is not quite as simple as it may appear, and here is where many shared savings programs break down.

Before the current bill can be compared to the base year, the current billing structure of the customer's power company must be entered into the computers that handle the billing. Then the current bill must be recreated to verify that the proper billing structure is being used. Once that is done each month, the base year bill can be created, compared to the current bill, and the savings figured.

With customers stretching across the country, the consultant must be able to work with the billing structures of over 100 power companies. Each one is different. And they change frequently. All changes, of course, must be entered into the firm's billing computers in order to properly compute the savings. Therefore, it is important for billing purposes to have the ability to do computerized simulation of power company billing structures.

## The Future of Shared Savings
## Financing for the Smaller Firm

As stated earlier, there are approximately 1,200,000 buildings in the private sector that are between 10,000 and 200,000 square feet. These buildings are prime candidates for shared savings financing of energy management systems.

Many companies, however, postpone energy conservation projects for lack of funds; they assume that sooner or later the economic balance will tilt in their favor, bringing lower interest rates and ready money. However, as reported in *Energy Management Magazine,** an article entitled "Comparing Financial Alternatives in Tough Times," by David Brown and Robert Ranch (two Time Energy executives) suggests otherwise.

They use discounted cash flow models to show that, for most situations, opting for shared savings financing immediately is superior to delaying the project for more than a few months. Furthermore, companies with capital available for other investment opportunities can "eat their cake and have it too." By utilizing their own capital

---

*
*Energy Management*, November/December 1982, Penton/IPC, Cleveland, Ohio.

for non-energy projects and using shared savings financing for energy efficiency projects, they can enjoy the benefits of both.

Educational institutions and government agencies are also ideal candidates for shared savings financing of energy conservation projects. Lacking available capital, these institutions can still enjoy the cost-avoidance benefit of shared savings which will provide them with additional money to educate students or offer more services to the taxpayer.

High schools and colleges, in particular, with their acute capital shortage and large potential for energy waste (classrooms are unoccupied much of the day), can benefit from this approach. Despite the advantages, however, educational institutions and local, state and federal governments have been slow to adopt shared savings financing for energy management, primarily because of their inability to sign long-term contracts.

Several states (among them, New York, New Jersey and Rhode Island) are beginning to change their laws to allow state agencies and institutions to sign multi-year shared savings contracts. The federal government is also seriously studying the shared savings concept. Nevertheless, the political process is slow, even though the benefits are obvious.

### Shared Savings Considerations

For companies that are considering shared savings as a way to finance energy conservation projects, here are several points to keep in mind.

1. *Engineering expertise.* Engineering capability is perhaps the most important consideration. Engineering affects every stage of an energy conservation project. One advantage of selecting an energy services company that can offer both engineering expertise and shared savings financing is the profit motive. With the return of its investment at stake, the energy services company will work hard to achieve maximum savings for both parties.

2. *Day-to-day management.* Unless a firm has a qualified engineer as a facilities manager, it should consider the day-to-day management offered by telecommunication, such as is available through Time

Energy's Energy Control Center. Regular monitoring and the reports generated from the data can provide the equivalent of a full-time building engineer.

3. *Custom-designed systems.* The firm selected should be able to provide the size and type of system required by the building, rather than forcing a particular piece of equipment to fit the building. The system should have sufficient capacity to control all the necessary loads on as many different schedules as needed, but it shouldn't be oversized.

4. *Control strategies.* Control strategies relate both to engineering ability and to custom-designed systems in that the facility should be analyzed to determine how energy is used and the best way to reduce consumption and demand. In some buildings, lighting may be a significant factor in energy usage with a wide margin for reducing illumination to acceptable levels. In another building, waste heat generated by various pieces of equipment (e.g., air conditioning compressor) may be recovered to heat water for the building's use. Be sure that the energy services company can analyze and provide the control strategies needed.

5. *Experience in shared savings financing.* Success in shared savings financing means more than just finding the required capital. As discussed previously, calculation of an equitable base year and billing procedures that ensure accuracy in the monthly bills received are equally important. And experience counts.

6. *Continuing service and maintenance.* Without guaranteed service and maintenance over the life of the contract, an energy management system may prove worthless to both building owner and the energy services company. A good track record is essential.

7. *Contract terms.* The shared savings contract should fully cover the obligations of each party over the term of the contract, including:

• Type of equipment to be installed.
• Location of the facility in which the equipment is to be installed.
• Percentage of the savings split to the customer and the energy services company.

- Terms of payment of the monthly savings to the energy savings company.

- A mutually agreed upon base year for each facility under contract.

- Provisions for restating the base year if an error is found by either party or if energy usage increases or decreases beyond a predetermined percentage.

- The right of termination of the contract (usually when a minimum amount of savings has not been achieved during a previous 12-month period).

- Disposition of the system at the end of the contract period based on the customer's preference (i.e., renegotiation of the shared savings contract, purchase of the system at fair market value, or removal of the system).

- Ask the company that is offering any or all of the above services to furnish customer references. If a dozen or more references from satisfied customers are not available, you may be a guinea pig! Customer references are as important in shared savings financing of energy management systems, as in the lease or purchase of such systems.

# Chapter 6

# Characteristics of Cogeneration System Financing

Barry Sedlik

### Qualifications for Cogeneration Facilities

A cogeneration facility under the Federal Energy Regulatory Commission (FERC) rules is a facility that produces (1) electrical or mechanical energy, and (2) useful thermal energy (such as process steam) so that the reject heat of one process becomes the energy input to a subsequent process.

*Ownership.* Less than 50 percent equity interest can be held by an electric utility or its affiliates. However, gas public utility holding companies may own cogeneration and small power production facilities under FERC rules. (The ownership restriction is currently under debate in Congress. The Humphrey bill allows electric public utilities to own more than a 50 percent share of a cogeneration facility.)

*Operating standards.* Topping Cycle: useful thermal energy output must be at least 5 percent of total energy output (on a calendar year basis. Bottoming Cycle: none.

*Minimum efficiency standards.* Topping Cycle: The useful power output of the facility plus one-half of the useful thermal energy output must be no less than 42.5 percent of the total energy input, or must be no less than 45 percent of total energy input if the useful thermal energy output is less than 15 percent of the total energy output of the facility.

Bottoming Cycle: The useful power output of the facility must be no less than 45 percent of total energy input, if oil or gas is used for supplemental firing (i.e., reheating waste steam before electric generation).

*Fuel Use Act exemptions.* FUA's goal is to reduce the unnecessary use of oil and gas used by industry. To burn oil and gas in a new cogeneration facility, an exemption must first be obtained from the FUA. Effective August 6, 1982, new rules have been designed to reduce the exemption process red tape so that energy efficient cogeneration will be encouraged. This makes it easier for cogenerators to prove they will actually save oil or natural gas. Cogeneration facilities are now eligible for an FUA exemption if generated electricity constitutes more than 5 percent and less than 90 percent of the useful energy output of the facility.

*Diesel-powered cogeneration.* Qualifies under PURPA where not restricted by air quality regulations.

*Incremental gas pricing.* Qualified cogenerators are exempt from the incremental pricing of natural gas under Title II of the Natural Gas Policy Act of 1978.

### Financing Options Available for Cogenerators

*Sponsor's own capital structure.* The conventional method of financing new plant and equipment has been for the sponsor to seek needed investment funds based solely on the sponsor's capital structure. Usually, such financing is composed of both equity and debt. The project and its associated debt financing appears on the sponsor's balance sheet. All tax benefits accrue to the sponsor. Risks associated with the project fall almost entirely on the sponsor.

*Project financing.* Funding from multiple sources is applied to a well-defined project. Such financing is intended to be catalytic in organizing debt financing and risk-sharing under an overall project financing structure.

Objectives obtained under project financing:

- Financing on a highly leveraged basis (80–100 percent debt) reduces the need to dilute the sponsor's existing equity and permits reductions in the cost of capital by substituting lower cost, tax deductible interest for higher cost, taxable returns on equity.

- Achieves off-balance-sheet treatment for the debt issued to finance major new facilities. Maintains or improves the firm's financing position.

- Possibility of limited recourse financing upon the occurrence or nonoccurrence of certain specified circumstances. Sponsors would be relieved of any obligation to support the project debt.

Characteristics of project financing:

- A separate project company is established for the ownership of a new facility. The project company borrows most, if not all, of the capital requirements from lending institutions.

- The sponsors themselves are not legally obligated to pay the debt of the project company and generally do not guarantee repayment of that debt. Instead, lenders rely on the ability of the project as a whole to generate enough cash flow to meet the debt obligations of the project and to meet other operating expenses.

Benefits and disadvantages of project financing:

- Reduction of sponsor's credit dilution by spreading certain costs and risks to others, including lenders. This arrangement enables the sponsor to enter into other projects requiring debt leverage, or to maintain or improve the sponsor's financial position while benefiting from a cogeneration facility.

- Retention of tax benefits or the ability to sell these tax benefits to tax-oriented investors.

- Setting up a project financing requires much more planning and time than conventional financing.
- Overcoming project participants' differences in objectives and willingness to assume additional risks may be difficult.

Risks associated with project financing:

- All risks and risk limitations must be explicitly worked out before entering into an agreement.
- Different types of project financing vary in their diffusion of these risks.

Types of risks include:

*Completion risk.* One project-related risk that lenders are most reluctant to take. Lenders generally view completion as an equity risk and are more willing to assume this risk when confident of the technological and cost aspects of the project. The form of completion risk that has been accepted by banks more often has been the establishment of a dollar limitation on the obligation of the sponsors to invest equity in the event of cost overruns.

*Cost overrun risk.* Inadequate financing may lead to troublesome renegotiations for lenders and sponsors, resulting in project delays, imposition of higher interest rates and tighter debt support provisions, and the need to fund a higher percentage of equity than was originally anticipated. Planners must develop conservative budget estimates and err on the side of realism by using relatively high cost estimates when developing the project financing structure.

*Market risk.* Most lenders will not enter into a project financing agreement unless market operations have been worked out. A market purchasing contract should be entered into that explicitly states who will purchase the output, at what price, and for what period of time.

*Operating risks.* Operating management, maintenance and expenses should be established at the onset of the project financing.

*Supply risks.* Contracts for the supply and costs of crucial fuels and supplies should be established at the onset of the project financing.

*Technological risks.* Should the venture prove to be a technological failure or reach early obsolescence, the risk must be assumed by the sponsors or lenders.

*Legal risks.* The risk of any legal or government constraints to efficient operations, changes in existing cogeneration regulations, or fuel use need to be delegated.

*Force majeure risk.* Costs arising from the risks of natural disasters or uninsurable risks must be delegated.

## Specific Types of Project Financing

Creation of a new legal entity owned by a group of investors, operated for their benefit, and jointly controlled by them. Types include:

*Corporate joint ventures.* Organized as a corporation; investor liability limited to the amount of investor's investment.

*Non-corporate joint venture.* Organized as a general or limited partnership or trust.

*Undivided interests.* Ownership arrangement where two or more parties jointly own property and each party's liability extends to its percentage ownership.

Arrangements not requiring creation of a separate legal entity. Types include:

*Production payment.* Right to receive a specified share of the production, in cash or in kind, until an agreed amount has been received. It is payable solely out of the project's production and is not otherwise secured.

*Unconditional purchase obligations.* Types include:

*Take-or-pay contracts.* Sponsor or user agrees to purchase a specified quantity of product each period. The purchaser must make specified minimum payments even if it does not take delivery of the contracted product. Designed to cover the supplier's debt service requirements.

*Leases.* The principal advantage of leasing is the economics from the indirect realization of tax benefits otherwise lost. If the sponsor is unable to generate a sufficient tax liability to fully utilize the investment tax credit or accelerated depreciation, the cost of owning the new equipment will be effectively higher. Leasing will be a less costly alternative, as the lessor utilizes the tax benefits from the acquisition and passes on most of these benefits to the lessee through a lower lease payment.

Guarantees of project debt:

*Direct guarantees.* Sponsor agrees to cover debt liabilities of the project.

*Indirect guarantees.* Sponsor agrees to make payments to a project if the project's working capital, income, or coverage falls below a specified amount.

## Obtaining Cogeneration Financing

*Credible information gathering.* Available technologies and legislative and legal rules governing cogeneration are still developing. These vary according to the location and type of facility. Generic cogeneration studies are of minimal use in evaluating plant-specific financing.

- Detailed feasibility study. The first step in project financing is to engage in a feasibility study. Qualifications for cogeneration, regulatory climate, capital cost estimates, and technical and operating characteristics must all be determined. In addition, a feasibility study should assess the appropriateness of financing alternatives to the sponsor.

- Preliminary technical study. Should the feasibility study prove encouraging, a preliminary review and assessment of the types of cogeneration systems appropriate to the sponsor should be undertaken. The technical study should include all aspects of constructing, operating, and maintaining the cogeneration system.

*Economic evaluation.* A rate of return on 100% equity investment should serve as a reasonable basis for project evaluation. This type of evaluation comes closest to simulating a project's worthiness from a lender's viewpoint. As long as the ROR is greater than the after-tax cost of interest (i.e., 50% interest rate), leverage will increase the rate of return.

An economic evaluation should consider both the cash and non-cash benefits from cogeneration. These benefits include tax benefits and technical gains in efficiency.

An evaluation of financing alternatives should be made by a financial institution consulting firm.

*Sensitivity analysis and scenario development.* This will indicate the effects on the project of changes in the economy and technology. Changes in assumptions must be consistent. Several scenarios may be necessary to determine an acceptable range for the project.

*Internal marketing to upper management.* Once the feasibility and economic soundness of the project is established, the plant manager will need to present cogeneration to upper management. Most critically, the plant manager should stress to upper management the benefits engaging in project financing, i.e., the minimal debt requirements necessary to implement cogeneration from project financing.

# Chapter 7 ————————————

# Financing and Ownership Alternatives for Cogeneration Projects

## Philip M. Huyck

The markets to which industry must turn to finance the transition to a more appropriate energy infrastructure are themselves in disarray. Today's markets are characterized by great volatility and instability.

The bulwark of the U.S. long-term, fixed-rate capital market, the life insurance companies, are themselves undergoing a sea change and are not likely to reemerge in the foreseeable future as purveyors of 20 or 30 year fixed-rate debt. The maturity will be shorter and some form of equity participation a likely requirement to get their attention.

### Financing Alternatives

With the stipulation that any information on the situation in the capital markets has a very short useful life, financing and ownership alternatives for cogeneration projects will be discussed. The first point is that cogeneration as a generic category is so diverse that it is difficult to generalize. A diesel generator in the basement of a yogurt factory in Queens has very little in common with a synthetic fuel multi-hundred megawatt heavy oil recovery project in California.

The second point is that in dealing with third-party financing, there are significant differences in lender/investor attitudes depending on the type of financial institution we talk about—e.g., commercial banks vs. insurance companies, etc.

### Relevant Factors

In looking at financing and ownership alternatives, a number of key factors must be kept in mind. Each time the structure is altered by one element, each of the other elements must be reviewed. The list is not exhaustive, but is certainly illustrative.

Remember that a number of these concerns are relevant whether examining a wholly-owned project or one that is jointly owned and/ or third-party financed. Both the client and any third-party investor are engaged in a risk/reward assessment and allocation process. The only difference between the client and third party is the willingness to accept certain risks.

*Financial.* One of the key questions in this area is the capital constraint position of the cogenerator. In most situations, even those companies who can get budget allocations for two or three projects begin to run into resistance when they find another five or six good potential cogeneration projects in their system.

In brief, nearly everyone will be in a capital constraint mode, if only in the competition for internally available funds. It is common to find the energy manager in the situation of recommending an investment but losing out in the budget battle to the mill manager, because the latter is in the main line of business.

Some energy managers are scoring points with the argument that the cogeneration investment is absolutely necessary not so much because of the potential return as much as the insurance factor. Utilities are increasingly telling their big industrial customers that electricity curtailments are a very real possibility in the next few years. Without in-house capacity, a refinery, paper mill or petrochemical facility could face curtailment of electricity and cutback or elimination of its operations.

The traditional wisdom in finance has been that first comes the investment decision, then comes the financing decision. Increasingly the financing decision is part of the investment decision. No money means no equipment, regardless of the payback and energy saving arguments.

One way—perhaps the best way—to help break the capital constraint logjam is to make the projects directly self-supporting. This would involve setting up a new entity which would own the cogeneration facility and sell steam to the industrial and electricity to the utility. The entity would issue its own debt, which would be recourse only to the assets and cash flow of the project and not to the parent participants. This concept will be developed in more detail later.

A second issue in this area is the present and projected tax position of the cogenerator. This assessment has a major impact on the decision whether to transfer the tax benefits under the new tax law. This theme will also be covered in more detail later.

*Legal.* Perhaps the most critical legal concern is the status of the Public Utility Regulatory Policies Act (PURPA) and its implementation in the particular state of operation. PURPA is significant from the perspective of a third-party investor, particularly an institutional lender which may also take an equity interest in a cogeneration facility.

The decision by the Circuit Court of Appeals for the D.C. Circuit is an example of the type of unfortunate development that casts doubt on the PURPA framework. Confusion can be as fatal to mobilizing third-party, non-recourse capital as bad project economics.

Keep in mind that PURPA exemption means the facility is not public utility property under the Internal Revenue Code, since it is not regulated as to the rates it may charge for power. Public utility status is not one to which you should aspire. It results in the loss of the energy tax credit (to the extent that survives at all) and puts you at best in the 10-year and probably the 15-year property category under the new accelerated cost recovery program instead of being 5-year property.

In short, the financial deck is stacked against utility ownership of more than 50% of a cogeneration project.

*Indenture.* Any financing structure should be examined from an indenture standpoint, particularly to assess the treatment of project finance debt and indirect credit supports. Interest coverage and other limitations can be a major barrier to mobilizing the financing necessary for new investments. These limitations are particularly relevant for utilities which are coming close to the allowable limits on issuance of mortgage bonds.

*Tax.* The tax area is a critical one and unfortunately one of the least stable. At one point recently there was some realistic hope that the cogeneration tax credit would actually be expanded. Now it looks as though the Administration may be pressing in the opposite direction. This kind of unpredictable treatment of tax benefits contributes very little to the decision-making process.

The author's experience is that the tax credit is often not viewed as a reliable benefit and is appropriately discounted. The cogeneration tax credit itself (as opposed to the alternative energy or specially defined property credit) is relatively modest even when available.

In some cases cogeneration may qualify for tax-exempt financing, for example a wood-fired facility that could qualify as a solid waste disposal facility. However, the revenue bond area is continually under attack, along with tax benefit transfers and the energy tax credits, and investors cannot be sure that any of these options will continue to be available.

The provisions of the Internal Revenue Code prevent the end user from getting the energy tax credit and tax-exempt financing on the same property. Under the provisions of the Windfall Profits Tax Act, the energy tax credit is not allowed on that portion of the investment which is financed by "subsidized" financing, which includes tax-exempt financing. The full energy tax credit was lost after December 31, 1982.

Also remember the "public utility property" issue. Public utility property does not qualify for the energy tax credit (with the exception of hydro). Public utility property also falls into a longer depreciation category under the new accelerated cost recovery program.

*Accounting.* One should not overemphasize the significance of where an obligation appears in a company's financial statements. But accounting treatment is seen as important in many circles, and getting an obligation off balance sheet is often a goal. There are two basic areas of concern in the accounting area. The first is how you can achieve equity accounting, i.e., avoid consolidating project debt and keep it off balance sheet. Solutions to this problem are determined by GAAP principles of consolidation.

The second area of concern is embodied in Statement of Financial Accounting Standards No. 47, which deals with disclosure of hell-or-high water purchase agreements. "Hell-or-high water" means agreements to pay for product (steam, electricity, etc.) even if it is not delivered.

Where an obligation resides in the financial statements should not affect in any substantive way the financing decision. But there are times when indenture requirements (e.g., coverage requirements for debt issuance) which incorporate generally accepted accounting principles by reference can pose a real problem, and accounting treatment can become a substantive issue.

*Nature of the facility.* The nature of the particular facility can vary enormously. One question to ask is, who is using the output? Is the steam for a sole user or are there multiple users within steam transmission distance? Can we assume, as is usually the case, that the steam need is continual, not intermittent? As to the electricity, is the entire amount for internal consumption or is there excess capacity available for someone else? That someone else would logically be the local utility, but it might also be another industrial consumer.

If it is decided to sell energy to a utility, it may be decided to sell only excess capacity. Another alternative, depending on how the local regulatory authority has implemented PURPA and the level of avoided cost, it may be decided to simultaneously purchase and sell (arbitrage). If it is decided to arbitrage the full amount, there are some pitfalls for the unwary. One of these is taking the full capacity payment.

One thing to avoid is sacrificing the insurance factor by contractually dedicating the capacity of the facility so that it is unavailable to you in the event normal deliveries from the utility supplier are interrupted. There are a number of techniques for coping with this problem.

If the local utility has a low avoided cost, review the wheeling alternatives which may be available. Problems may be encountered in forcing wheeling, but if the local utility is cooperative, the option should be explored.

*Fuel source.* The fuel source is a critical element. First of all, assuming the present energy tax credit and tax-exempt financing system survives intact, there are some major tax benefits for the right fuel source. Also be sensitive to the problems of preserving the investment tax credit for oil- and gas-fired cogeneration. Review early with a tax counsel the investment tax credit and accelerated depreciation implications of oil- and gas-fired cogeneration projects.

A second critical aspect of the fuel source is how much to rely on its availability and what the price will be. For example, if the cogenerator does not control the complete amount of projected waste wood, how does the cogenerator plan to obtain it and at what price? A boiler that can burn coal also can be flexible to accommodate a shift in fuel supply, but there may be environmental limits on how far the shift can go.

For natural gas, be sensitive to the availability and pricing policies of the local regulatory authorities. Again, most gas turbine units can be dual-fueled, so there is an alternative. Obviously that alternative also places an effective lid on the prices which a gas utility can charge without triggering substitution. However, if gas prices are abnormally low in your particular area, you may face a major increase as prices are decontrolled.

*Rating agencies.* Any financial officer is going to be concerned with the reaction of the rating agencies, particularly in the context of whether non-recourse third-party financing has any real benefit. Rating agencies will look at each situation on its own merits. It's safe to say that their concern over the risk elements in a project and sources of cash flow are very much the same as yours should be.

## Ownership and Financing Alternatives

### Direct Ownership

The simplest mode is the vanilla own it and use it approach. Here the elements mentioned above are all relevant, but there is nothing on the financing side that gives you any edge in the investment decision. Let's review a few variations on the base case to try to minimize the financial impact.

*Tax benefit transfers.* To any cogenerator which is unable to take timely advantage of tax credits or is in a low marginal bracket or loss carry-forward position, optimizing tax benefits is critical. Leasing should be explored as an option. With the demise of the safe harbor leasing provisions, leasing today provides a little less flexibility, but is still an option worth reviewing.

*Tax-exempt financing.* Another way to optimize the financing is to take full advantage of tax-exempt financing options. This approach is under attack, is not always available (depending on fuel source, etc.) and can result in loss of energy tax credits, but must be analyzed in each case as to its availability and value. A present value analysis can tell whether you are better off with the spread between taxable and tax-exempt financing or the tax credit.

*Arbitrage under PURPA.* The next technique that can be used to optimize project economics is to arbitrage electricity sales under PURPA. PURPA may not have been effectively implemented in a particular state or the avoided cost is too low to make it worthwhile. Some companies have decided not to arbitrage as a matter of policy.

But this option should be examined to determine if a satisfactory relationship with the utility by selling at a price somewhere in between full avoided cost and the industrial rate can be reached. Remember if it is decided to arbitrage not to get too greedy for the capacity credits if it can be anticipated that there is a possibility of an electricity curtailment and that such a loss can not be tolerated. In short, be judiciously aggressive, but not foolishly greedy.

*Non-recourse financing.* Lastly, non-recourse financing for the facility should be sought. Even if a lender could be persuaded to lend to a separate subsidiary set up solely for the purpose of owning the cogeneration facility and financing non-recourse to the parent, this should still be shown on the balance sheet under consolidation principles. So most financial officers are not overly intrigued by this option.

## Project Financing

Project financing is a catch-all rubric which for this purpose means some sort of third-party financing.

Leasing can help with tax planning, but the lease obligation is still a credit obligation. In the eyes of many analysts, it is a debt equivalent even if it can be kept off balance sheet. There is also the fair market purchase requirement that some view as a deterrent.

What is meant by project financing? Much too simply, rather than owning the asset directly and financing it with internally generated capital and funds borrowed by the parent company, a separate entity is established to own and finance the particular asset.

Normally, the new entity is a joint venture, in part to share the risks of the project and also the benefits, but also because of one of the goals discussed above—equity accounting. Under principles of consolidation, if any partner or shareholder of an entity "controls" the entity, debt of that entity goes on that controlling parent's balance sheet.

In a general partnership in which no one partner controls, the debt goes on no one's balance sheet; you make a one-line entry to reflect the equity investment and adjust it to reflect the project entity's earnings.

The optimum financing arrangement could be a project partnership which would own and operate the cogeneration project. In an ideal situation, the equipment would be acquired under a lump sum, fixed price, date certain contract with the entire payment on completion. This eliminates financing during construction and any completion risk.

The partnership would sell steam to the industrial partner under a long-term take-if-available contract and electricity to the local utility under the same type of arrangement, i.e., a long-term PURPA avoided cost contract to pay for product when available.

The partnership would borrow some major percentage of the capital cost from an institutional lender on a long-term, fixed-rate basis recourse only to the project itself and the revenues from the sale of steam and electricity. The project revenues would comfortably amortize the debt, and some flexibility would be built into the loan arrangements to accommodate unexpected outages.

The lender may well demand an equity participation if the project is attractive. In the perfect world, the industrial partner might have an option to buy out his partner's interest at some point in the future, e.g., when the project debt has been paid off. In the meantime the industrial partner would have complete operating control and responsibility under a project management agreement.

If this were feasible, you might have the best of all possible worlds. You must look at each structure in light of the various concerns. You would have financed the project without affecting the parent company's financing capability. The debt would not appear on the balance sheet. The partnership structure allows flow through on a timely basis of the tax benefits to the parent participants.

A substantial portion of the cash flow to service the debt would come from a third party, the utility. The steam purchase contract is not a full take-or-pay, so you will not be compelled to disclose the contract obligation in your footnotes as a debt equivalent under the FASB's Statement No. 47. Since the debt is non-recourse and much of the cash flow to service it is from the utility, the rating agency view of transaction is likely to be benign.

All the variables reviewed earlier can be incorporated into this approach. The partnership is the optimum vehicle from a tax standpoint. First, the tax benefits are flowed through directly to the partners. Second, there is flexibility to allocate tax benefits disproportionately to ownership within the partnership framework.

The critical question is whether lenders could be attracted to lend on such a basis. Obviously the answer revolves around a risk and reward analysis. If you want to attract institutional fixed-rate debt in today's competitive capital markets, you are probably going to have to share the rewards of project ownership.

A financial institution could be the ideal project partner. Other potential partners or owners exist. For example, many engineering firms and equipment manufacturers are helpfully aggressive in providing financing for cogeneration projects.

The local utility could also be a partner, although they are likely to have capital constraint problems of their own and with rare exception have generally shown themselves to prefer simply buying electricity, the cost of which is flowed through immediately to their ratepayers under a purchase power adjustment clause.

With a finance partner, you are under no constraint to use particular services or equipment, as might be the case if equipment manufacturers were supplying financing. Money is delightfully neutral in this regard.

There is no potential interference in project operation as might be the case with a utility which might prefer to operate on an economic dispatch basis.

Having a major financial institution as a partner can help in the negotiating process with the utility and in building a constituency that would have an interest in maintaining the existing deregulated and avoided cost framework.

For projects too small to attract institutional attention, limited partnerships for individual investors may offer some potential, but be careful of the "at risk" limitations in the new tax provisions.

If structured and financed correctly, cogeneration projects instead of being a capital drain could actually be a source of capital. Lenders which may no longer be interested in lending on any basis to the parent company might be intrigued by opportunities as a project lender. Cogeneration projects, instead of being a problem could turn out to be an opportunity.

Third-party financing of a cogeneration project is a real option but will have to be integrated carefully. The sooner that the analytical process is started, the more likely an innovative solution to the financial constraints impeding the desired development of cogeneration will be found.

# Chapter 8

# Balancing Risks and Benefits in Cogeneration System Financing

Robert N. Danziger, Esq.

Roger R. DeVito, Esq.

For the past half century, one's energy needs were purchased in a marketplace which consisted of a single energy-producing and distributing utility. Statutory changes directed at the marketplace, in the past five years, have greatly enhanced the energy options available to the sophisticated corporate or governmental manager. Specialization and expertise in the technical, legal, and financial areas, have become critical components when exploring the myriad of considerations inherent in alternative energy technologies, and the adaptability of such technology to a particular setting.

The successful implementation of any major energy project requires a highly skilled and experienced development and management team. This team must have the requisite capabilities to handle the interconnections between legal, regulatory, financial, technical, and management considerations involved in each project.

Financing energy projects closely resembles a hybrid of real estate and major equipment financing. Essentially, there are two financing orientations: Tax-oriented financing and non-tax oriented financing. Of course, different energy technologies have different tax implications under both state and federal law. As a result, there is some degree of difference as to how each individual technology is financed. For example, solar, wind, biomass, geothermal, and other renewable energy technologies are eligible for significant state and federal tax credits. Cogeneration in California, where both natural gas and oil cogeneration systems predominate, fails to qualify for significant energy tax credits.

Figure 8-1 is taken from the Internal Revenue Code and shows the degree of energy tax credits available to various energy technologies. Cogeneration, specially-defined energy property and some of the other technologies fall under the general rule category. In addition to the energy tax credit, the Regular Investment Tax is often available.

**[Code Sec. 46(a)(2)(C)]**

"(C) ENERGY PERCENTAGE.—For purposes of this paragraph—

"(i) IN GENERAL.—The energy percentage shall be determined in accordance with the following table:

| "Column A—Description<br><br>In the case of: | Column B—<br>Percentage<br><br>The energy percentage is: | Column C—Period<br><br>For the period:<br>Beginning on: | And ending on: |
|---|---|---|---|
| I. GENERAL RULE.—Property not described in any of the following provisions of this column | 10 percent | Oct. 1, 1978 | Dec. 31, 1982. |
| II. SOLAR, WIND, OR GEOTHERMAL PROPERTY. —Property described in section 48(l)(2) (A)(ii) or 48(l)(3)(A)(viii) | A. 10 percent<br>B. 15 percent | Oct. 1, 1978<br>Jan. 1, 1980 | Dec. 31, 1979.<br>Dec. 31, 1985. |
| III. OCEAN THERMAL PROPERTY.—Property described in section 48(l)(3)(A)(ix) | 15 percent | Jan. 1, 1980 | Dec. 31, 1985. |
| IV. QUALIFIED HYDROELECTRIC GENERATING PROPERTY.—Property described in section 48(l)(2)(A)(vii) | 11 percent | Jan. 1, 1980 | Dec. 31, 1985. |
| V. QUALIFIED INTERCITY BUSES.—Property described in section 48(l)(2)(A)(ix) | 10 percent | Jan. 1, 1980 | Dec. 31, 1985. |
| VI. BIOMASS PROPERTY.—Property described in section 48(l)(15) | 10 percent | Oct. 1, 1978 | Dec. 31, 1985. |

Figure 8-1

The focus of this article is on cogeneration, although all the investment vehicles reviewed here apply to the other technologies as well. Some of these investment vehicles are better than others for optimization of tax benefits. These will be especially useful in tax shelter-oriented financing for some of the renewable energy projects.

Cogeneration is unique in that it is both a conservative and novel technology. While cogeneration has not been in widespread use for the last 35 years, cogeneration has been around since the late 1890's. Although, of course, there are exotic ways of doing cogeneration in a non-tested fashion, virtually every viable application of cogeneration has available some conservative technology.

Cogeneration, in fact, may be used as part of a solar, wind, biomass or other renewable energy system because cogeneration is simply the production of two forms of useable energy from a single energy input, whether that energy input be wind, solar, natural gas, coal, etc. The most economic cogeneration approach for the next 15 years or so is to use natural gas, oil, or biomass when it is readily available. Cogeneration does not require technical, engineering or production development. All cogeneration requires is implementation.

Cogeneration systems may be owned by local governments, both public and private utilities, private individuals, third-party entrepreneurs, leasing companies, banks, and industry itself. The major difference in one ownership versus the other is that the risks and benefits are allocated differently. There is a certain pie of tax benefits, capital gain and ordinary income flowing from the system. In addition, in each form, a different party is bearing risks of cost overrun, technical underperformance, unforeseen circumstances and accidents.

The act of packaging a good deal lies in the proper allocation of risks and benefits.

This report will highlight several critical areas pertaining to the necessary balance required between the risks and benefits when financing a cogeneration energy project. These areas include:

A. Financial/Regulatory Interrelations
B. Financing Risks Involved in an Energy Project
C. Security Expectations
D. Investment Vehicles
E. Creative Financing
F. Financial Implications of Power Sales Negotiating

## A.  Financial/Regulatory Interrelations

The Federal Energy Regulatory Commission rules implementing the Public Utility Regulatory Policies Act (PURPA), passed in 1978, are most critical to any financial analysis relating to a cogeneration project.

The Public Utility Regulatory Policies Act, which makes cogeneration possible, is founded on the premise of improving the efficiency of electric generation. Stated very simply, the PURPA rules call for an overall efficiency that significantly exceeds the electrical efficiency of modern-day, central-station utility plants.

Going back to the origin of PURPA, we see that the purpose of that act is not to increase the efficiency of the use of a rare feedstock, gas and oil, but to increase the efficiency of electrical generation in the United States by *eliminating some of the regulatory barriers* to cogeneration and small power production implementation. To summarize briefly, the efficiency standard states that the electrical efficiency plus one half the thermal efficiency must exceed 42½% for systems where the total thermal output to be used in process heat or other thermal applications is less than 15%, the electrical efficiency plus one half the thermal efficiency must equal 45%.

PURPA puts electric generation on a new footing, declaring that the most economically efficient producer of electricity will reap the greatest reward. Efficiency is used in the sense of not just energy efficiency, but capital efficiency as well. In addition, PURPA provides a guaranteed market which is cogeneration's greatest incentive. Generally speaking, a cogeneration system can increase electrical generation efficiency from its conventional 30 percent to a possible 75 percent fuel efficiency, thereby frequently cutting the plant's energy costs by more than half.

As to the most desireable type of cogeneration system to be installed, the combined cycle, electrically efficient systems are much less risky from a regulatory viewpoint, though they are somewhat higher in cost than other types of cogeneration systems. The economics of cogeneration and in particular a combined cycle system can be extraordinary by anyone's standards. However, the force that drives the economic in any project can be stated very simply—the system heat rate, or stated another way—the electrical efficiency of the system. There just isn't anything more important than the heat rate in cogeneration economics, both long-term and short-term. It is that simple. The lower the heat rate the better.

The available heat rate is a function of three things. *First:* pressure requirements. The higher the pressure requirement, the fewer options one has in designing systems to achieve the lower heat rate. *Second:* demand load. If the load isn't sufficient, the efficient equipment is probably going to be too large and will not be able to be operated for one of many reasons. *Third:* we have reliability, durability and deliverability. Electrically efficient systems are relatively new and are not the most conservative of all cogeneration technologies. As a result, a balance must be struck between reliability, durability and deliverability. But from a financial perspective, the technological risk is outweighed significantly by the regulatory risk, particularly since there are ways of contractually ameliorating operation and maintenance risk for aircraft derivative type of systems.

The heat rate has a significant effect on the size of a cogeneration system. The higher the heat rate, the smaller the system necessary to supply the thermal load. This is because a greater percentage of the total fuel input is available to be used to satisfy thermal requirements. Likewise, electrical and thermal income varies significantly with different systems. The higher the heat rate, the more thermal income there is from the system. However, the higher the heat rate, the lower the electrical income.

Although it is beyond the scope of this paper to discuss the variations in cogeneration technology, it should become apparent that as the heat rate goes up and electrical efficiency goes down, the more important the question of relative price of oil and gas becomes.

## B.  Financing Risks

In a recent letter to Sunlaw from a major California bank, it was stated: "A few comments about the lender's perspective of project financing may be helpful. Project financing is a method of identifying risks, and then finding ways of minimizing and allocating the risks among the parties to the transaction in a mutually acceptable way. In almost every project, the first risk of concern is *completion risk.* Lenders must be satisfied that sufficient technical and financial resources are available to bring a project to successful completion. The second issue is *operating performance risk.* The projected operating efficiency and reliability of a project after completion must be achieved in order to assure the proper retirement of project debt. Finally, the lender must be assured that an *adequate market* exists for the product output at a price that supports the project economics. The use of long-term sales contracts commonly mitigates this marketing risk.

"The question now arises as to who might appropriately take these risks. We do not believe that lenders are available to assume a lot of these risks, which are generally too large relative to the expected returns. Interested third parties (consumers, suppliers, host governments) are often called upon to assume some project risks. In the absence of third party support, a lender must ultimately look to equity support from a strong sponsor group to bear the risks outlined above."

From this statement it is noted that there are essentially three risks to deal with from a financial institution's perspective. There are, of course, risks in a risk management sense going to liability for injuries and other forms of insurable risks, but from a project financing standpoint, these are the risks that must be addressed.

*Completion risk.* Completion risk may be ameliorated by showing that there is a competent team to complete the project. There are, of course, legal, regulatory, and financial risks in addition to the technical risks. A competent team in all areas is required. The larger the project, the more expansive the team. Lobbying, for example, is often a part of major energy investments by utilities. Technical capability of the project personnel internal to the company is also important as well as the engineering and construction staffs retained to do the actual work.

In today's real world climate, a major risk in terms of completion is whether or not the permits will be obtained. Delay increases project cost. The question arises: Is the underlying investment group strong enough to support the types of cost overruns that can occur in energy projects? This is a major question that must be addressed in order to successfully complete the project, let alone obtain financing.

*Operation and maintenance risk.* The operation and maintenance risk can be defined as impacting several aspects of the project operation. In summary, however, operation risk goes to either underperformance or cost overrun associated with operation. A major consideration is that of heat rate. For example, has the electrical efficiency through improper operation and maintenance been allowed to increase in some respects so that the actual operating heat rate is well above that for which the project was designed?

Of course, when there is either cost overruns or underperformance, there is danger that an insufficient amount of money will be left to adequately compensate all parties to the transaction. Also, if the operation and maintenance is being done under contract and warranty by one company, the financial entities must be assured that the operation and maintenance company is sufficiently strong to avoid bankruptcy.

*Marketing risk.* The marketing risk in cogeneration is particularly simple yet subtle. Cogeneration has two outputs: heat and electricity. Heat is to be consumed by the host entity and the electricity to be consumed by an electric utility. Of course, there are variations and combinations, but this is essentially the case.

The sale of electricity under long-term contract is, of course, very attractive, stable, and substantially reduces marketing risk. As to the thermal output of the system, however, the major risk is that the host entity itself will go out of business. Of course, from a private sector point of view it can be argued that some of these companies may go out of business if they do not implement cogeneration.

A company can go out of business due to mismanagement, economic times, fire, theft, natural disaster, a million different reasons, many of which are under no one's control. The only real protection that the investors and lenders have is that the host entity is sufficiently strong to survive the trials and tribulations of the marketplace. In particular the industries such as concrete, textiles and carpet mills, as well as the fashion industry will have a major problem when they have guessed wrong on fashion, or when the construction industry goes through a slowdown. Guess wrong on fashion a few years in a row and you are out of business.

## C.  Security Expectations

There are only three things that investors can look at in assessing their desired or needed security in any given project. First is historical. Historical security simply means that the company has been in operation for a long time, has a good track record, and is likely to remain strong for the foreseeable future.

In situations where a company's history is in fact this strong, non-recourse financing of various sources is available. "Non-recourse" means that the lender looks to the project for full repayment and not the specific credit of the entities involved. Leasing is a classic example of non-recourse financing.

The second level of security is where the investor has a right, in the event of failure, to repossess the equipment, to enforce the contract, or to have recourse to other assets of the entities involved, such as a building or equipment that can be mortgaged and sold or repossessed and sold.

The third level of security could be called "future security," and that is where the individuals and/or corporations involved in the project put their balance sheets on the line promising to pay on their general credit in the event there is some level of project failure.

## D.  Investment Vehicles

There are five different vehicles for financing cogeneration: corporations, joint ventures, partnerships, trusts, and estates. Each has its own advantages and disadvantages.

Partnerships are particularly good in situations where a series of individuals are getting together to finance solar, wind, or other tax shelter oriented energy projects.

Corporations, on the other hand, have the advantage of being able to issue both debt and equity, while joint ventures can have both characteristics. Corporations and limited partnerships have the advantage that the liability of the investors is limited to the extent of their investment.

## E. Creative Financing

Financing of a cogeneration project may be done through several different means, such as:

1) Equipment Sale
2) Sale and Leaseback
3) Simple Lease
4) Leverage Lease
5) Equity Lease
6) Third-party Ownership
7) Tax-exempt Financing

The last of these options may be the most attractive to municipalities and local governments.

*Equipment sale.* This is the classic situation where the ultimate user goes out and buys a piece of equipment. The users issue whatever RFPs are required to purchase the system and operate and maintain the energy equipment. They typically pledge their corporate balance sheet or their corporate history usually in conjunction with some form of ongoing relationship with the bank financing the equipment.

Typically, if it is a big ticket item, one does not buy it all for cash. The three things that the borrower will be looking to are the length of the loan, the interest rate that has to be paid, and the percentage of the capital cost the lender will finance.

The two key factors are the percentage that the lender will finance and the length of the loan. The interest rate is the third level of consideration in this regard.

It is interesting to note, however, that in large conglomerates, the parent company typically provides financing for the subsidiary companies, thus allowing the parent company to issue major debt and get an overall better rate of interest in terms for financing all the aspects of their business divisions.

*Sale and leaseback.* This can take many different forms. Typically, sale and leaseback may be described as occurring where an entity purchases an installed system from an industry and then leases it back to the industry for the industry to operate. This can also, in fact, work the other way where an industry purchases some equipment on its balance sheet and then leases it to a third party operating organization that then sells energy back to the lessor host industry. This is an extremely effective method of working for certain forms of tax-exempt organizations, such as municipalities and others.

*Straight lease.* The straight lease is essentially just a loan. An industry pays a fixed amount to a company which represents a certain number of investors or a bank. The loan amount is typically calculated as a percentage of the total capital cost and is generally a good way of doing off balance sheet financing. It should be noted that there are numerous leasing organizations other than banks and conservative lending institutions looking specifically for energy projects. For example, some companies now offer to come in for a percentage of the savings to do certain energy functions for your company. This can be construed to be a lease. There are some things to be concerned about in this regard and some legalisms, so attorneys should review any lease agreements.

*Leverage lease.* This is very much like a straight lease except that a portion of this lease cost is borne by some equity investors. Such transactions involve three parties: a lessor, a lessee, and a lender to the lessor. Usually these are net finance leases (i.e., the lessee is responsible for all maintenance, insurance, and taxes). The lease term covers a large portion of the useful life of the leased property, and the lessee's payments to the lessor are sufficient to discharge the lessor's payments to the lender.

*Equity lease.* Equity leasing is an innovation in financing that is becoming more and more prevalent as time goes on. Here, the bank pays for the equipment and installation at the site, and then leases the equipment to the cogenerator. However, instead of getting a fixed amount for the lease on a monthly basis, the lease payment is a percentage of the profits on the system. This allows the bank to profit from its lease investments which are particularly risky. The bank incurs the liability in the event that the venture goes sour, but there is a greater potential reward.

*Third-party ownership.* This is very much a utility type of function that occurs today. Here, instead of the host entity investing in the plan, an entity either pre-existing or newly formed purchases the equipment, installs the system, and then sells heat and electricity to the utility and host entity. Third-party ownership, to be effective, must come as an all-encompassing package. An ongoing legal and regulatory capability (to see that the system is not interfered with), an ongoing technical management capability, and an ongoing technical review are all part of what is necessary to run these projects over a period of years. Organizations with strength in only one of those areas may not have complete understanding of these projects and may face a crisis downstream.

At this point, it would be most helpful to digress and include a few additional comments about project financing. Project financing may be described as a combination of warranties, guarantees, construction contracts, power sales agreements, and insurance contracts, which in the aggregate will provide financial guarantees, and eliminate the need for a credit-worthy party. The process of project financing, in simple terms, is to devise, negotiate and document a myriad of uniquely complex relationships. If done properly, the financing of the project will not appear as a balance sheet liability to the actual consumer of the energy, thereby enhancing borrowing power.

Project financing has become quite popular because outside capital is employed, but from a practical viewpoint this method has become an extremely difficult process of coordinating and setting in motion the wide range of multi-party negotiations necessary to consummate this type of arrangement. It is imperative that the financing team implementing the necessary tasks within this type of financing have all the requisite legal, technical, financial and management skills needed to effectively ameliorate virtually all the risks to the debt-holders.

Project financing has also become known as "third-party financing." This alternative title is sometimes used because the necessary investment funds for the project are procured from sources outside of the host entity. It should be noted that in a third-party financing arrangement, an inherent disadvantage exists in that the profits and overhead of the third-party organization will lessen the profits or savings to the using company.

However, this disadvantage is often viewed as more than compensated for in that the third-party investor has incurred all the risks associated with the project. Typically, the responsibility of the host company is to assure simply that they will take or pay for a specified amount of energy over a period long enough to adequately amortize the debt.

*Tax-exempt financing.* This sort of financing can be extremely attractive in entities such as municipalities, state governments, state universities, and other non-profit tax-exempt or government institutions. It does not make much sense to use this form for technologies with very high tax benefits such as solar and wind, but for cogeneration and other non-tax oriented technologies, tax-exempt financing can be quite attractive. The legal aspects of putting together tax-exempt financing are extremely complex. State governments, municipalities, and other non-profit, tax-exempt institutions or entities have used the tax-exempt form of financing for many years. Tax-exempt financing for such entities has come in the form of industrial development, revenue for general obligation bonds or municipal lease-purchase arrangements. The latter method of financing, municipal leasing, is becoming an increasingly significant financing tool for the governmental unit. A political subdivision or governmental unit may lease a wide range of needed equipment and facilities.

Most states and local governments are finding it more and more difficult to raise funds to implement new capital intensive projects. This economic state of affairs makes financing the critical factor for a governmental unit when implementing an energy production facility. The lease form of financing has proven most beneficial for the governmental entity wanting to increase revenues and reduce energy costs by the implementation of an energy project.

The lease form is used to help governmental entities acquire an ownership interest in the leased equipment which it cannot afford to purchase with one payment. The cost of the leased property is amortized over the lease term, interest is charged on the original obligation and the lessee receives title at the end of the lease term for a nominal sum. A significant advantage offered by the lease form is that it may allow the governmental entity to finance acquisition at tax-exempt rates without incurring debt within the meaning of state or local law.

## Financial Implications of Power Sales Negotiating

The power sales agreement between a private power producer and an electric utility is a critical and essential element of any energy-producing project.

For the small power producer, the power sales agreement may be considered the cornerstone to a successful implementation of an energy-related project. The power sales agreement, in general terms, is the foundation of the financing of any dispersed energy project where more power is being produced than is required on-site. The agreement will contain a price term which indicates what the utility is going to pay for power to the small power producer, and it delineates the regulatory, technical and operational risks to be assumed by each of the parties. The critical aspect in financing an energy-related project is the degree of inherent risk to the investor. If upon close scrutiny, the power sales agreement does not ameliorate most if not all of the completion, operation, or marketing risks inherent in a dispersed energy project, then you must look to other creditworthy parties.

The small power producer will find himself facing higher interest rates, shorter loan terms, and higher equity requirements if the technical, operational, marketing, and completion risks associated with this type of project have not been eliminated within the structure of the power sales agreement. Traditionally, banks and institutional lendors will only invest monies in a "sure thing," and therefore, the more risk that can be ameliorated in the context of a power sales agreement, the lower the financing costs, and the higher the corporate or investor interest. In general, the project will be facilitated and a higher level of reliability will be attached to the project in a technical as well as financial and legal sense.

From the view of a completion problem, the need for or possibility that the Public Utility Commission will not approve the power sales contract becomes a risk. The risk of contract approval has come into play in California under the Public Utility Commission's order OIR-2. This order now involves the PUC in the approval of all nonstandard contracts entered into with the utilities. And while there is a fairly advantageous means of getting expeditious review of the contract, this has become a risk that perhaps can be dealt with in the context of the power sales agreement.

The other problem areas under the heading of completion risks, such as schedule delays and cost overruns, could be considered standard problems in all energy projects. Therefore, it will be most appropriate to cover this type of risk, delay in construction time, within the terms of the power sales agreement with the utility.

Most, if not all of these operational risks, can be successfully dealt with within contracts outside of the power sales agreement. It appears that the only way to deal with these operational risks within the parameters of the power sales agreement itself would be writing that agreement as a take-or-pay contract where the utility is in actuality guaranteeing the debt service and/or return of equity. However, since we do not know of any utility willing to enter into a take-or-pay contract, which they are not legally obligated to enter into, there will be a considerable cost to the utility for contracting in this manner. Therefore, it is more likely that these operational risks will have to be dealt with within other contracts outside the power sales agreement.

Within the operational phase, utilities have broad experience in carrying out the operation and maintenance. Sometimes, therefore, entering into an operation and maintenance agreement with the utility is a very good idea and mutually beneficial. Be sure, however, that the utility does not exculpate itself from all risk during the operation phase and it would be incumbent upon the promoter here to see to it that the utility is intimately involved in the engineering and the construction of the project so that there is a very high degree of mutual confidence when they undertake operation and maintenance of the plant.

But the most important risk that can be dealt with is to look at relative escalation rates where operation cost is an important factor in the economics of the facility. For conventional cogeneration or other projects using coal, oil and gas as feedstock, minimum pricing is not going to do the job. Minimum pricing will provide assurances for solar, wind and other projects that do not depend on feedstocks control by other parties. For conventional cogeneration, therefore, tying the escalator and whatever energy price is paid to the feedstock cost in some way is a very, very important factor.

The third problem area would be the marketing risk. This is primarily a function of whether the escalation rates for the electricity being sold or other power being sold are high enough to account for escalations in operating costs. In addition, it is extremely important that the utility in fact continue to take the energy produced.

The extent to which the utilities take all or part of the power produced is very clearly a matter of contract. Most power sales agreements today call for the utility to take all power produced except during system emergencies or periods of minimal load. These periods tend to be extremely short in duration and account for typically less than two to three percent of the total hours in a year. Whether the percentage of time, particularly of minimal load, will increase, is a matter of great concern and should be addressed within the power sales agreement.

Perhaps the most important risk to be ameliorated in the contract is freeing the qualifying facility from the vagaries of future public utility commissions. If the Public Utility Commission can order readjustment or renegotiation of the contract, then the marketing risk will be placed squarely on the qualifying facility. There is no risk to the utility whatsoever in that case. However, if the utility bears some of this risk by allowing perhaps for advance approval of the contract by the PUC and no more, this appears to be a reasonable compromise so that the utility has some assurance that it will not be exposing its shareholders and its ratepayers while at the same time providing a forum for review of the contract to protect the shareholders and ratepayers as well as the cogenerator or small power producer.

For certain projects such as wind or solar, the utilities have on occasion provided the land for the project. When this is done, they have also occasionally provided guarantees that solar insolation at the site or the mean average wind speed will be sufficient for the project to reasonably amortize debt. In effect, the utilities are guaranteeing, usually within a band, the availability of sun or wind at that site. Now this is an extremely important risk, particularly with what must be characterized as more "exotic" technologies.

In sum, it is extremely important to remember that power sales agreements by themselves do not ameliorate all the risks involved in a project. Above all, there is no substitute for good system design. And remember that project financing (so popular in the dispersed energy field) is just a combination of contractual agreements that in the aggregate provided debt service guarantee instead of one creditworthy party. Therefore, we as lawyers have the responsibility to devise, negotiate, and document a myriad of uniquely complex relationships. The fluidity of these relationships cannot be overstated. Positions, changing with time, cause ripple effects ranging from insignificant to major. Often technical, financial, and management skills together with legal insight must remold the whole range of agreements entered into based upon minor variations in any one of the agreements but particularly the power sales agreements.

Essentially, a power sales agreement is documentation of a business deal between two parties negotiating within a highly complex regulatory framework. It is not an arms-length negotiation in a private enterprise sense. It is not a willing buyer and a willing seller. It is a willing seller and a regulated entity that has grown up as a government-sponsored monopoly. PURPA, OIR-2, and the state laws all over this country simply have defined a regulatory framework that establishes the beginning point for negotiation between two interested parties, one of whom may have been brought to the table kicking and screaming.

This is not to say that the negotiating power is necessarily one-sided in any sense. It should not be. Power sales agreements within the context of PURPA are supposed to be economically neutral. And in that sense perhaps the best definition of a good power sales agreement is a record of it as a good business deal for the cogenerator, small power producer, ratepayers and utility shareholders.

It must be noted at this point that the power sales agreement is not the only component to the financing picture, but the project manager or coordinator must include an analysis of the fuel supply contracts, insurance contracts, contractors' performance and completion bonds, equipment specifications and warranties, and many other documents that will complete the financing puzzle.

## Conclusion

A well-designed system is the bottom line. Poor equipment, engineering, operation and maintenance can never be contracted away. We must design the systems to be used with a view of the future that is grounded solidly in operational experience. Legal, regulatory, financial as well as technical risks must be designed out of projects.

Creative financing is just what it says, a creative, innovative, or perhaps even artistic approach to deal-making that identifies the requirements of all the parties involved and then creates a legal, financial, regulatory structure that will accommodate the myriad economic and other needs of the entities.

Most entities are not in the utility business. Diversification into that business requires expertise. Creative financing can be an answer to struggling companies' problems, particularly where they have other capital obligations or process-related plans that should be instituted.

# Chapter 9

# Leveraged Lease
or Limited Partnership?
A Cogeneration Case Study

Project Finance Group
Dean Witter Reynolds Inc.

If management is to assess alternative energy system financing methods properly, it needs detailed analysis of the various options available.

Such an analysis has been prepared for Parsons Brinckerhoff Development Group (PBDG) by the Project Finance Group of Dean Witter Reynolds Inc. for a combined cycle cogeneration facility of 25 megawatts. The project will cost approximately $27 million; project completion is expected by 1984.

One part of the Parsons Brinckerhoff Development Group financing report reviews the pros and cons of leveraged leasing versus a limited partnership arrangement. It is presented here as an example of the complex individual financing structures which must be created and evaluated before energy projects can be undertaken.

### Leveraged Lease

*Purpose*

A leveraged lease will enable PBDG to obtain a low financing cost by transferring to an external party the tax benefits of the project which PBDG cannot directly utilize. The project assets and related debt will not be recorded on PBDG's balance sheet. PBDG will obtain any development fees and operating profits from the project.

### Structure

A tax-oriented investor purchases the completed project from PBDG. The purchase price is financed in part by the investor's own funds (approximately 20%) with the balance borrowed from outside lenders (approximately 80%) on a non-recourse basis.

The project is leased back to PBDG by the investor (i.e. the lessor) for a rental sufficient to cover debt service and to provide a cash return on investment. Upon expiration of the lease term, the project belongs to the lessor and PBDG must negotiate a further lease or purchase if it wishes to continue to use the project. The lease is on a net basis with all maintenance and operating expenses paid by PBDG. PBDG will unconditionally be obligated to make all lease payments even if the plant is not operating. Sample lease terms and flow diagram are shown in Figures 9-1 and 9-2.

This lease should be distinguished from the ground lease between the site owner/energy user and the lessor. Under these documents, the lessor will have the right to remove the project upon the expiration of the ground lease terms.

PBDG obtains operating control of the project and sells at "avoided cost" the electricity generated by the project to the local public utility pursuant to a power sales agreement. This contract will probably consist of a firm capacity payment supported by a PBDG performance guarantee and an energy charge paid on a take-if-delivered basis. The lenders will be given an assignment of the power sales agreement as well as a security interest in the project.

### Tax Treatment

The lease of the project will be structured as a "true lease" which will meet Internal Revenue Service Guidelines. Under this type of lease, the lessor is treated as the owner of the project and obtains the tax benefits of ownership.

The available tax benefits include the 10% regular investment tax credit (ITC) on all property.

## SAMPLE TERMS OF LEVERAGED LEASE

| | |
|---|---|
| **Project:** | Combined-Cycle Cogeneration Facility located in California. |
| **Project Cost:** | Approximately $27 million. |
| **Project Completion:** | Expected by 1984. |
| **Lessee:** | PBDG |
| **Lessor:** | An Owner Trust to be established for the benefit of the equity investors (the owner participants) located by the investment banker. |
| **Lessor's Cost:** | Equal to the Project Cost. The Owner Participants will provide equity equal to approximately 20% of Lessor's Cost. |
| **Long-Term Debt:** | Long-Term Lenders arranged by the investment bankers will provide approximately 80% of Lessor's Cost by making loans to the Owner Trust (the Long-Term Debt). The Long-Term Debt will likely be fixed rate debt from the outset of the Lease. The Long-Term Debt will be secured by an assignment of the Owner Trust's rights under the Lease (i.e. primarily the rental stream) and a first lien on the Project. |
| **Lease:** | Twenty years. |
| **Net Lease:** | The Lessee will have the entire responsibility for maintenance, repair and operation of the Project and all expenses and liabilities in connection therewith, and will keep the Project free of all liens and in compliance with all applicable laws and regulations. |
| **Insurance:** | The Lessee will provide insurance with financially sound and reputable insurers covering such risks. |
| **Event of Loss:** | If the Project is destroyed, an event of loss will be deemed to have occurred, whereupon the Lessee will pay the Lessor an amount equal to the stipulated loss value of the Project. Title to and legal responsibility for the Project will immediately pass to the Lessee. |
| **Option to Renew:** | The Lessee will have an option to renew the Lease for a renewal term at the fair market rental value. |
| **Option to Purchase:** | The Lessee will have the option to purchase the Project at the end of the Lease term or any renewal term for fair market value. |

Figure 9-1. Leveraged lease

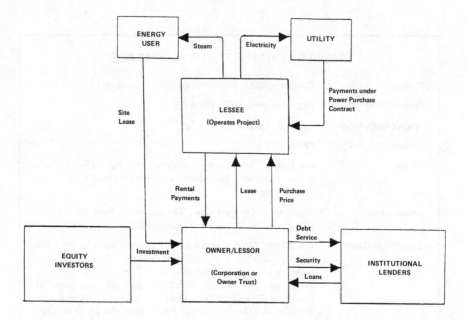

Figure 9-2.  Leveraged lease

Property "owned" by a municipality is not eligible for the investment or energy tax credits. While the project will be located on
municipal property, the project is physically moveable and the
terms of the various leases will be such that the lessor will have the
right to remove the project assets. Therefore, the assets will not be
considered as owned by the municipality and will be eligible for the
tax credits. However, a review of the ground leases involved will be
required to confirm this treatment.

The project also qualifies for accelerated cost recovery (ACRS)
depreciation deductions, in all likelihood over the five year schedule.
These tax benefits enable the lessor to quote a rental to PBDG at a
rate substantially less than the pretax rate PBDG would pay if it had
financed the project cost directly. In addition, PBDG can deduct the
rental payments as they accrue.

## Accounting Treatment

The financing is designed to comply with Statement No. 13 of the Financial Accounting Standards Board (FASB 13). This enables the project assets and the related debt to not be reflected on PBDG's balance sheet. The obligation to pay rent would be recorded in a footnote.

## Regulatory Treatment

The project will be considered to be a "topping cycle" cogeneration facility. Five percent or more of the energy produced in a topping cycle facility must be in the form of steam supplied to the user, and the system must meet certain efficiency standards. Also, as noted above, the project must receive an exemption from the requirements of the Fuel Use Act of 1978 on the basis that it is a cogeneration facility meeting certain required efficiency standards. It is assumed that PBDG has made the necessary calculations and that the project qualifies as a cogeneration facility entitled to a Fuel Use Act exemption.

Under current provisions of PURPA, the utility is required to purchase electricity made available from the project at an "avoided cost" rate. PURPA also exempts the project from rate regulation.

The utility has published "standard offers" to purchase power at the avoided cost rate, but it is believed that these do not have to be accepted "as is." Rather, they can form the basis for negotiations between the utility and PBDG.

## Sources of Funds

Lease equity for the project is provided by a tax-oriented corporate investor. Currently, there are relatively few conventional leveraged lease equity sources willing to commit to a transaction which will not be in service until 1984. However, when the project is scheduled to be placed in service, lease equity funds should be available. There should exist a variety of sources including closely held corporations which are subject to the "at risk" requirement. In the interim, prior to the long-term financing, the investment banker can place a construction loan for the project on behalf of PBDG.

Debt for the project will be obtained from institutional lenders through a private placement. The lender will obtain a lien on the project assets, the rental stream and the power sales agreement.

### Advantages to PBDG

- Financing cost reflects the transfer of the tax benefits of project ownership.
- Probable off-balance sheet treatment under current accounting practices.
- PBDG retains the development fee and operating profits from the project.

### Disadvantages to PBDG

- Loss of project residual value.
- Potential necessity for PBDG to indemnify against loss of tax benefits.
- PBDG is obligated to pay rent even if the utility purchases no power from the project.

## Limited Partnership

### Purpose

A limited partnership enables PBDG to transfer the tax benefits of the project to third parties to the extent they are not usable by PBDG. PBDG retains a share of any project residual value and can have an option to buy back the balance from the limited partners.

### Structure

A partnership is formed to purchase the completed project from PBDG. The purchase price is financed in part by partners' equity contributions (approximately 20%) with the balance being borrowed by the partnership from third-party lenders on a fixed-rate basis (approximately 80%). PBDG acts as general partner and individuals located by the investment banker invest as limited partners. The general partner invests in the partnership in an amount of 1% of the equity, while the limited partners contribute 99% of the equity.

The liability of each limited partner is limited to the amount of his investment in the partnership plus any amount required to satisfy the "at risk" requirement discussed below. The general partner is personally liable for all obligations of the partnership and has control of all business activities of the partnership subject to the terms of the limited partnership agreement. In addition, the general partner must have a net worth of at least 15% of the partnership equity to satisfy tax law requirements. Sample terms for a limited partnership and flow diagram are shown in Figures 9-3 and 9-4.

The partnership sells electricity on an "avoided cost" basis to the public utility pursuant to a power sales agreement. This contract, as in the leveraged lease case, will probably consist of a firm capacity payment supported by a PBDG performance guarantee and an energy charge paid on a take-if-delivered basis.

The lenders are secured by a first lien on the assets and have a senior call on all revenues generated by the project. The debt is recourse to the partnership to the extent necessary to satisfy the "at risk" requirement. The amount that is recourse can vary each year according to a variety of factors including the level of realizable tax benefits, partnership income, and the initial equity infusion.

Revenues from the project are allocated in the following order of priority:

1) to the payment of principal and interest on all loans to the partnership;

2) to the payment of operating and maintenance expenses;

3) to the general partner and the limited partners as follows:

a) until the sum of the previous cash distributions and tax benefits to the limited partners exceeds the limited partners' capital contribution, 1% to the general partner and 99% to the limited partners; and

b) when the sum of the previous cash distributions and tax benefits to the limited partners exceeds the limited partners' capital contribution, 30% to the general partner and 70% to the limited partners.

## SAMPLE TERMS OF LIMITED PARTNERSHIP

**Project:** Combined-Cycle Cogeneration Facility located in California.

**Project Cost:** Approximately $27 million.

**Project Completion:** Expected by 1984.

**Owner:** A Partnership to be formed for the purposes of investing in the Project.

**General Partner:** PBDG

**Limited Partners:** Investors seeking equity participation in alternative energy projects.

**Nature of the Partnership:** The liability of each Limited Partner will be limited to the amount of its investment in the Partnership. The General Partner will be personally liable for all obligations of the Partnership.

**Capital Contributions:** The General Partner will be required to invest in or pledge assets to the Partnership in an amount at least equal to 1% of the equity provided by the Limited Partners. The Limited Partner share is to be determined subject to the availability of Debt.

**Term of the Partnership:** The Partnership will likely terminate on December 31, 2003 (i.e., after no more than 20 years) unless dissolved sooner.

**Debt:** The Partnership will borrow approximately 80% of the cost of the Project. The Debt will be secured by a first lien on the assets and will have senior call on all revenues generated by the Project. The Debt will be recourse to the partnership to the extent necessary to satisfy the "at risk" requirement; it will otherwise be non-recourse.

**Debt Amortization:** Level repayments of principal and interest will commence when the plant is placed in service.

**Allocation of Revenue:** Revenue will likely be allocated in the following order:
1) to the payment of principal and interest on all Debt of the Partnership;
2) to the payment of operating and maintenance expenses;
3) to the General Partner and the Limited Partners, as follows:
    (a) if the sum of the previous cash distributions to

the Limited partners do not exceed the Limited Partners' capital contribution and tax benefits, 1% to the General Partner and 99% to the Limited Partners; or

(b) if the sum of the previous cash distributions to the Limited Partners exceed the Limited Partners' capital contribution and tax benefits, 30% to the General Partner and 70% to the Limited Partners.

**Insurance:** The General Partner will maintain at the expense of the Partnership such liability and casualty and other insurance as necessary to protect the Partnership's property and in accordance with prudent industry practice.

**Dissolution:** The General Partner may elect to dissolve the Partnership by purchasing the Limited Partners' interest at any time after the fifth year if the Limited Partners have received previous cash distributions in excess of the Limited Partners' initial capital contribution and tax benefits.

If prior to December 31, 2003 the Partnership has not been dissolved, the affairs of the Partnership shall cease and its assets liquidated as promptly as practical. Liquidation proceeds shall be distributed to pay Partnership debts, to pay the General Partner a liquidation fee and the balance to the Limited Partners in proportion to their respective capital accounts. Upon termination of the partnership, the General Partner shall contribute to the Partnership any deficit balance in its capital account.

Figure 9-3. Limited partnership

Payments to the general partner and their approximate amounts are as follows:

1) Management Fee. Compensation for services rendered in managing the operations of the partnership. Normally, this fee will equal 5% to 6% of gross revenues of the partnership.

2) Distributions. When the limited partners have received previous cash distributions and tax benefits in excess of their initial capital contributions as described above, the general partner

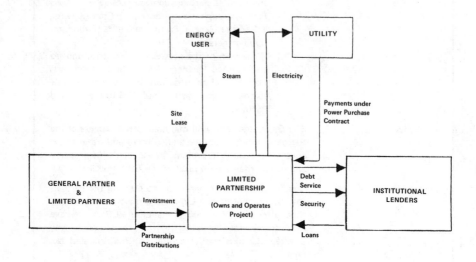

**Figure 9-4. Limited partnership**

will receive distributions equal to 30%. Prior to that point, the general partner will receive 1%.

3) Liquidation Proceeds. Upon dissolution of the partnership, assets will be liquidated and net proceeds after payment of any liabilities will be distributed. Liquidation distributions would be made in accordance with the partner's capital accounts which would have been adjusted to reflect income and losses, contributions and distributions allocated to such partner.

It should be noted that other allocation, fee and capital percentages can be established depending upon market considerations and PBDG needs, though the figures cited above may be considered typical.

*Tax Treatment*

Under the revenue allocation procedure described above, 99% of project distributions and consequently 99% of project tax benefits are received by the limited partners as long as the sum of previous cash distributions and tax benefits to the limited partners do not exceed the limited partners' capital contribution. As in the leveraged lease case, the tax benefits include ITC and ACRS depreciation deductions. The limited partnership format thus enables the bulk of the project's tax benefits to flow to the limited partners rather than PBDG.

A limited partner's share of the taxable loss of a partnership which may be deducted on the limited partner's individual tax return cannot exceed the tax basis of the partnership interest (which includes accumulated partnership income distributions) and, with respect to noncorporate partners, the aggregate amount with respect to which the limited partner is "at risk" as of the close of the applicable tax year. Similarly, the ITC would be limited to the taxpayer's amount "at risk." Nonrecourse loans are not included in a partner's "at risk" amount.* As discussed previously, one of the structuring goals of the limited partnership will be the need to keep "at risk" recourse loans at a minimum.

## Accounting Treatment

Each partner reflects its own pro rata share of ownership including income, assets, and liabilities in the partnership on its balance sheet and income statement.

## Regulatory Treatment

As in the leveraged lease alternative, the project will qualify as a cogeneration facility under PURPA and receive commensurate benefits, as long as the conditions cited earlier are met.

Since the partnership interests will be considered "securities," their offering and sale will be subject to the Securities Act of 1933. This Act requires the filing of a registration statement with the Securities and Exchange Commission (SEC) in connection with the offering and sale of any securities. Filing, however, may be avoided if the partnership interests are offered and sold only to a limited number of sophisticated investors in a private placement.

---

*For ITC purposes, up to 80% of asset cost may be financed by a non-recourse loan from a bank or other financial institution.

## Sources of Funds

Limited partners for the project are individual investors who have higher risk profiles and tax rates than institutional investors. The investment banker will market the project to individual investors through its extensive retail brokerage system.

As in the leveraged lease alternative, debt for the project is obtained from institutional lenders through a private placement. The lenders obtain a first lien on the project assets and have a senior call on project revenues. The debt is recourse to the partnership to the extent necessary to satisfy the "at risk" requirement.

### Advantages to PBDG

- PBDG can transfer, to the extent it desires, the tax benefits of project ownership to the limited partners.

- PBDG can receive fees and some project revenues from a relatively small investment.

- The partnership retains control of any project residual value and PBDG therefore controls its share.

### Disadvantages to PBDG

- Debt is recourse to the partnership to the degree necessary to satisfy the "at risk" requirement.

- Have risks of ownership as general partner including the unlikely event of no utility payments, without full benefits of ownership (benefits also flow to the limited partners).

## Ownership

### Purpose

Although PBDG has indicated that it would like to transfer the tax benefits of project ownership to third parties, nonetheless, the case was considered in which PBDG owned and financed the project directly. Under this structure, all benefits of the transaction—the development fee, operating profits, tax deductions and credits, and project residual value—flow to PBDG.

## Structure

The project is built and owned by a newly-formed subsidiary of PBDG. Construction and permanent financing is provided by borrowings from institutional lenders, possibly on a non-recourse basis.

## Tax Treatment

All of the tax benefits of ownership discussed in the previous sections flow to PBDG's subsidiary and, through the filing of a consolidated return, to PBDG.

## Accounting Treatment

The project assets and liabilities are recorded on PBDG's financial statements.

## Regulatory Treatment

As in the preceding cases, assuming that the necessary conditions are met, the project will qualify as a cogeneration facility under PURPA and receive commensurate benefits.

## Source of Funds

Equity for the project will be provided by PBDG. As in the preceding cases, debt for the project is obtained from institutional lenders through a private placement. The lenders again obtain a first lien on the project assets and have a senior call on project revenues.

## Advantages to PBDG

- PBDG obtains all benefits of project ownership.
- PBDG is not required to satisfy needs of lessors or limited partners.

## Disadvantages to PBDG

- PBDG assumes all risks and is unable to spread them to other participants.
- PBDG may be unable to use tax benefits in the early years of the project.

## Financing Costs

### Leveraged Lease

The effective financing cost to a lessee (i.e., PBDG) in a leveraged lease is typically expressed as a lease rate which is defined as the discount rate at which the present value of the lease rental payments equals the cost of the leased project.

The lease equity market, since it is relatively small, tends to function less "perfectly" than other financial markets. Often, wide variations in lease rates will be experienced among competing lessors. Lessors differ in their investment yield which is principally determined by the rental stream paid by the lessee, the residual value at the end of the lease term, the tax benefits associated with the project and the lessor's ability to utilize them, and the rate on the debt. The debt rate, in turn, is a function of the overall level of interest rates for the desired term, the collateral value of the project, the credit of the lessee, and other credit support mechanisms such as power purchase contract with the utility.

A computer program is typically used to calculate the lease rate and rental stream, given fixed values for all other variables. Using the lease model, the cost to PBDG as a lessee in the leveraged lease is estimated to be 11.45%. Key assumptions in determining this rate include:

- Lessor target pre-tax yield of 30%.
- ITC is 10% combined with a depreciation basis reduction of one-half of the ITC.
- 15% pre-tax debt rate.
- Five year ACRS property.
- 20 year lease and debt terms.
- Zero residual and salvage value.
- 1984 in-service date.
- Semi-annual rentals and debt payments in arrears.

These assumptions reflect recent market conditions and several elements may vary for the actual financing.

## Limited Partnership

The financing cost to a general partner in a limited partnership is difficult to determine accurately as it depends on many variables such as cash distribution percentages, management fees, and amount of debt used. Furthermore, the cost to a lessee of a leveraged lease is not directly comparable to a partnership cost as risks and rewards are allocated differently under each structure. PBDG's role as a general partner would be quite different from that of a lessee. Nevertheless, the cost to a general partner in a limited partnership can be estimated on a very rough basis by a method similar to that used for the leveraged lease alternative.

Under this method, the cost to PBDG of the limited partnership financing alternative is estimated to be 10.03%. Key assumptions in determining this rate include:

- Investor target after-tax yield is 12.25%.

- ITC applicable is 10% with depreciation basis reduction of one-half of the ITC.

- Investor has a 50% tax rate.

- 15% pre-tax debt rate.

# Chapter 10

# State Policy Initiatives for Financing Energy Efficiency in Public Buildings

John C. MacLean

*Editor's Note:*

The Higher Education Energy Task Force is developing a College and University Energy Management and Financing Program. The continuing program, which began in November 1981, has been made possible by a grant awarded by The John A. Hartford Foundation of New York City. The Higher Education Energy Task Force is jointly sponsored by three higher educational associations: The American Council on Education, The National Association of College and University Business Officers, and the Association of Physical Plant Administrators.

The program is designed to help U.S. colleges, universities, and non-profit institutions reduce their current energy consumption by giving administrators the management, financial, and technical information necessary to make energy conservation decisions which can increase the present 10 percent savings by another 20 to 25 percent.

This chapter reflects HEETF's research into financing options, which focuses on the present financing barriers an institution faces when considering an energy efficiency program, and on methods for providing institutions with access to the capital markets available for energy efficiency investments. The financial options are internal funding, development fund raising, leasing, tax-exempt bond financing, the use of energy service companies, and financing mechanisms which encourage expanded use of private capital by allowing private investors to receive the tax deductions and tax credits from investments in campus facilities.

---

### Energy Efficiency

Energy cost is a predictable annually recurring building operating expense. An energy efficiency investment can be conceived as a means to restructure this liability. By substituting capital for energy, the least cost energy system can be achieved.

For example, one major New England medical center was built with a design energy consumption rating of 955,000 Btu/square foot/year, the equivalent of a barrel of oil for every seven square feet of floor space annually, an incredible quantity even for medical buildings which normally are very energy intensive. Operations and maintenance improvements and low cost conservation measures lowered energy use to 552,000 Btu/sq ft/yr in FY 81. Plant staff have identified $3 million in major mechanical system improvements that could reduce consumption down to an estimated 360,000 Btu/sq ft/yr, saving $1.3 million in the first year. Given an energy price escalation rate of 10 percent annually, over $23 million of state taxpayer monies could be saved over ten years from this project alone. Yet, it has awaited funding for over a year.

All states face the same problem: (1) rising energy costs, (2) excellent investment opportunities in efficiency improvements, yet, (3) limited capital resources to make the investments. The legislative response to this problem we recommend is threefold:

- improve the use of internal resources by making changes in budgeting and accounting procedures,

- utilize bonding capacity for financing energy improvements, recognizing their long-term investment attributes, and,

- access private sector capital as a substitute for limited public resources.

States should adopt a policy of promoting all feasible energy efficiency projects when they are cost-effective and can reduce long-term energy expenditures. Energy efficiency offers numerous public economic benefits: jobs in the conservation industry, a reduced loss of purchasing power from the local economy to pay for energy "imports," the healthy economic multiplier effects of increasing the local circulation of goods and services, and lower costs for public services.

State legislators have a choice: to continue to pay ever increasing energy costs or organize financing to take advantage of dollar saving energy efficiency opportunities. A dollar saved on energy is one additional dollar that can be spent on libraries, staff salaries, research, program development, etc.

Energy efficiency investments (EEI's) can substantially improve the long-term financial viability of an institution. Many public managers do not take an investment perspective when analyzing a conservation project. A $100,000 EEI with a three-year simple payback may have an excellent return on investment and be economically very sound but it is viewed as an expense. The budget must be balanced this year, so the item is cut.

The lack of long-term outlook derives in part from the political and electoral process. Once an energy saving opportunity has been identified, delay in implementation results in lost potential savings. The process of implementation and capital budgeting needs to be expedited and streamlined. The loss of potential savings due to delay represents an opportunity cost that should be quantified and used in the financial analysis of alternative funding mechanisms. This direct equation between energy and dollars needs to be made in the minds of public administrators.

## Fiscal Impact of Energy Costs

State legislatures need to be concerned with energy efficiency in the buildings which the state owns and operates and have particular fiscal or public responsibility for schools, hospitals, colleges and universities, and municipal facilities because these facilities are operated in the public purpose.

High energy costs have taken their toll on municipal budgets. A 1980 survey of 1,550 local governments by the International City Management Association revealed that energy expenditures were the second highest line item in the annual operating budgets of 56 percent of the local governments surveyed.

Nationwide, higher education spent an estimated $3.2 billion on energy costs in FY 1981/82. This amount is equivalent to the salaries of 129,000 full-time faculty, $363 for every full-time student, or one-and-one-half times the budget of college libraries nationally. A dollar spent on energy is one less dollar available for academic programs. The estimated energy expenditure for public schools (K–12) is $4.5 billion; for hospitals, over $3.4 billion, equating to $2,517 per bed per year.

These costs will continue to rise, especially in the wake of natural gas deregulation. For example, two-thirds of the nation's hospitals use natural gas as their primary fuel. Given that natural gas prices double by 1986, which is expected under the current Natural Gas Policy Act deregulation schedule, $900 million will be added to hospital fuel bills. Even though the price of oil has fallen recently, from approximately $34 to $28 per barrel, the economic incentive for improved energy efficiency is still as great as ever. Remember that in 1979 oil prices were $14/barrel; in 1972 they were $1.50/barrel.

### Decline in Federal Support

The Department of Energy's Institutional Grants Program, popularly known as the Schools and Hospitals Program, is being phased out. Funding for its fourth grant cycle (FY 82) was reduced to $48 million, with the Reagan Administration supporting elimination of funding altogether. Whatever funding level is achieved for the fifth cycle, it will be grossly inadequate to finance all the cost-effective EEI's that are being identified within these sectors. DOE is searching for policy initiatives which will promote the financing of energy conservation, work with the private sector and market forces, and require a minimal budgetary commitment from the federal Treasury.

This decline in federal support further shifts responsibility for energy financing to state and local initiatives.

## Improving the Use of
## Current Resources

All public agencies follow formal budgeting procedures for allocating capital funds. Several changes in budgeting and accounting procedures could improve the use of public funds for financing energy projects.

### *Policy Initiative #1: Develop Incentives*

Individual public agencies typically do not have incentives to save energy. If energy savings are achieved these saved dollars revert back to the state general coffers. Few, if any, dollars are returned to the institution which generated the savings. This problem has been emphasized repeatedly during our consulting with public higher education institutions.

If future energy budgets are based on historic energy expenditures, the agency may have a positive disincentive to conserve. One institutional manager, in anticipation of a governor's mandate to cut utility costs by a fixed percentage of existing expenditures, deliberately refrained from implementing all energy conservation measures in order to protect future budget allocations.

The solution is to localize the incentive to conserve energy with the end user by allowing individual agencies to retain all or part of their energy savings. If made available, these savings could be used by the individual agency for reinvestment in further energy efficiency measures or for program-related expenditures. Such a policy needs to be balanced with the need for central agencies to retain control of appropriations. Three important issues have to be addressed in designing an incentive program: how far into the future should energy costs savings be calculated, how should subsequent years' energy budgets be calculated, and what stipulations should be placed on the use of saved energy dollars.

In the higher education sector, a small percentage of avoided energy costs are being distributed back to the individual campus administrations within the State University of New York system. California, Utah, and North Dakota are also investigating such a policy. The Iowa Board of Regents used to receive energy savings, and invested it 100 percent in further energy projects, but the program was rescinded by the state legislature under budgetary pressures.

Considerable savings also comes from how well a building is operated and maintained. Incentives need to be developed for on line managers. The value of increased physical plant personnel devoted to energy conservation needs to be recognized. Often additional personnel can save annually several times the costs of their salaries in saved energy costs. These opportunities should be taken advantage of.

### *Policy Initiative #2: Provide Budget Flexibility*

If an agency has identified an energy conservation measure which will repay its initial costs in one year or less, it should be allowed to spend or transfer funds out of its utility/fuel account to implement this measure. This practice is not allowed in many state institutions and prevents expeditious implementation of conservation measures. Massachusetts is considering taking this logic another step further by allowing funds to be spent from the fuel account budget line for lease, debt service and other forms of energy efficiency financing payments *if* the transaction creates a positive cash flow, that is payments are less than energy savings. This policy would encourage use of innovative financing programs and give institutional managers the budgetary flexibility to initiate such transactions.

Budget issues are especially critical in the hospital sector, where over 70 percent of revenue derives from medical insurance reimbursement, Medicaid/Medicare, and Blue Cross/Blue Shield. If reimbursement formulas are based on cost, and energy costs are reduced, a hospital's revenue will suffer.

### *Policy Initiative #3: Present Energy Projects Separately*

EEI's compete directly for funds with projects that are vital and directly related to an agency's mission. Many agencies operate under an annual capital budget ceiling. Even when cost-effective EEI's have been identified and engineered, they are not always submitted for appropriation. At one public university a ceiling had been imposed on total capital budget requests. Administrators knew that utility bills would be paid, no matter their amount. They therefore had no incentive to submit all identified EEI's in their capital request.

Presenting energy efficiency improvements separately for capital budgeting will encourage them to be brought up the line. Further, it will allow their financial returns to be highlighted and other funding sources to be explored.

If internal funds are lacking a state government should consider long-term bond financing or avail itself of the many sources of private capital that are rapidly becoming available for financing energy improvements. A properly financed energy efficiency investment will match debt service payments with the flow of energy cost savings and thereby generate an immediate positive cash flow back to the energy-using institution.

## Tax-Exempt Bonds

Tax-exempt bonds (TEB's) are the traditional method for public institutions to finance capital projects. The two types of government bonds are: (1) general obligation (GO) bonds, and (2) revenue bonds.

### General Obligation Bonds

General obligation bonds are secured by the full faith and credit and taxing powers of the issuing government. Many states have reached their limit to GO bonding or otherwise cannot afford to utilize their general obligation bonding capacity for energy efficiency. Bonding capacity is a scarce resource that must be husbanded for other essential government projects. GO bonds also require voter approval, a process that can delay project financing.

However, because they are an established available method for general purpose capital expenditures, general obligation bonds are the first option for long-term financing of public building energy improvements.

*Policy Initiative #4: Grant and Loan Programs Financed with General Obligation Bonds*

The federal schools and hospitals program remains an excellent model for grants programs operated at the state level. This program could be assumed and expanded by state governments using state general obligation bond financing.

New Jersey issued $50 million in general obligation bonds in November, 1980 to finance energy improvements in the 40 million square feet of state-owned buildings. A bill is pending currently for a $25 million issue for conservation grants program to local school districts.

Massachusetts is considering an innovative program for financing energy efficiency projects for state and municipal facilities to be funded by general obligation bonds. The original bond principal would establish a revolving loan fund. Individual loan terms would be arranged so that debt service payments would be less than annual energy savings. Debt service would be deposited back into the loan fund for reinvestment in additional projects. $45 million was originally proposed to initiate the program; this amount has been reduced to $10 million in a bill now before the state legislature.

Nebraska has committed $5 million per year for the next five years for a public schools energy conservation grants program. The state grant covers 75 percent of the project costs, requiring a 25 percent matching local contribution. The funding derives from oil and gas severance taxes, which, of course, all states do not enjoy.

Herricks School District, Long Island, N.Y., and Jefferson County, Colorado, recently gained voter approval for bond issues solely to finance energy conservation projects. These issues were presented to the voters in terms of the total saved tax dollars which the school districts would experience as a result of the EEI's. The debt service on the bonds was designed to be less than the energy savings, thus generating a positive cash flow from the project. Voters apparently understood this logic.

*Revenue Bonds*

Revenue bonds typically are secured by the revenues of the project being financed where the cash flow from operation of the project serves as security and source of bond debt service. Because energy efficiency projects save costs rather than generate revenues they are not eligible for a strictly self-supported project financing.

Two exceptions exist to this rule. First, if the project generates power (electricity or steam) for sale, then those revenues could be used as security. Second, a private business entity could intervene between the bond authority and the public institution. Using the bond proceeds, the private firm would make energy efficiency improvements under one of several contractual arrangements. The payments from the institution to the private firm would serve as the revenue stream to secure the bonds. The advantage of project revenue financing is that it is "off credit" for the institution; the institution's capacity to borrow for other purposes is not diminished by the transaction.

Many state governments have established health and education facilities authorities which can issue revenue bonds for capital projects and equipment for hospitals, colleges and universities, and schools. The issuing authorities have no taxing power. Bonds issued by these authorities are not a debt of the state or local government which established them. No government obligation is created by these bond issues. These authorities are an ideal and identifiable vehicle for energy project financing.

*Policy Initiative #5: Encourage financing of energy projects via state health and educational facilities authorities and other bond authorities*

All established state bond authorities that can issue bonds for energy projects should be identified. Legislation may be required to extend an authority's mandate to include energy project financing.

The key to these bond issues is creating adequate security for the bonds. Most often a bond beneficiary, e.g., a college, must offer its "full faith and credit" to secure a bond. Specific sources of institutional revenue can also be pledged: a set portion of tuition revenues, special compulsory student fees, e.g. a plant improvement fee, dormitory revenues, state government revenues, etc. The revenue stream being pledged need not be directly related to the project being financed.

Secondary security—assets which can be used to repay bond debt in event of institutional default—also must be arranged. Bond insurance, letters of credit, or collateral, e.g., a first mortgage on real property or escrowed cash and securities, are the common sources of secondary security.

*Limitations to widespread use of TEB's.* Three major disadvantages exist which limit widespread use of TEB's for college and university energy improvements. First, for most underwriting firms and issuing authorities, $2 million is the minimum size bond issue due to the high transaction and administrative costs involved. Small institutions may not be able to assemble this large an energy efficiency investment program. Second, many institutions cannot qualify for the minimum credit rating required to make a bond issue marketable. Third, not all private institutions have access to a bonding authority.

*Bond fund pools.* Creation of a bond funds pool may be a solution to these first two problems. A bond funds pool is a means to offer tax-exempt bond financing for numerous smaller projects, and minimize the expense and inconvenience of issuing a bond by utilizing the proceeds of a single issue. Funds could be made available to institutions which otherwise would not take the initiative themselves to finance energy programs.

Bond proceeds would be loaned to individual institutions by the issuing authority. The main key security of the issue lies in the required terms of the loan agreements which the issuing authority enters into with each borrowing institution. The loan standards are clearly spelled out in the bond indenture. They generally require that the borrowing institution have an investment grade rating, an irrevocable letter of credit from an approved financial institution, or have escrowed certain collateral to secure the loan.

There are two types of bond fund pools: a blind pool and a composite pool. A blind pool does not identify specifically the projects to be funded or the borrowers of the bond proceeds before the issue. A composite pool, on the other hand, assembles all the borrowers and projects before the issue, thereby providing an opportunity to prescreen all credits and create, with greater certainty, a secure issue.

In the interim period between the time the bond proceeds are received and the time the loans are made, the authority is able to arbitrage the funds. The issuing authority has three years to disburse all the funds according to I.R.S. regulations.

Typical interest rates currently range from 10–13 percent with a term of six to ten years. The authority lends at a rate slightly higher than the bond issue, the income from the interest spread going to fund the administrative costs of the pool. The period of the loans will range from three to ten years. No loans can be outstanding past the term of the bond issue.

*Working models.* Authorities in California, Colorado, Illinois, and Missouri have issued bonds to create blind pools to finance major equipment purchases for hospitals. The Maryland Energy Finance Administration is assembling a composite pool to finance commercial and industrial energy efficiency projects.

*Advantages of tax-exempt bonds.* Interest income from TEB's is tax-exempt to the bondholder and, therefore, they carry lower interest rates. The term of bond financing for renovation purposes is normally 10 years. Bond proceeds can be used for any type of energy efficiency improvement. This combination of lower interest rates, longer term, and flexibility in use of funds makes TEB's an attractive source of capital.

## Utilizing Private Capital

Fiscal pressure on states and localities due to cutbacks in Federal appropriations, tax revolt, lower tax revenues, higher borrowing costs and debt limits are severely restricting the amount of current tax revenues and bonding capacity that state and local governments can devote to energy projects. Several financing mechanisms exist which can fund energy efficiency improvements in public buildings utilizing private sector capital. Although none of these options have been much used to date, the fiscal constraints are spurring more experimentation.

Accessing private capital for energy efficiency projects offers several important advantages. It can:

- relieve the burden of funding from state and local budgets,
- generate an immediate positive cash flow to the state,
- free scarce state resources and preserve borrowing capacity for other purposes,
- expedite acquisition of energy saving equipment and thereby avoid losing potential energy savings which delayed implementation causes, and,
- make use of the project development expertise of the private sector.

In order to utilize private capital public agencies must continue to identify energy projects and develop procedures and standards for procuring financing. In many cases, procurement law will have to be changed. For example, exemptions allowing multi-year contracts must be extended to energy projects.

*Policy Initiative #6: Inventory Energy Efficiency Projects*

It is critical that public agencies continue to collect energy data on their buildings and to identify efficiency projects. This is the initial phase of project development which only the building owner/manager can undertake. Accurate data is needed to prioritize projects, attract private financing, negotiate sound contracts and independently monitor results. Funding for audits and engineering feasibility studies should continue aggressively.

As an aside, one possible source of funds for energy audits or even minor improvements is reserve repair and replacement funds which are established by bond indentures for buildings originally funded by bonds. For non-state owned public buildings, state energy offices (SEO's) could continue to assemble proposed energy efficiency projects as they have under the Federal schools and hospitals program.

*Policy Initiative #7: Develop Procedures for Procuring
Private Sector Financing*

State governments should develop procedures for utilizing private capital financing of energy efficiency improvements. There may be economies in centralizing financing expertise in one state office and then making it available to other state agencies and public purpose institutions. State energy offices, purchasing, general services, public works—all these may be the appropriate office to undertake the task.

After researching and qualifying financing mechanisms and specific plans offered by private business, the energy financing office could serve to connect these institutions needing financing with firms that can provide it. By assembling cost-effective energy projects the SEO could attract investor interest in this market. The office's goal would be to provide information that would open up the marketplace and assist both public institutions and private businesses in engaging in mutually beneficial transactions.

*Debt limitations.* Many public institutions must live within strict constitutional debt limitations and cannot incur debt liabilities, except bonded indebtedness, for more than one year. This restriction may place limits on their ability to use these private financing mechanisms.

Each state has its own laws which act as barriers to the procurement of energy project financing from private sources. For example, in Massachusetts, school districts can only lease certain property—buses, computers—and are not currently authorized to lease energy equipment. Identifying legal barriers and revising the laws to permit private financing necessarily will be an individual state-by-state process.

*Transfering tax benefits.* One goal of utilizing private capital is to allow for-profit businesses to capture the tax benefits of equipment ownership which public and other tax-exempt organizations cannot utilize. The investment tax credit, energy tax credit (available for some energy property), accelerated depreciation and other business expense deductions from tax liability can make these investments particularly attractive for private investors.

Institutions considering private financing should conduct independent research into the tax benefits that can accrue to the investor in order to negotiate the most favorable contract. If the value of these tax benefits is passed through to the energy user, the net cost of capital of private financing can approach that of tax-exempt bond financing. Some uncertainties concerning tax benefits exist. When contracting private financing, the public agency should make sure that any risks of taking an aggressive tax position are totally assumed by the private party and that it is protected contractually in event of an adverse I.R.S. ruling.

### Private Capital Financing Mechanisms

These mechanisms come in many combinations and variations. For ease of discussion, they are herein classified as leasing, energy management companies and third-party financing. A brief description of these three private capital financing mechanisms follows.

#### *Leasing*

A lease is a means to convey the right to use a piece of property without conveying ownership. Thus, leasing is an alternative to the direct ownership of energy saving equipment. The main attraction of leasing is that it can allow an institution to acquire the use of energy savings equipment without incurring large up-front costs. Monthly lease payments can be made less than the monthly energy savings, giving the user a positive cash flow from the beginning of an installation.

A lease transaction allows another party, the lessor, to maintain ownership of equipment while it is being used by the lessee. The lessor is able to claim all the tax credits and depreciation expenses associated with ownership.

*Types of lessors.* A lessor can be a number of different entities in a lease transaction. The two most common types of lessors are equipment manufacturers and leasing companies. Major corporations, recently motivated by the search for tax benefits, have also become lessors. Many vendors offer financing plans, including leases, to their customers.

There are two types of leasing transactions applicable to tax-exempt organizations: a "true" lease, and a financing lease. A special type of financing lease for public institutions is a municipal lease.

*True lease.* Under a true lease agreement, the lessee cannot specify the terms of the purchase option other than at fair market value. The term of the lease must be shorter than the useful life of the asset and the lease usually carries cancellation clauses. Current Federal tax law does not allow investment tax credits to be taken by the lessor on property leased to tax-exempt institutions, although the lessor is eligible for accelerated depreciation deductions. This reduces the attractiveness of the transaction to the lessor and results in a higher lease rate.

*Financing lease.* A financing lease is really an installment or conditional sales contract. Lease payments are set by amortizing the full value of the equipment over the term of the lease. The purchase option at the end of the lease term is set at a nominal amount.

*Municipal leasing.* A municipal lease is a straight financing lease where the lessee is a state or political subdivision, such as a state university. The cost of the leased equipment or property is amortized over the lease term with interest charged on the original cost. At the end of the lease period, ownership must pass to the lessee with nominal payment. Interest income on the lease is tax-exempt to the lessor, making it an attractive instrument for tax-motivated investors.

The terms of a municipal lease can be structured to meet a state institution's legal and budgetary requirements. The lease generally must be renewed year-to-year to accommodate restrictions against multi-year liabilities. Thus, a municipal lease is risky for the lessor because the lease may not be renewed. This additional risk can raise interest rates on municipal leases up to 2 percent above the tax-exempt bond rate. The transaction is made more secure for the lessor if the leased property is essential to the lessee, such as a central boiler plant, or if the property has substantial market value in and of itself.

A number of states are turning to municipal leasing to finance needed acquisitions without incurring debt as defined by state and local law. State laws and opinions of attorney generals often state that "debt" does not include future lease payments under specific prescribed conditions. For a public institution to consider municipal leasing, state law research must be conducted to determine: if the institution is qualified to issue tax-exempt obligations; if the standard municipal lease transaction is lawful or must be modified; and if the proposed lease agreement violates any state debt limitations.

Municipal lease-purchase agreements have functioned successfully for financing energy management systems for state and county higher education institutions.

*Limitations of leasing.* Leasing energy efficiency equipment can involve some difficult and/or gray areas in tax law. Legal counsel should be consulted prior to entering major lease contracts. One limitation that is of primary importance is that not all energy efficiency improvements can be leased. Many EEI's can only be classified properly as structural additions to real property. Installation costs can represent such a high proportion of total costs than an energy improvement has no economic value elsewhere. Consequently, as defined by the I.R.S., the property is "limited use property," i.e., at the end of the lease period it has no value except to the lessee, and it is not eligible to be leased under the traditional leasing laws.

*Energy Service Companies/Share-the-Savings Plans*

A number of private companies now exist that will pay for energy efficiency capital improvements in exchange for receiving, as their compensation, a portion of the energy cost savings that accrue. The energy savings potential is large enough to provide a fair return to all parties involved in the transaction. Under these contracts the private firm retains operating and maintenance responsibility for the equipment after it is installed in the user's premises. The equipment is the firm's business property, allowing it to claim the full tax benefits of ownership. The question remains, however, whether the private contractor can in fact retain ownership of the energy efficiency improvements if they become permanent fixtures to the real property of the energy user's building.

The energy management business is being conducted under two main types of contractual arrangements: shared savings, and energy services contracts.

*Shared savings.* The share of savings required by the investor to make the contract economically attractive will vary from a 50 percent up to as high as a 90 percent. Typically the share accruing to the building owner increases after the first years of the contract. If no savings accrue, then the energy user is not liable to make payments. A shared savings contract can be entered to purchase single pieces of equipment and has most commonly been used to purchase energy control systems.

*Energy service companies (ESC's).* An ESC is a full service company which contracts to provide given levels of heating, cooling, lighting and equipment use. The ESC assumes responsibility for utility bill payments and makes its profit on the spread between its costs and its fees. The ESC will make capital improvements to provide energy services most efficiently, at no expense to the building owner.

Besides financing of conservation improvements, ESC's offer a mix of several other services: engineering energy audits, professional consultation on improving plant operations and maintenance procedures for energy efficiency, project and construction management, and on-going operating and maintenance services. For facilities managers that lack both the initial capital and the in-house expertise or organizational momentum to implement an energy management program, the use of an ESC is an alternative that should be seriously considered. The ESC is most perfectly and fairly matched with a client who needs, requires, or simply wants to buy *both* kinds of services, management and financial.

*Contractual considerations.* The energy services contract must address several key issues.

- *Purchase option.* At the end of the contract term, how are the improvements disposed of? Can the contract fix a purchase option or could the improvements be donated? Can the contract be bought out prematurely?

- *Calculating savings.* How are energy savings calculated? The energy user should establish a means to independently monitor the energy savings results.

- *Contract contingencies.* Contingencies in the contract should be provided for in event of damage to the building or if the energy user adds or subtracts an energy load.

If an energy services or share-the-savings contract is entered into by a public institution, several additional legal issues arise.

- The institution may not be able to enter into a long-term contract or financial obligation.
- The state requirements for competitive bidding must be complied with.
- What account will the energy services payments come from? Hospitals using shared savings financing could face problems in obtaining reimbursement to apply to annual shared savings payments. Reimbursement formulas may need to be restructured so that hospitals can take advantage of these energy saving contracts.
- Since an ESC must assume plant operating responsibility, what will its relationship be with the existing unionized or civil service staff? Displacement of union jobs would be a major barrier to these contracts. While it is not necessary that the ESC hire non-union workers or even that plant operating staff be under their direct employ, the ESC does require that certain O&M standards be met in order to meet their energy saving targets. How will existing staff respond to the possible supervisory intervention of the ESC into existing management relations? These concerns are resolvable but must be handled sensitively and creatively.

*ESC procurement activity.* The State of Delaware recently issued a request for proposal (RFP) for procuring energy services for state buildings and hospitals. The RFP requires a guarantee of energy savings and a ten-year contract term subject to yearly state legislature funding. All operation and capital improvements are to be paid for entirely by the energy savings.

The New Jersey Energy Office has published a set of procurement standards for energy service and shared savings contracts.

A bill has been introduced in the New York State Legislature (S. 9181 A) to develop procurement regulations that authorize and encourage ten-year performance management contracts to meet state building energy needs. California's General Services Department is preparing to develop similar procurement procedures.

*Disadvantages and advantages to shared-savings and energy services contracts.* Most ESC's will not consider implementing energy efficiency improvements which have over a three-year payback period. Many limit themselves to two and even one year payback measures, leaving many cost-effective measures unimplemented. Thus, full reliance on an ESC for energy management could result in underinvestment in energy efficiency and lost potential savings.

An ESC involves substantial intervention in a building's operation and management. The ESC contract must be supervised very carefully and results independently monitored. All contract contingencies need to be anticipated and addressed in the original contract.

The industry is new. Each individual firm must be scrutinized carefully for professionalism, ability to perform over the term of the contract and track record. It may also be appropriate to investigate the firm's source of financing for capital improvements.

An energy services or shared savings contract can offer substantial advantages. No upfront costs are required. At the end of the contract term, all the capital improvements revert to the building owner. Guarantees are offered by some firms, assigning to them the risk of technical performance. Management assistance, even training, is provided.

Use of an ESC can be viewed as a *transition* energy management strategy. By shifting some responsibility to the ESC for the first few years of a comprehensive energy management program, plant staff can develop additional knowledge about operations, maintenance and investment for energy efficiency. At the end of the contract term, internal staff can take over the functions that the ESC provides, if they choose.

### Third-Party Financing of Central Plant Facilities

Many state institutions operate large central plants. Rising energy prices have made major modifications to central plant facilities, particularly cogeneration and boiler conversion to alternative fuels, economically attractive. These projects are excellent candidates for private capital financing.

*Working mechanism.* A private for-profit party is contracted for which can provide for the combined financing, design, construction and possibly the operation of central plant facilities. The private party can lease the facility back to the state, similar to current state lease-purchase agreements for office buildings, or it can assume plant operational responsibility and enter into long-term contracts for the sale of steam and electricity. In the latter case, the real property on which the plant is sited would be leased to the private party. The private party is typically organized as a limited partnership and utilizes debt leverage to maximize the tax benefits to the investors.

The California Department of General Services recently issued a request for proposal to procure third-party financing for ten cogeneration plants. Because the overall cost and form of financing is a key influence on a project's design and feasibility, it was deemed critical that the financing entity become involved in the projects from their inception. The program has just begun (June 1982) and the state remains flexible in considering all types of financing approaches.

The University of Texas has utilized this method for financing the construction of conventional boiler plants. Dade County, Florida is considering leasing a cogeneration plant in a similar arrangement. The County will operate the plant and sell electricity to the local utility. Thermal output will be used to power absorption chillers for cooling. The county estimates a first-year net profit of $700,000 from electricity revenues and saved energy costs. After ten years, Dade County can purchase the plant for a nominal sum. The Navy has engaged in third-party financing of cogeneration facilities and soon will be issuing another RFP to acquire these services.

*Utility participation.* The state's role as public utility regulator is important in developing small power projects. Regulations requiring utilities to interconnect with small power producers and purchase power from them at rates approaching the utility's "avoided cost" should be enforced at the state level to create a positive regulatory climate for such projects. Utilities can also play a major role in financing energy efficiency projects as an economic alternative to the construction of new generating capacity.

## Conclusion

As the above report indicates, there are many options for financing cost-effective energy efficiency investments. Implementing these projects constitutes sound fiscal policy and need not languish for lack of public funds.

# Chapter 11 —————————————

# New Approaches to Financing Industrial Energy Conservation Projects

Anthony M. Carey, P.A.

This chapter, while concerned with investment by industries in Maryland, contains information on financing of industrial energy projects which can apply in any state.

It also indicates the distinctive nature of individual state influences—regulatory, legal, financial, and political—which govern the development of any similar project.

A complete knowledge of existing—and pending—conditions in each state is of course necessary.

This chapter underlines the complexities encountered when energy conservation projects move beyond what is now the comparative simplicity of engineering and technology, and into the challenging world of enactment.

For industrial firms, energy is expensive and going up, escalating now at a higher rate than many other costs. Some managers tend to think of energy in terms of the cost of petroleum, which has remained more or less flat for the past year, but for many companies, oil is a relatively small fraction of the energy mix. The costs of electricity or natural gas may have far larger impacts on operating budgets. With industrial gas projected to rise in this area by 15% over the next 12 months and electricity at a rate in excess of the rate of inflation, there is some truth to the statement that you pay now or pay double later.

It is now well recognized that plants with energy intensive operations can usually reduce fuel expenses by at least 10% to 20% through investments in energy efficiency retrofits. Paybacks of two years or less in saved energy costs are not uncommon. Thus, a company paying $2 million a year in fuel bills might be able to save 15% or $300,000 a year in current energy costs with a capital investment of $600,000. When you put conventional fuel cost escalators to this first year savings, substantial increases in cash flow can be projected in future years.

Investments in energy efficiency equipment are not the only approach. In some cases, conversion of boilers to burn alternative fuels, such as coal or trash, can be cost effective, and, in addition, provide greater long-term fuel reliability. For example, 1% sulfur steam coal is available in the Baltimore area at a delivered cost of somewhere between $2.00 and $2.40 per mmBtu, less than half the price of 1% sulfur No. 6 oil at $5.18 and interruptible natural gas at $5.24 per mmBtu.* Commercial trash contains less energy than coal (an average of 4500 Btu's per pound v. 23,000 Btu's per pound), but the additional savings in disposal costs—landfilling trash in the Baltimore area exclusive of collection costs is now $18 a ton and is projected to go over $30 a ton by 1985—can more than make up for the lower energy content.

The problem for many firms is not so much lack of understanding of the value of increased energy efficiency but lack of capital. The purpose of this chapter is to describe two new and more cost-effective approaches to the financing of industrial energy projects. The first is tax-exempt industrial development bond financing through the Maryland Energy Financing Administration, a new program sponsored by the State Department of Economic and Community Development. The second is so-called "shared savings" financing in

---

*
Assumes 1% sulfur coal at a delivered cost of $50 to $57 per ton; oil and gas quotes from BG&E as of November 5, 1982.

which third-party investors pay all costs associated with a project and then share the savings from the investment with the industrial user for a term of years, at the end of which the company has the option of purchasing the equipment at fair market value.

Each of these approaches is either cheaper than or has other advantages over conventional debt or lease financing. For the company that is prepared to take on debt and that can use the tax benefits associated with an investment in capital equipment, tax-exempt financing is probably more advantageous than any other financing method available.* For a company, on the other hand, that is not prepared to expend credit for an energy conservation or alternative fuel investment, a shared savings arrangement can immediately increase cash flow with no encumbrance of its balance sheet or risk to the industrial user.

Let's examine these two approaches in more detail.


## Tax-Exempt Financing Through the Maryland Energy Financing Administration (MEFA)

MEFA is a division of the State Department of Economic and Community Development, which can issue industrial development bonds to finance a wide range of industrial energy conservation projects. The proceeds of the bond issues are to be used to fund individual loans to businesses, the security for the loan being the credit of the borrower and liens on the equipment or facilities financed. To induce local banks to post letters of credit behind individual loans, which are necessary for such loans to serve as security for a larger bond issue, the act establishing MEFA provides for loan insurance by a sister agency, the Maryland Industrial Development Financing Authority (MIDFA).

Interest on these loans will be tax exempt to the lender, provided the borrower and the project meet the terms of the so-called "small issue" exemption for industrial development bond financing under

---

*For a company that cannot use the tax benefits associated with a capital investment but is prepared to take on a fixed obligation, leasing is an alternative that should be explored.

Section 103 of the Internal Revenue Code.* MEFA estimates that its financing will be available at less than a 13% fixed interest rate for a term of ten years. It will require a cash investment by the borrower of approximately 5% of the cost of the project.

In general, a private business can qualify for small issue tax-exempt industrial development bond financing if the proceeds are to be used for industrial energy conservation projects and the face amount of the loan and prior outstanding tax-exempt borrowings by the business or related businesses for facilities in the same political subdivision do not exceed $1 million. Tax-exempt IRB financing of up to $10 million is available to a business but in this case the borrower is normally subject to a $10 million limitation on capital expenditures of any type for three years prior and three years after the tax-exempt borrowing for any facility or plant used by the borrower or related parties in the same political subdivision.

Application for MEFA financing can be made through local commercial banks that have agreed to participate in the program or directly to MEFA. The borrower must first submit a pre-application to MEFA that will be used to determine program eligibility. Final loan applications must be accompanied by financial statements and other credit information, a feasibility study, estimation of the project payback period, performance ratings of the proposed technology, track record information concerning the proposed contractor, a budget for the project, and an appraisal of the property, and equipment offered as collateral on both an "as is" and "completed" basis.

The local bank will screen the credit, provide construction and interim financing, if necessary, and furnish a ten-year letter of credit as security for the loan. The loan application papers must also be reviewed by MIDFA and MEFA. It is expected to take no more than a week to screen a pre-application and about 60 days to process a final application, once the program is in full operation.

A company using MEFA financing will thus have to pay for a feasibility study, and the costs of preparing and submitting the loan

---

*Some industrial energy conservation projects may also qualify as "exempt facilities" under Section 103 and thereby not be subject to the dollar limitations that apply to small issue IRBs. Exempt facilities include air or water pollution control facilities, and plants which use solid waste as a fuel to generate steam.

application and related documents, although the engineering and feasibility study expense can be financed from the loan proceeds. Most of the data for the application will probably come from in-house sources.

MEFA does not provide construction financing but that should be available at normal rates from the bank furnishing the letter of credit based on a long-term MEFA and MIDFA loan and insurance commitment. MEFA's buy-out will be conditioned upon receipt of a certification from a competent engineering firm that the equipment installed will perform according to specifications. Reflected in the interest rate charged for a MEFA loan will be the cost of underwriters, MEFA bond counsel, the fees charged for letters of credit posted by banks and MEFA's own fee, which adds about 4 points to the market rate for a triple A rated tax-exempt bond.

### Shared Savings Financing

In the shared savings approach, a third-party investor audits the industrial facility at its own expense. If the company meets credit standards and its plant offers opportunities for conservation projects which meet the investor's payback criteria, usually less than three years, a shared savings proposal will be made.

This financing method normally requires the investor to pay the cost of an engineering study which describes the equipment to be installed and which establishes a monthly base of energy use in units of energy for a representative period before the installation of the energy conservation equipment.

The investor will pay the full cost of equipment installation and share the energy cost savings over a term of years with the industrial user and will bear all responsibility and expense for insuring the equipment and providing for repair and maintenance. At the end of the contract term, the industrial user has the right to buy the equipment at fair market value.

The industrial user assumes no debt or lease obligation. The agreements typically are structured as service contracts and thus need not appear on the user's balance sheet. The investor is entitled to all tax benefits associated with equipment ownership and its share of savings consists of the reduction in energy units multiplied by the then current unit cost of such energy, so that the dollar value of the share is indexed to the escalation in fuel costs.

The only recourse the investor has to the user is for its share of energy savings. That share, however, will be a real dollar payment over and above then existing utility bills, assuming a savings has been produced. The risks of overstatement of energy savings by the engineering firm, decrease in the level of production or energy use by the industrial user, or malfunction in the performance of the energy equipment are all assumed by the investor.

Shared savings financing is by now relatively well known. There are a number of firms in the business and a good number of industrial companies, including a number on the list of *Fortune* 500 companies which are either going ahead with programs or have them under serious consideration. These investments were stimulated by the additional 10% energy tax credit to which investments in many of the usual industrial energy conservation devices are entitled.

These credits expired at the end of 1982. Even without the energy tax credits, however, it appears these investments are now sufficiently well understood and well regarded by certain sophisticated investors that they will continue to be sought after in 1983 and beyond.

### Comparison of the Two Approaches

Shared savings and tax-exempt financing have the following comparative advantages and disadvantages:

*Shared Savings*

(a) Advantages

- No credit impairment or cost
- No project risk
- Fast increase in cash flow
- Contracting and documentation simpler than tax-exempt financing

(b) Disadvantages

- User gives up the opportunity to reap a larger share of energy cost savings for a substantial period of time

- Can only be used for projects with short paybacks

*Tax-Exempt Financing*

(a) Advantages

- Higher bottom line cash flow, particularly where tax benefits can be used
- Can finance investments with longer paybacks

(b) Disadvantages

- Debt obligation for ten years; security interests in property must be given and loan agreement entered into
- Front end costs for engineering studies and 5% cash down payment
- Longer processing time, more complicated documentation, and periodic reporting requirements

Set forth on an attached exhibit is a somewhat simplified financial comparison between the two approaches.

The example assumes a $500,000 investment with an estimated two-year simple payback in fuel savings and a ten-year life. It is assumed the project is completed and began operation on January 1, 1983.

The tax-exempt financing example assumes debt at 13% for ten years, amortized in equal annual amounts of principal and interest, and an annual equipment, repair and maintenance cost of 5% of the capital cost of the investment. 100% debt financing has been assumed. It is further assumed the property is five year ACRS property for which the owner receives a 10% investment tax credit in the first year of operation and straight-line depreciation deductions over the ACRS life of the equipment on a basis reduced by one-half of the amount of the investment tax credit as provided in the 1982 Tax Act. It is assumed the corporate owner is in the 46% tax bracket for purposes of calculating the cash flow benefit of the depreciation and debt interest deductions.

For purposes of the shared savings example, it is assumed the investors share savings on a 50-50 basis with the industrial user over

## TAX-EXEMPT FINANCING

|  | 1983 | 1984 | 1985 | 1986 | 1987 | 1988 | 1989 | 1990 | 1991 | 1992 |
|---|---|---|---|---|---|---|---|---|---|---|
| Value of Energy Savings | 250 | 250 | 250 | 250 | 250 | 250 | 250 | 250 | 250 | 250 |
| Less Expenses: | | | | | | | | | | |
| Maintenance | 25 | 25 | 25 | 25 | 25 | 25 | 25 | 25 | 25 | 25 |
| Interest | 65 | 61 | 57 | 53 | 48 | 42 | 36 | 28 | 20 | 11 |
| Depreciation | 48 | 95 | 95 | 95 | 95 | 48 | | | | |
| Additional Taxable Income | 112 | 69 | 73 | 77 | 82 | 135 | 189 | 197 | 205 | 214 |
| Income Tax @ 46% | (52) | (32) | (33) | (35) | (38) | (62) | (87) | (91) | (94) | (98) |
| Less: ITC | 50 | | | | | | | | | |
| Net Income | 110 | 37 | 40 | 42 | 44 | 73 | 102 | 106 | 111 | 116 |
| Add Back Depreciation | 48 | 95 | 95 | 95 | 95 | 48 | – | – | – | – |
| Less: Principal Repayment | 27 | 31 | 35 | 39 | 44 | 50 | 56 | 64 | 72 | 81 |
| Net After Tax Benefit | 131 | 101 | 100 | 98 | 95 | 71 | 46 | 42 | 39 | 35 |

## SHARED SAVINGS

|  | 1983 | 1984 | 1985 | 1986 | 1987 | 1988 | 1989 | 1990 | 1991 | 1992 |
|---|---|---|---|---|---|---|---|---|---|---|
| 50% of Gross Savings | 125 | 125 | 125 | 125 | 125 | 125 | 125 | 125 | 125 | 125 |
| Income Tax @ 46% | 57.5 | 57.5 | 57.5 | 57.5 | 57.5 | 57.5 | 57.5 | 57.5 | 57.5 | 57.5 |
| Net After Tax Benefit | 67.5 | 67.5 | 67.5 | 67.5 | 67.5 | 67.5 | 67.5 | 67.5 | 67.5 | 67.5 |
| Purchase Option* | | | | | | | | | | (50) |
| Net Benefit | | | | | | | | | | 17.5 |

*Residual value is assumed here to be 10% of original purchase price.

the life of a ten-year contract. For both approaches no escalation in the value of the annual energy savings has been assumed.

As can be seen, the tax-exempt approach produces substantially more bottom line cash flow in the early years, primarily as a result of the tax credits, interest, and depreciation write-offs. Once the depreciation has been utilized, shared savings produces more net income—in this example $67,500 per year compared to amounts ranging from $46,000 in 1989 to $35,000 in 1992 for the tax-exempt approach. In the final year under shared savings, the exercise of a purchase option at an assumed 10% of original cost would drop the net for that year to $17,500. The analysis, however, does not reflect the additional income the firm using shared savings would receive by having $500,000 in unencumbered credit to invest.

# Chapter 12 —————————————

# Creative Financing for Commercial Facilities

## Jack W. Caloz

Owners, operators, lessors, and managers of commercial facilities are well aware of the effects escalating energy costs have had on operating costs and lowered profit margins. Many have already taken simple steps, such as lowering thermostat settings and reducing excessive lighting levels in their facilities in an attempt to reduce their energy consumption. Depending on the types of HVAC (Heating, Ventilating and Air Conditioning) systems installed in their facilities, some of these measures could actually increase consumption. The best approach to energy conservation in a facility is to improve or modify the existing systems so that they operate more efficiently.

The improving or modifying of energy consuming systems in a facility is known as retrofitting. Retrofitting a facility for energy management conjurs up in the minds of most nontechnical managers large capital costs, highly technical energy management techniques, and sophisticated hardware installations. The truth of the matter is that energy management is the application of the same basic techniques of planning, organizing, actuating and controlling that one would apply to administration, marketing, or production on a daily basis in running any business venture.

Through personal experience and research on successful and unsuccessful programs, a number of constraints have been identified.

These constraints have significantly hampered the implementation of energy conservation projects on a large scale.

Many owners are unwilling either to part with their cash or reduce their available credit to invest in energy conservation. Lack of capital is the single most frequently given reason for not investing in energy conservation.

However, more often than not lack of capital is an excuse as opposed to a reason for not investing. This has recently become evident with the advent of creative financing plans. Reluctance, although significantly reduced with creative financing, still exists indicating that additional motivation factors are still necessary. In cases where a true lack of capital problem exists, the financial marketplace is presently addressing the demand for energy conservation capital. Financing is available which will neither deplete existing liquid assets nor reduce available credit, for any energy conservation program with a payback period of less than three years.

There are approximately four million commercial buildings in the United States which contain more than 32 billion square feet of space.[1] Rough estimates of annual energy costs incurred in office buildings range from $0.80 to $1.30 per square foot.[2] DOE estimates an investment of $1.00 per square foot would reduce commercial buildings' energy cost by 35 percent.

A 35 percent reduction in energy costs, assuming an average energy cost of $1.00 per square foot, yields a payback of less than three years. This meets the financing criteria of not requiring capital or reductions in available credit. Expanding the $1.00 per square foot average cost and 32 billion square feet of commercial space in the United States, yields a total of $32 billion of available energy conservation projects with a less than three-year payback.

The capital for energy conservation projects is available. If not provided internally, it can be provided externally.

The creditability of real savings from energy conservation is believed to be the most pertinent constraint deferring the implementation of energy conservation programs.

While there are many projects and services available in the energy management marketplace which will reduce energy consumption and costs, there are also some which are worthless. The "con" in energy conservation makes for newsworthy articles in general and trade publications. This adds to an owner's reluctance to invest his money or a building manager to risk his name.

Additionally, savings from otherwise proper application of valid products and services frequently have their real dollar savings masked by rising utility rates or changes in building use or occupancy. This creditability gap is a major stumbling block.

There are, however, a number of methods which can be utilized to overcome skepticism, including education, experience and allocation of risk.

*Education* is the most obvious but also the most difficult process. Many energy conservation strategies are highly technical and require an engineering background and practical experience with operating systems before they can be understood properly. Increasingly, professional management firms realize these needs and we are seeing more technically competent on-staff personnel today.

Small owners and management firms cannot afford the luxury of in-house engineering staffs; they appreciate the fact that they are at the mercy of the marketplace.

*Experience* is the most effective method of answering the question, "Are energy savings real?" Those owners and managers who have been successful in implementing energy conservation programs know first-hand the benefits of reduced energy consumption and its effect on their bottom line. From our experience, however, these successful owners and managers frequently are technically competent themselves or have technically competent engineering staffs on the payroll or on retainer.

*Allocation of risk* appears to have the greatest potential for rapidly alleviating the credibility gap. By placing the burden of proof of savings through energy conservation programs on vendors, manufacturers, and energy conservation companies, owners and managers can gain experience without financial risk on their part.

Creative financing of energy conservation programs can be structured in such a way that owners and managers will only have to pay for programs which are successful. And they will pay for them out of the savings which have been achieved. Removing the financial risk from owners should alleviate skepticism and significantly overcome the reluctance to the implementation of conservation programs.

Approximately 50 percent of all commercial buildings are owner-occupied, single-purpose buildings.[3] There is a clear, quantitative motivation for the owners of these buildings to implement energy conservation. The owner pays his own utility bill and has control over all the energy consuming equipment on site.

A decrease in the monthly utility bill has the effect of directly increasing cash flow and profit in the same amounts. Assuming that sufficient capital or access to sufficient capital to cover implementation is available, there exists more-than-adequate motivation for the owner to implement all economically justifiable energy conservation strategies that are available to him.

Tenant-occupied buildings, on the other hand, have either no incentive for the owner to decrease energy consumption, or have a disincentive. In tenant-occupied buildings, the owner charges the tenants for the utilities either through submetering or a method of pass-through.

In a submetered building, the tenant pays the utility company directly or pays the landlord for the amount of energy consumed in his respective space. When the tenant pays the landlord or owner, based on submetering, the rate structures are frequently such that the owner can profit from the utility revenues he collects.

In this case, the more energy the building consumes the more revenue and subsequent profit the owner can generate. Thus there is a disincentive for the owner to implement an energy conservation program. The more that energy consumption is reduced, the lower are the owner's revenues.

In the case of pass-throughs, the owner passes the cost of utilities on to the tenants either on a pro-rata basis (usually rented square footage) or in annual escalation clauses written into the lease and based on the owner's increased maintenance costs, which include utilities.

The only incentive then for an owner who is able to pass energy costs on to the tenant to reduce consumption, is the rentability of the space. Tenants, when looking for space, would logically look at total lease costs including utility rates when renting space. A more efficient building could offer space at a reduced rate thereby making the economically-logical assumption that energy-efficient buildings would be rented first. At lease-renewal time, tenants would likely move to the most efficient building with the lowest total lease cost for comparable space.

The economical decision is not normally the prime consideration. The prime consideration in commercial office space is location. With total commercial office space in short supply, the tenant is frequently forced to accept what space is available at a preferential price.

The disincentive for tenant-occupied or speculative commercial facilities to institute energy conservation programs is recognized by trade associations such as Building Owners and Managers Association (BOMA). Energy conservation subcommittees have been set up by BOMA, and new lease arrangements have been discussed. Provisions, such as passing energy conservation improvement costs on to tenants or allowing owners to share in savings realized by improvements they make, have been proposed. To date, there has been little acceptance of these suggested lease changes. We have, in fact, seen a trend toward submetering in the design of new speculative office buildings.

The lack of background knowledge about heating, ventilating and air-conditioning systems and their associated central systems adds to the skepticism prevalent in the marketplace. The task of educating present owners, managers, and vendors has been assumed by their respective trade associations: Building Owners and Managers Association (BOMA), Mechanical Contractors Association (MCA), National Electrical Manufacturer Association (NEMA). These and many other smaller associations have undertaken the task of providing programs to enlighten their respective members. All of these associations have made and are making significant contributions to increasing the general awareness and educational level of the marketplace as a whole.

In discussions with owners and managers nationally, we find that there exists the misconception that conservation is contrary to a quality or first-class office building image. This is especially true in the speculative real estate market. In this market owners are very sensitive to tenant perceptions of their space. Speculative owners depend on tenant satisfaction for their revenues. An energy-efficient building is useless if the tenants begin cancelling leases and moving out.

There does not have to be a sacrifice in tenant's comfort levels when implementing a conservation program. More often than not, if the conservation program is properly implemented, tenant comfort conditions can be improved while energy consumption levels are reduced. The energy conservation strategy for the purposes of this analysis includes only improvements in building efficiency which do not adversely affect tenant comfort levels. The concept that energy efficiency and tenant comfort are completely compatible should be conveyed to management to reduce its reluctance to implement a conservation plan.

Utility bills, such as gas, oil, electric, coal, or purchased steam are traditionally paid by the accounting departments of building owners or managing agents. Energy-consuming systems are controlled by the building maintenance staff. Rarely do these two diverse departments interface. Escalating utility rates have been accepted as a fact of life and a cost of doing business.

Maintenance staff's responsibilities are to provide adequate comfort levels. The normal measure of the effectiveness of a maintenance staff is the number of complaints received from tenants. This is frequently counterproductive with respect to energy conservation. It is usually easier to provide greater comfort conditions for an occupied space by increasing the energy consumed by an existing inefficient system, than it is to modify that same system to provide the comfort conditions efficiently. As long as maintenance staffs are not held accountable for the energy consumed by the systems under their control, an effective conservation program cannot hope to succeed.

The accounting department, utilizing generally accepted cost accounting procedures, should develop an on-going procedure to measure the operating efficiency of the facility, just as it would to measure a production or marketing department's efficiency.

By coordinating the accounting and maintenance departments, a single source of responsibility can be established thereby eliminating the otherwise contradictory role of the maintenance department. A revised objective of the maintenance department might read as follows: Provide adequate comfort conditions throughout the facility, in the most economically feasible manner, during normal occupancy hours.

The developed accounting procedure would not be a one-shot

program. To be effective, reporting should be on a monthly basis, and with the shortest possible time lag between receipt of utility bills by the accounting department and issuance of the efficiency report. If too much time passes between consumption of energy and issuance of report, the person who has been given the responsibility of controlling the energy consumption is unable to take required remedial action until it is too late.

Large consumers of energy have traditionally had a disincentive to conserve because of utility rate structures which provide lower bulk rates to large users. This is due to the utility companies' economies in providing large quantities of energy to single points. Charges for that energy are marginally less for each additional increment of energy. Therefore, when conservation projects are implemented, the consumption units they conserve are the least expensive.

Nationally, rate schedules are constantly being revised. The trend we are seeing is away from the traditionally beneficial rates for large consumers. A prime example of this is New York's Consolidated Edison electric rate schedule for large commercial users. They have implemented time-of-day rate schedules for commercial users who consume in excess of 1000 kilowatt hours (kw) of demand. Time-of-day rate schedules charge more for energy consumed during normal working hours (peak period) and less for energy consumed during weekends and at night (off-peak period).

In addition, summer kw demand charges, under this particular rate schedule, have risen from their previous level of approximately $10.00 per kw to approximately $24.00 per kw. This charge, which is in addition to a consumption charge, is significant. For example, a building with a demand of 2000 kw would be charged $48,000 in one month for demand in addition to the charges for consumption. Consolidated Edison is not alone in these rate structure revisions. They are following a trend already established by others such as Long Island Lighting Co. and Potomac Electric Power Company.

Rate changes for all energy sources are now being implemented nationally. This will tend to discourage the previous advantages which were enjoyed by large utility consumers.

The financing of energy conservation projects has been a major constraint to their implementation. The utilization of internal sources of capital is highly competitive. Although energy conservation projects may have a high rate of return, they have to compete with acquisitions, marketing, manufacturing and other processes which are likely to be closer to the hearts of top management. Energy conservation projects may make significant impacts on year-end financial statements, but they don't make exciting presentations at stockholders' meetings.

Constraints on using traditional financial institutions for funding energy projects are the same as those faced when internal funds are sought. These sources of money are expensive. Present interest rates detract significantly from the returns that energy conservation projects yield.

Energy management product and service organizations have become acutely aware of the constraints faced by their clients. Mr. Ray Wendel of Fred Wendel Co., an energy conservation contractor, was recently quoted in *Contracting Business* Magazine as saying, "It's almost as if energy conservation contractors have something so good they can't even give it away."[3]

Energy conservation product and service companies have provided funding to owners on a limited basis. This has traditionally taken the form of a share in the savings. The obvious motivation of energy conservation companies is to promote their respective products or services.

The concept of share-in-the-savings is that an owner would allow an energy conservation company to install its respective equipment or service in a building and the owner would pay for this equipment or service out of the savings generated over a time of from 3 to 10 years. The owner would therefore realize a percentage, traditionally 50%, of the savings without the risk of investment. The concept has been a tremendous marketing tool for those companies with the financial wherewithal to implement them. The only problem for the owner is that his choices of products and services has been significantly limited to those firms which offer these financial services.

These limitations can disappear as new financial instruments are developed to meet the $32 billion market that is presently available. Organizations are now providing financial instruments for the implementation of economically viable energy conservation projects without regard to the manufacturer or service company. This allows the owner to develop his own program utilizing the products and services which best fit his needs and also avail himself of third-party financing which neither requires up-front investment and associated risk nor reduces the owner's available credit.

## References

1.  DOE, *Expansion of the Residential Conservation Service Program to Multi-Family and Small Commercial Buildings* (Washington: U.S. Government Printing Office, Nov. 1980) pp. 2-3.

2.  Marketfacts—Washington, Report to DOE on Commercial Building Sector, (Washington: U.S. Government Printing Office, Sept. 30, 1981) IV-17.

3.  Stephan, Ed, *Contracting Business* (New York: Penton, April 1982) Vol. 39, No. 4, pg. 31.

# Chapter 13

# Financing Alternative Energy Projects

David Seader

Alternative energy projects are becoming increasingly attractive as sound investment opportunities for the 1980s.

Alternative energy projects are essentially industrial projects. As such, they are conceived, engineered, and developed with sophisticated technological orientation. They are also evaluated as investments in the same way as business' other capital investments.

Often, a firm's investment analysis of an energy project doesn't measure up with its other uses of funds. In that case, energy projects may be dropped or deferred. But many of those projects are proving profitable to special purpose development companies which have the experience and expertise to implement and finance such projects as a main source of business. The product of this nascent industry is either a turnkey project delivered complete to a firm, or the sale of power as a discount "across the fence" delivered to the user "off-the-books" (that is, without the application of scarce internal capital).

The list of alternative technologies is long. They range from bio-mass conversion, to oil shale recovery, to wind power, to small-scale hydro power, to cogeneration. Some, like oil shale recovery and synthetic fuel development, require massive financial resources that only major energy companies can muster.

Others, such as garbage-to-energy or cogeneration, can be developed on a project-by-project basis with relatively modest investments that can come from a mix of corporate and private sources.

## An Economic Incentive

The economic viability of many alternative energy projects is largely the result of a 1978 law intended to encourage development of small-scale energy resources—The Public Utilities Regulatory and Power Act (PURPA). PURPA exempts small power production facilities (under 80 megawatts) from federal regulation and mandates that local power companies buy energy from them at the utility's avoided cost (what it would cost the utility to generate the additional power from its most expensive plant or to build new facilities for increased generating capacity).

The Act, in effect, provides guaranteed markets for power from alternative energy projects and ties the price of their output to the rising price of a utility's source of power—i.e. imported oil, nuclear or coal.

With national policy encouraging investment in alternative energy development through federal regulations and the tax code, investors are now being attracted to an increasing number of projects. Successful investing will depend on a variety of factors, including sound technology evaluation, reasonable projections of energy prices, secure revenues through long-term contracts, stringent cost controls, and a reliance on reputable developers.

## Financial Benefits to
## Private Investors

The opportunities for private investors are in equity syndications through limited partnerships.

For a cogeneration plant the total capital costs could range from $5-$50 million; a small hydro facility $1-$25 million; a garbage to energy plant $3-$30 million. The offerings will usually involve less than 35 individuals, with 20-40 percent of the capital cost raised as equity and the rest derived from conventional debt financing, or through industrial development bonds.

Private investors may be able to realize depreciation deductions, cash flow, capital gains and enhanced tax credits from a given project. The primary incentives for investment are usually the tax credits and potential cash flow. Depreciation for facilities and equipment will follow the same schedule under the Economic Recovery Tax Act of 1981 as that of any industrial capital investment. While capital appreciation is possible in certain instances, energy projects are not often undertaken primarily for long-term capital gains.

As a result of several recent pieces of federal legislation—e.g., the Energy Security Act of 1980 and the Crude Oil Windfall Profits Tax Act (COWPTA)—the available tax credits for investing in alternative energy development are substantial. Because project revenues are tied to the escalating price of energy, a significant amount of cash flow may also be generated after the startup of a facility.

Hypothetically, in the first year of operation of an energy plant, a 30 percent equity investment might result in a 10 percent Investment Tax Credit, and a 15 percent depreciation write-off for a facility under a five-year schedule. Additional Business Energy Tax Credits are still available for alternative energy projects (e.g., 11% for small hydro; 10% for biomass conversion). Thus, the first year write-offs (of the total capital cost of the facility) may practically allow an investor to break even.

## Financing Approaches

Some of the methods we anticipate using to finance alternative energy projects follow:

• Large financial institutions (insurance companies, pension funds) which traditionally invested in long-term fixed rate investments now prefer endeavors that can promise escalating returns—e.g., energy projects, since most would agree the cost of energy will continue to escalate. These firms would provide permanent financing as well as up-front capital. In return for sharing some of the risk, they would ultimately participate in the financial rewards of operating revenues and capital appreciation, and could immediately realize a tax benefit for their investment. Traditional venture capital firms also show interest in well-structured alternative energy projects.

- Joint-venture undertakings can be put together as a means of establishing a wider source of capital. Several companies can combine to finance the development costs and provide the teams of technical experts necessary to complete these complex projects.
- A company can undertake the front-end work on a given energy project using in-house technical capabilities to develop the basic concept. When the project has reached the stage of economic promise, it can be transferred to a larger energy concern that can more efficiently capitalize, implement, and operate the facility.
- An alternative energy equity fund can be established to provide front-end development monies for a diversified portfolio of new energy projects and technologies. The fund would attract passive investors through public or private offerings that would provide investors with immediate tax benefits, as well as eventual capital appreciation and operating revenues.
- Foreign corporations and investors with technological capabilities can be enticed to participate in projects in the United States because of our large and dependable energy market. This process would provide a beneficial proving ground for technological know-how, as well as profitable investment opportunities.

## Financing for Three Types of Alternative Energy Systems

Three types of alternative energy systems appear to hold great practical opportunity for development, given today's tax and financial climates—waste-to-energy, small hydropower, and cogeneration (either from conventional or unconventional fuels). Each has a growing list of successful applications and a variety of proven technologies.

### Financing a Resource Recovery Plant

To finance the construction and operation of a garbage-to-energy facility for the city of Pittsfield, Massachusetts, a limited partnership was formed by Vicon Construction Company (the general partner) with solicitations made to individual private investors through an investment banker. The project involves a plant and equipment to process 240 tons/day of municipal solid waste through incineration.

It is designed to produce 700,000 pounds of steam per day that is sold to a local paper manufacturing concern. Total capital expenses amounted to approximately $10.8 million, with $6.2 million coming from an industrial development bond issued through the city. Twenty units of limited partnership interests were offered at $171,250 each.

The plant has been in operation since March of 1981. Limited partners have been able to take advantage of a 10 percent investment tax credit (ITC) on $10,631,000 of the facility's assets. Because of the use of industrial development bonds, it only qualified for a 5 percent energy tax credit (ETC) on $9,593,000 of eligible property. Depreciation for the bulk of the plant ($10.5 million) is over an eight-year period.

(Note: If syndicated currently, the ETC would not be available and the depreciation would be 5-year ACRS based on the $10.5 million less one-half of the ITC.)

The financial projections for the project indicate that in 1981, the first year of operation, the individual investor receives tax credits of $77,138 for one unit of investment, as well as a tax loss of $106,100; there is no cash flow. In the succeeding two years, additional tax losses of $111,700 flow through the partnership, and the project yields cash flows of $50,300. Thus, over the first three years, one unit of investment at $171,250 produces for an investor a tax benefit of $186,038 (assuming a 50 percent marginal tax bracket) and cash of $50,300.

Additionally, the schedule of paying in the one unit of investment is geared to the schedule of tax losses and cash flows to minimize the net exposure of the investor. In succeeding years, the investor enjoys escalating cash distributions which continue to be sheltered through the eighth year of the project. The net result of the investment is a substantial tax deferral benefit, significant cash flows and ownership of a highly productive asset.

## Financing Cogeneration Systems

A great deal of cogeneration development will take place over the next decade, requiring substantial capital. The cost of typical cogeneration systems ranges from $300/kw to $800/kw; $300,000/mw to

$800,000/mw. Systems being considered for development range in size from 25 kw to 25 mw.

The current rebirth of interest in cogeneration does not just derive from individual and/or collective interest in energy conservation per se. Cogeneration systems are being installed in increasing numbers because they save money or make money.

Heightened interest also stems from financial incentives now provided by a number of public electric utilities because installation of cogeneration systems in their service areas will help to alleviate shortages of generating capacity.

For cogeneration to produce savings or cash flow and profit commensurate with the requisite capital and owning and operating costs, the following conditions must prevail:

• The proposed site must be in a geographic area served by a public electric utility that cannot achieve an increase in capacity with hydro, nuclear power, or coal in a reasonably short time, or a utility that has enough generating capacity but gets 60% or more of its power from expensive oil or gas.

• There must be a demand for some form(s) of thermal energy (steam, hot water, chilled water, etc.) which is consistent and fairly coincident with the demand for electric power.

• There must be a high usage factor. The entity contemplated for service by cogeneration must require a continuous supply of both electric and thermal energy for a majority of the 8760 calendar year hours.

Because investment in cogeneration generally ranges from a minimum of hundreds of thousands of dollars, to more typically millions of dollars, very detailed analyses are required to establish economic viability. The initial phase of these engineering and economic analyses is directed toward establishing the configuration of a system which provides optimum savings in utilities' costs. Factors to be considered include energy demand and consumption, potential future demand, and the total costs of system installation, operation and maintenance.

The availability of investment tax credits and revenue derived from the sale of excess power to a utility can often provide for a rapid payback. The feasibility analyses we are routinely performing indicate that where cogeneration is applicable, ROI is in the realm of 29% to 30%.

Any process industry that has a fairly constant demand for thermal energy—process steam, hot air for drying processes, combustion air for boilers, heaters or hot gas generators, hot water and/or refrigeration—is a candidate cogenerator. According to the U.S. Department of Energy, industries with the greatest potential for cogeneration include: petroleum refining and related industries; textile mill products; paper and allied products; chemicals and wood products; and metals. For the various industries, return on investment hurdle rates vary. The spectrum ranges from chemicals (20%–25%), to food (20%–30%), to paper (16%–19%), to textiles (15%–30%).

For cogeneration systems being developed for municipalities, financing is usually arranged through tax-exempt bonds. In the case of larger systems, industrial revenue bonds are providing the required capital. Of more particular interest is the leveraged lease option; here an equity participation of at least 20% provides such tax benefits as investment and energy tax credits, depreciation and interest on the debt portion of the capitalization provided by the bank, and the residual value of the cogeneration property at the expiration of the financing term. Revenue bonds in combination with equity is another financing option, the bonds being either taxable or tax-exempt depending upon individual circumstances.

With proper financing secured, a potential cogenerator has several procurement options. He can:

• Contract with a consultant who will perform the feasibility studies, establish the configuration of the optimum system and have the system designed and constructed, either on a turnkey basis or by competitive bidding against plans and specifications prepared by the designer.

• Lease the system from a firm that will design and build it on a turnkey basis.

• Procure the electric and thermal output of the system under a long-term contract with a firm that will design, build, own, and operate the system and furnish utilities at stipulated costs sufficiently lower than the costs which would accrue if the facility continued to operate in the conventional mode.

- Exercise the latter option with the provision that the system may be purchased at some stipulated time.

Cogeneration can clearly be an attractive investment option. But it will only represent a sound investment if the following conditions are met when evaluating a potential system:

- The economic and engineering analyses which established the system's feasibility and defined the payback period are accomplished without prejudice in favor of any single option.
- These analyses are based upon realistic installed capital costs.
- Realistic, all-inclusive projections are made for owning and operating costs.
- The system is reliable and does not experience uncalled for, unscheduled shutdowns.
- All the system components are designed for continuous-duty operation, and have an adequate service history to prove it.

### Small Hydropower Development

Recently, government and private developers have begun to examine the energy-producing potential of small hydroelectric sites. Economics strongly favor rehabilitation of abandoned hydroelectric facilities (as opposed to developing new sites with full facilities, or adding power-generating capability to existing hydraulic facilities).

If a dam exists and only remedial work is required, the development cost for a 3000-kw facility would be between $3 million and $6 million. A 3000-kw plant operating at only 50% capacity would generate approximately 13 million kwh/year. With an average power value of $.06/kwh, the total revenues from this project would be $780,000/year. In addition, substantial tax credits are available to companies for investing in alternative energy development.

Financing techniques reviewed earlier in this chapter apply as well to small hydropower development projects. There are, however, certain precautions which must be noted if the large up-front investments needed are to be based on full and realistic appraisals.

The cautions also apply to waste-to-energy and cogeneration projects which rely on PURPA for electrical revenues and COWPTA for tax credits.

PURPA and COWPTA offer favorable legislation and tax advantages in developing small hydropower; however, aspects of these laws have also created an adverse climate for small hydropower development which must be guarded against. Under PURPA, utilities are now required to purchase the output of a small hydropower facility at the utility's avoided cost. What the law does not mandate is that the utility offer the long-term contracts needed for long-term financing; nor is there a guarantee that a utility's PURPA rate shall continually escalate at the rate oil costs escalate.

Currently, the requirement for a utility to purchase power from qualified small power producers at full avoided cost is under challenge in the courts.

Many development schemes assume rapid escalation in the power purchase agreement with the utility. However, these "contracts" are presently projections and may not materialize. In practice, utilities may only offer long-term contracts substantially below the PURPA rate, often on a levelized (non-escalating) basis.

Some developers are suggesting investors take the risk of building the project without long-term contracts. On multi-million dollar projects this is not a practical approach. Any projects without long-term contracts might suddenly find themselves unable to meet project obligations. PURPA has not been the ultimate solution in making small hydropower projects viable. Anyone who thinks otherwise has not fully researched the ramifications of the regulations.

Tax incentives applicable to small hydropower under COWPTA supposedly offer a windfall to project development. However, after a thorough investigation of the regulations, many of these incentives look less inviting. There are no Internal Revenue Service opinions concerning treatment of the cumulative 21% tax credit on small hydropower projects. Anyone developing these projects runs the risk of convoluted proceedings with the IRS in resolving differences of opinion concerning tax law. What facilities, or portions thereof, qualify for the tax credits is a confusing issue. For example, facilities requiring new dams are clearly disqualified, while rehabilitation of an old dam qualifies for the credits.

Besides institutional and financing problems, small hydropower projects are subject to severe cost overruns and time delays which are a common disease to these types of projects. Two private developers who put their projects on line in 1980 both experienced cost overruns in excess of 40% of the initial estimates. When there's a cost overrun on private work, unlike public works, the developer, or investors, must be prepared to supply monies or the project will not be completed.

The time required from beginning to end in developing a small hydropower plant is aggravated by the license and environmental process. Even after getting a license, a project can be delayed for numerous reasons, adding escalation costs to the project. Any licensee ostensibly has behind them the power of the Federal government in resolving issues relevant to the project's development, including the condemnation of the land on which the project site is located. While this is what the law states, in practice the process involves costs and time delays, and in the case of condemnation, there is no precedent in condemning land not owned by the licensee.

Small hydropower plants may not be able to absorb large up-front investments nor the uncertainties of construction cost overruns and legal and environmental delays. The PURPA and COWPTA law offering development incentives through power purchase requirements from utilities and tax credits from Uncle Sam need to be better defined for an orderly development procedure. The positive attributes of developing small hydropower in an escalating energy environment must be weighed against the pitfalls common to these projects.

# Chapter 14

# Lease-Financing Energy Systems

Martin Klepper
Joseph Sherman
Megan Carroll

As interest rates come down to a more normal level, leasing as a method to finance energy systems grows. Leasing is being offered by an increasing number of equipment manufacturers and their affiliates. Other organizations, acting independently, will review leasing as one of the several energy system financing techniques available. Often, they will serve their clients by planning and carrying out leasing arrangements when this method is selected.

Leasing provides 100% financing to a property owner interested in acquiring energy equipment. The owner of leasable energy equipment obtains tax benefits that may include, depending on the owner and the type of equipment (1) a 10% regular investment tax credit, (2) accelerated depreciation of the equipment and (3) an alternative energy project tax credit. The lessor can pass the value of these tax benefits on to the lessee (property owner) in the form of reduced lease payments. As a result, monthly lease payments may be lower than the monthly payments on the funds borrowed from a bank to acquire the same equipment.

Lease financing may be attractive to both corporate and individual investors (lessors). Leasing is a well-known financing technique.

Banks, leasing companies and other financial institutions are engaged in the business of leasing cars, computers, xerox machines, typewriters and other equipment.

## Summary of Investigation

In preparing this chapter, lease financing was discussed with more than thirty different firms, including energy equipment manufacturers, engineering firms, banks, life insurance companies and independent leasing companies. From these conversations six firms were identified that have engaged in leasing energy efficiency equipment to building owners. Only one of those firms specifically focuses on leasing energy equipment. Table 14-1 contains a summary of the leasing activities of these firms.

There are hundreds of leasing companies operating in the United States. Some of these firms are affiliates of large insurance companies and national and international banks. Others are small companies that specialize in leasing one type of equipment. Most leasing firms use equipment vendors and distributors as a principal marketing source. Often the leasing company never even meets the lessee. The equipment vendor makes the "sale" and then assigns the lease to the leasing company. Sometimes the lessee does not even know who the real lessor will be until after the lease is signed.

One company was found that specializes in leasing energy equipment. That company, Energy Leasing Services, Inc., operating out of Boston, Massachusetts, was formed in the latter part of 1981.

A few firms were identified that engage in setting up separate limited partnerships which purchase various types of energy equipment and lease that equipment to an end user (building owner) or to an intermediary corporation (the lessee) as part of a shared savings plan. The lessee in these situations usually agrees to make lease payments consisting of (1) a very small fixed monthly fee and (2) a percentage of the energy savings. If the lessee is an intermediary, the lessee will retain an engineering firm to install the equipment in the building. The leasing partnership serves as nominal owner of the equipment.

## Table 14-1. Lease Financing

| Name of Company | Currently Leasing Energy Equipment | Owner of Equipment At End of Lease Term | Credit Criteria | Specific Building Sector |
|---|---|---|---|---|
| Energy Leasing Services, Inc | Yes | Negotiable | Credit Worthiness of customer; soundness of Company; value of energy efficiency equipment | Industrial and Commercial |
| Johnson Controls, Inc. | Yes | Johnson Controls | Credit Worthiness of customer | Primarily Commercial (few multi-family) few industrial |
| Equico Leasing Company | Yes | Equico Leasing (Lessee may purchase at 10% of cost or continue to lease at reduced rate) | Standard Credit Criteria | None Targeted |
| Barclays American Leasing | Yes | | | Hotels/Motels |
| Pacific Lighting & Leasing | Yes | Pacific Lighting & Leasing | Financial strength of customers & offers of guarantees | None Targeted |
| Lloyds Bank, Equipment Leasing Division | No | Lloyds | Standard Bank Credit Criteria | None Targeted |
| Performance Management Corp. | Yes | | | |
| TXL Corporation | No | TXL unless purchase option negotiated | Facility or lessee must have net worth 1X or 2X cost of equipment | None Targeted |
| Greyhound Leasing Corp. | No | | Standard Credit Criteria | None Targeted |
| Republic Financial Corp. | No | | Standard Credit Criteria | None Targeted |

## Types of Leases

There are two types of leases:

- Operating leases
- Financing leases

### Operating Lease

An operating lease is usually a short-term lease, often month-to-month. Lease payments do not amortize the full cost of the equipment. The lease term is shorter than the equipment's expected useful life. A lessee does not own the equipment at the end of the lease. The lessee can either (1) renew the lease for an agreed upon lease term, (2) buy the equipment for its value at the end of the lease, or (3) acquire other equipment. The tax benefits in an operating lease accrue to the lessor, except that in some circumstances the lessor can pass tax credits on to the lessee.

### Financing Lease

A financing lease is really an installment purchase. The lease payments amortize the full price of the equipment, plus an interest factor. At the end of the lease term the "lessee" purchases the equipment for a nominal amount. For tax purposes the lessee is the owner of the equipment and is entitled to the applicable tax credits and other benefits.

## Advantages and Disadvantages
## of Lease Financing

### Advantages of Leasing to the Property Owner

1. There is no capital requirement.

2. Lower cost of energy efficiency: The owner can obtain the benefits of acquiring equipment at a lower cost than with a bank loan, particularly if he does not want or need the tax benefits.

3. Pass through of operating costs: A lease may permit commercial property owners whose tenants are obligated to pay any

escalation in operating costs to include the costs of energy efficiency equipment as an "operating cost" and pass it through to the tenants. If the building's lease provisions only permit the owner to pass through energy cost increases, then energy leasing expenses could not be passed on to tenants.

4. Off balance sheet financing: Lease financing is deemed to be "off balance sheet financing." In other words, it does not directly reduce the net worth of the lessee. It is not a liability which will impinge on the lessee's credit worthiness.

5. Flexible payments: Unlike a bank loan, which usually requires equal monthly amortization payments of principal and interest, lease payments may start low and escalate over the term of the lease. That permits the lease payments to be structured to match energy savings, which are expected to increase annually as utility rates increase.

6. Flexible length of lease: Lease transactions generally range from three to five years. Energy efficiency equipment, however, could be leased for terms up to seven years. The longer the term, the lower the monthly payment.

7. Risk of obsolescence limited: By obtaining a short-term lease, a building owner can "hedge his bets" in the event the equipment becomes obsolete. Faster and more efficient equipment may become available at an attractive rate within a few years. An equipment purchase will usually require a longer holding period to justify the investment before acquiring more modern items. Under a lease, the owner can terminate the lease and lease new equipment. The lessor in this case would bear the risks of obsolescence.

*Disadvantages to Lessee*

1. Cost: The cost of leasing equipment will usually be higher than a loan if the lessee keeps the tax credits; however, that is not always true. Rates quoted for financing leases, which are leases where the building owner has the right to purchase the equipment for a nominal sum at the end of the lease term, ranged

between one and three points above the prime interest rate. See Table 14-2. It is unlikely that a bank loan for the same customer would be at a higher rate.

2.  No ownership of equipment: If the building owner enters into an operating lease he will not own the equipment at the end of the lease term. He will probably have an option to buy the equipment for its market value when the lease expires. The market value may be as low as 10% of its original cost, but may also be much higher. If the equipment has a high value at the end of the lease term, this would be a significant disadvantage.

## Tax Issues Involved in Leasing

The principal issues are:

1.  Is the energy equipment leasable equipment?

2.  What is the appropriate depreciation (capital cost recovery period) for the equipment? Is the item a structural component of the building or "tangible personal property"?

3.  Does the equipment qualify for the investment tax credit? Is the equipment used in commercial or industrial buildings and does it constitute tangible personal property?

4.  Does the equipment qualify for the energy tax credit?

5.  Will the "at risk" rules limit the availability of the deductions to investors who participate in the entity which owns the equipment and serves as the lessor?

6.  Can the owner of the building pass through to tenants the operating costs incurred in leasing energy equipment?

7.  Can the owner of a multifamily apartment building that is subject to a Section 8 housing assistance payment contract with the U.S. Department of Housing and Urban Development include the lease expense of acquiring energy equipment as an operating expense for which he is entitled to reimbursement?

8.  Is the equipment a fixture or personal property under state law?

9. Does equipment installed as part of the substantial rehabilitation of a nonresidential building qualify for a substantial rehabilitation tax credit?

## Financial Issues

There are a range of financial issues related to leasing energy equipment. They include:

### Lack of Adequate Collateral

The lessor will obtain a lien on the leased equipment. However, energy equipment is not viewed as valuable collateral. It has no established resale value. Its true value depends on its ability to save energy in a particular structure. The cost and difficulty of removing the equipment, if it were repossessed, is unknown.

### Small Transactions

Leasing companies, like banks, are most interested in either large transactions or a very large number of small transactions. While one or two of the leasing companies we talked with said they lease equipment that costs as little as $10,000, most companies said that the relatively small size of energy efficiency equipment leases gave it a low priority in their overall marketing strategy.

### Not All Energy Improvements Require Installing Leasable Equipment

Often an energy audit recommends a series of measures that are cost effective. Many of the conservation measures suggested will be low cost/no cost items which do not involve leasable equipment (e.g. caulking, weatherstripping, storm windows, etc.). Only a portion of the total projected cost savings will result from the installation of leasable equipment.

### Uncertainty Surrounding Existing Tax Benefits

Uncertainty regarding the availability of existing tax benefits makes it difficult for leasing companies and property owners to

**Table 14-2. Lease Financing**

| Name of Company | Type of Lease | Finance Rate | Disposition of Tax Credits and Depreciation | Length of Lease |
|---|---|---|---|---|
| Energy Leasing Services, Inc. | a) Operating Lease | 1) Prime interest rate<br>2) 6 or 7 points below prime | Customer receives Tax Benefits<br>ELSI (or investors) receive Tax Benefits | 5–7 yrs<br>(Min. 3 yrs;<br>Max. 10 yrs) |
| | b) Shared Savings Lease | Lease payment based on share of savings | Third party Investors | 5–7 yrs |
| | c) Positive guaranteed cash-flow lease | Lease payment guaranteed from energy savings | Third party Investors | 5–7 yrs |
| Johnson Controls, Inc. | a) Financing Lease | Interest rate varies as a function of credit worthiness of customer, & prime rate | Customer receives Tax Benefits | 3, 5 or 7 yrs |
| | b) Operating Lease | Interest rate varies as a function of credit worthiness of customer & prime rate | Customer receives Tax Benefits | 3, 5 or 7 yrs |
| Equico Leasing Company (Boston Office) | a) Financing Lease | Transactions less than $25,000: 1 to 3 points above prime<br><br>Transactions greater than $25,000: 1 point under prime | Customer receives Tax Benefits<br><br>Customer receives Tax Benefits | 1–5 yrs<br>(avg. 3)<br><br>1–5 yrs<br>(avg. 3) |
| | b) Operating Lease | 4 to 7 points under prime | Equico retains Tax Benefits | |

| Company | Lease Type | Pricing | Tax Benefits | Term |
|---|---|---|---|---|
| Barclay's American Leasing | a) Financing Lease | 1 to 3 points above prime | Customer receives Tax Beneftis | 5 yrs |
| | b) Operating Lease | 1) Prime or 1 point above | Barclay's receives Depreciation, Customer receives ETC & ITC | 5 yrs |
| | | 2) Prime to 4 points less than prime | Barclay's receives all Tax Benefits | 5 yrs |
| Pacific Lighting and Leasing | Operating Lease | Depends on who receives tax credits & depreciation | Negotiable | 3–7 yrs prefer 5 yrs |
| Lloyd's Bank, Equipment Leasing Dept. | Operating Lease | 1) 1 to 2 points above prime | Customer receives Tax Benefits | 5 yrs |
| | | 2) 5 to 7 points below prime | Lloyd's retains Tax Benefits | 5 yrs |
| Performance Mgmt. Co. | Shared Savings Lease | Depends on income stream produced by shared savings installation | | 7 yrs |
| TXL Corporation | a) Finance Lease | 1) Approx. 7 points below prime | TXL or Investors receive Tax Benefits | 5–7 yrs |
| | b) Operating Lease | 2) Not applicable to energy equipment due to marginally fungible nature of equipment | Not Applicable | |
| Greyhound Leasing Corp. | Operating Lease | Depends on disposition of tax credits, ACRS, dollar amount of transaction and credit worthiness of customer | Negotiable | 7 yrs (2 yr min.; 15 yr max.) |

*(continued)*

## Table 14-2. Continued

| Name of Company | Type of Lease | Finance Rate | Disposition of Tax Credits and Depreciation | Length of Lease |
|---|---|---|---|---|
| Republic Financial Corp. | a) Finance Lease<br>b) Single Investor Tax Leases<br>c) Multiple Investor Tax Leases | Depends on:<br>1) The credit and financial strength of the customer;<br>2) "tax appetite" of the customer; and<br>3) tax requirements of the equity raiser. | Negotiable | Negotiable |

accurately evaluate the relative attractiveness of leasing energy equipment.

### Uncertainty Caused by Proposed Changes in Tax Benefits

Uncertainty caused by the Administration's proposal to eliminate the energy tax credit acts as a depressant to the energy equipment market, preventing some leasing companies and other financial institutions from moving into this area.

### Availability of State Tax Credits

Many states have enacted very attractive tax credits for energy conservation and solar energy equipment. Of the eleven states we surveyed, five offered energy tax credits to commercial, industrial or multifamily building owners. Table 14-3 summarizes the tax credits available in these five states: California, Colorado, Massachusetts, North Carolina, and Oregon.

For example, Oregon offers a 35% tax credit for energy conservation improvements in commercial and industrial buildings. The credit must be taken over a five-year period. The Oregon credits can be used by investors in limited partnerships who purchase and lease energy equipment to industrial and commercial property owners in Oregon.

State tax credits can be combined with federal tax benefits to provide an attractive investment return for investors who purchase and lease energy equipment. If the partnership can obtain debt financing equal to 75% of the cost of the equipment, the tax credits will almost offset the equity investment and the investors will be able to charge a lease rate that is competitive with rates charged by leasing companies. However, if existing financial institutions decide to actively pursue the energy leasing market, they can provide quicker, easier and faster lease arrangements than private investors. They have both the available capital and marketing outlets (sales representatives) who have established relationships with manufacturers and vendors. The leasing companies do not need to form specific partnerships, prepare private placement memoranda and related financial projections, and sell a deal to investors to consummate each transaction. They can identify and close a deal within a few days.

Table 14-3. State Income Tax Incentives for Conservation and Alternative Energy Equipment*

| | California | | Colorado | | Massachusetts | |
|---|---|---|---|---|---|---|
| | Solar Credit | Conservation Credit | Write-Off for Alternative Energy System | Credit for Energy Property | Solar Credit | Solar Deduction |
| **Type of System** | | | | | | |
| Solar | X | | X | | X | X |
| Cogeneration | | | X | | | |
| Conservation | | X | | X | | |
| Other | X | | X | | X | X |
| **Bldg. Types** | | | | | | |
| Residential | X | X | X | X | X | X |
| Commercial | X | X | X | X | X | X |
| Industrial | X | X | | | | X |
| **Amount of Credit** | For all bldg. types: credit for 55% of costs up to $3,000<br><br>For systems costing more than $12,000 in non-residential buildings: the greater of 25% or $3000 | For systems costing less than $6,000: credit for 40% of costs, up to $1500<br><br>For systems costing more than $6,000 in nonresidential buildings: 25% of costs | Deduction or 5-yr write-off of costs | Credit for 10% of costs for expenditures up to $1.75 million in 1982; $2.25 million in 1983–6 | Credit for 30% of costs for expenditures up to $1.75 million in 1982; $2.25 million in 1983–6. | Deduction for system costs |

| | | | | | | |
|---|---|---|---|---|---|---|
| *Available to Lessors of Eligible Systems?* | NO | NO | ? | NO | NO | NO |
| *Termination Date* | 12/1/84 | 12/1/84 for some equipment; 12/1/86 for other equipment | 12/1/86 | 12/1/87 | 12/1/87 | None |
| *Other Requirements* | | | Cannot be used with state tax credits | | | Taxpayer must use property in business for 10 years after deduction is claimed; systems must be certified |
| *Other Relevant Program(s)* | Can be combined with 3-year write-off of solar energy equipment costs | Can be combined with 3-year write-off of conservation equipment costs | | | | |

*This represents a survey of eleven states. Credits that can only be claimed by taxpayers on their principal residences are not included. The other states surveyed are: Florida, Georgia, Maryland, Minnesota, New York, and Texas.

*(continued)*

**Table 14-3.  Continued**

| | North Carolina Solar Credit | Cogeneration Credit | Credit for Boiler Conversion | Industrial Credit | Oregon Conservation Credit |
|---|---|---|---|---|---|
| *Type of System* | | | | | |
| Solar | X | | | | |
| Cogeneration | | X | | X | |
| Conservation | | | X | | X |
| Other | | | | | |
| *Bldg. Types* | | | | | |
| Residential | X | | | | |
| Commercial | | | | | X |
| Industrial | | X | X | X | X |
| *Amount of Credit* | Credit for 25% of system costs (can't exceed $1000 per unit) | Credit for 10% of system costs | Credit for 10% of costs (limit of 15% of costs paid in any one year) | Credit for 20% of costs up to $8000 for "single instal-lation" | Credit for 35% of costs over 5 years |
| *Available to Lessors of Eligible Systems?* | NO | NO | NO | NO | YES |
| *Termination Date* | None | None | None | None | 12/1/85 |
| *Other Requirements* | | | | | Facility must be certified; only $40 million of facilities can be certified per year |
| *Other Relevant Program(s)* | | | | | |

Large financial institutions can be expected to make capital available to lease energy equipment when the demand for such leasing transactions becomes more evident. As the economics of acquiring energy equipment become more attractive, it is likely that more firms will begin to specialize in leasing energy equipment. The first entities that will move into this market will be manufacturers and vendors of energy equipment, followed by leasing affiliates of life insurance companies and independent leasing companies.

## Lease Financing for Industrial Buildings

Leasing is an economically feasible and attractive means of financing industrial energy efficiency improvements. Industrial firms are usually familiar with lease financing. They are likely to have adequate credit to qualify for a lease. The off-balance sheet aspect of leasing is important to industrial firms whose financial statements are reviewed by stockholders as well as banks and other lenders. Many of the energy efficiency items recommended for industrial buildings qualify as leasable equipment under traditional IRS guidelines. Industrial energy equipment also qualifies for the regular investment tax credit and accelerated depreciation. In addition, most of the existing energy tax credits apply to industrial energy efficiency improvements.

Despite these advantages, we did not find many examples of leased industrial energy equipment. Industrial firms that identify cost-effective energy investments do not appear to examine leasing on a regular basis as a financing alternative. They are more likely to either request budget authority to purchase the item, or defer acquisition until budget authority is available. Perhaps the engineering orientation of many corporate energy managers—and their lack of financial expertise—contribute to the dearth of innovative financing for industrial energy improvements.

If leasing companies targeted energy equipment as an area warranting a special marketing program, they could significantly broaden the use of leasing for industrial energy improvements. But most of these companies do not have sufficient evidence that the market demand exists. It is a little like the chicken and the egg. If the demand existed, the leasing firms could readily satisfy the need. If leasing companies aggressively marketed energy equipment leases, many industrial firms might choose lease financing.

## Model Lease Documents for Industrial Equipment

Model lease documents which can help implement industrial lease transactions are discussed later in this chapter. These model documents can increase the acceptance and use of energy equipment leasing by different types of property owners in different industries located throughout the United States, thereby increasing the rate and level of energy efficiency investment. These efforts also have the potential of generating support and participation from a broad array of financial institutions who have the resources to aggressively market an energy leasing program once its feasibility is firmly established.

Documents to implement an industrial leasing transaction include:

1. A lease for energy efficiency equipment;

2. Security agreements;

3. Cash flow and after-tax analyses of the relative benefits of leasing energy equipment to the user;

4. Financing agreements for acquisition of the equipment by the lessor;

5. Guarantees of energy savings, if needed, from the equipment manufacturer or installer;

6. Insurance agreements for the equipment and the energy savings, if necessary or desirable to create a program that would have wide acceptability.

Documents should include alternative provisions for a financing lease and an operating lease and should identify provisions needed to pass tax benefits through from the lessor to the lessee.

### Lease Financing for Commercial Buildings

Lease financing for commercial buildings is not as attractive as industrial buildings because the available tax benefits are more limited. Commercial building owners are also less willing to provide credit or separate collateral for the loan. Nevertheless, there appears to be a large potential market within the commercial building sector to lease energy equipment, particularly:

1. In buildings where the equipment lease payment becomes an operating cost that can be passed through to the tenants;

2. Where the building owner has good credit; and

3. Where the owner seeks to acquire a computer-controlled energy management system, which usually qualifies for the 10% regular investment tax credit and accelerated capital cost recovery.

Individual owners of commercial buildings may personally benefit by using tax credits from leasing transactions. The individual can borrow 80% of the money needed to acquire the equipment and lease the equipment to the entity (partnership or corporation) that owns the building. This transaction must satisfy other specific IRS guidelines. Model documents to demonstrate the economic feasibility of leasing computer-controlled energy management systems—for the lessor and lessee—can increase the number and availability of such leasing transactions. Banks, insurance companies, utilities and real property managers would probably participate in these transactions as sources of debt financing and as general partners.

## Lease Financing for Multifamily Buildings

Energy items recommended for multifamily buildings do not often lend themselves to leasing. In multifamily buildings there is usually no collateral available to secure the lease. The credit of the property owner will probably not be satisfactory. Those factors will make it difficult for an investor to provide or obtain financing for the equipment which might be leased to a multifamily owner.

Despite the above cautionary comments, leasing could play an important role in multifamily buildings as the energy savings available from different types of equipment increases. The willingness of more engineering firms and equipment manufacturers to guarantee energy savings will encourage financial institutions to make loans based on economic value of the equipment. The lessor, as owner of the equipment, would be the beneficiary of the savings guarantee if the equipment were repossessed and installed elsewhere.

Large financial institutions, including banks and life insurance companies, could play a vital role in developing and encouraging lease financing for energy equipment in commercial and multifamily buildings. These institutions, as mortgagors, have a long-term financial interest in large numbers of buildings. Improved energy efficiency of these buildings increases the owner's cash flow. Increased cash flow will benefit the lender if the lender's interest payments vary depending on the owner's cash flow.

Mortgagors could encourage and provide financing for energy efficiency equipment lease transactions. With prior approval of certain transactions from large lenders, property owners who might otherwise be reluctant to install certain types of equipment will be more willing to "follow the leader." They would know the lender approves of the improvements. However, leasing is an important option which can be expanded and utilized to provide significant financing for energy equipment.
equipment.

### Leasing Solar Equipment

We have examined the feasibility of leasing solar energy equipment to multifamily property owners in California. In northern California, the utilities provide a rebate of $8 per unit per month for 36 months to building owners who install solar domestic hot water heaters. There is also a 25% California state tax credit for solar systems owned by a business.

The combination of those state subsidies with available federal tax benefits could be expected to create solar leasing transactions that would be attractive to tax shelter investors. However, there are three drawbacks:

1.  Returns available to investors in private partnerships in real estate, oil and gas and other activities have become more attractive as a result of the 1981 Economic Recovery Tax Act. When compared to the risks of a solar energy investment, the potential return from the solar energy equipment was offset

by greater risks that the equipment might not operate as promised and a lack of certainty regarding the value of the solar system in the future (its residual value).

2. The economics of the solar equipment, the long payback required because of the rather limited real dollar savings resulting from solar domestic hot water systems, prevented transactions from having real economic viability, beyond the tax subsidies.

3. Debt financing was difficult to arrange and expensive. For equipment with a payback of 15 years, a 7- or even 10-year loan was not sufficient to provide a monthly positive cash flow from energy savings.

Our experience examining the feasibility of leasing solar domestic hot water systems to multifamily owners in California underscores the importance of the economic viability of the investment. Even with very large tax credits, if the equipment does not have a payback of a few years, it is unlikely that viable financing transactions can be arranged without public sector support.

The City of Oceanside, California, is providing the necessary public sector support to develop a solar leasing program through funds from the California Energy Commission. The City has established the Oceanside Municipal Solar and Conservation Utility (MSU) which arranges for private firms to lease domestic solar hot water systems to building owners within the City.

Under special provisions of state law, the lessors of the solar equipment are entitled to take the state solar energy tax credit, even though they do not own the structures upon which the solar equipment is installed. We have been advised that a few building owners have recently signed leases for this program.

The role of the MSU includes establishing standards for equipment and installations, establishing an arbitration board to settle disputes, and disseminating energy information and lists of qualified installers. The MSU also collects all lease payment and is a party to all leases of energy equipment between private leasing companies and property owners.

## Lease Financing by Energy Service Companies and Other Energy Efficiency Professionals

Leasing energy efficiency equipment deserves special treatment in the context of energy service company and energy management company financing. In a survey of companies offering energy management equipment and/or services, it was inquired whether lease financing was offered to customers as an alternative to shared savings or direct purchasing. Most of the vendors, distributors and manufacturers, as well as a few energy service companies, offered to arrange third-party leasing or, as an alternative, directly lease-finance equipment, systems and/or services themselves.

### Financing Leases

Two of the six manufacturers we contacted permit customers to finance energy efficiency equipment by lease purchasing, known as a "financing lease."[1] A financing lease plan is similar to an operating lease, except that after the last payment in the lease term, the lessee may purchase the equipment for a nominal sum, usually one dollar. No large initial capital outlay is required from the user.

The user's right to purchase the energy equipment at the end of the lease term for a nominal sum often means that the lease payments will be higher than under an operating lease. A five- to ten-percent commitment fee is usually required at the beginning of the lease term. Lease purchasing permits the lessee, unlike a conventional lease, to be treated as the property owner for tax purposes. The lessee can take depreciation deductions and the available investment and/or energy tax credits.

### An Example of An Energy Financing Lease Program

International Energy Conservation Services (IECS) offers three-year and five-year lease-purchase plans for its Energy Master room motion sensors. At the end of the lease term the owner buys the equipment for $1.00; the owner/lessee also takes the depreciation and tax credits. IECS connects the sensors, which are used in hotels,

---

[1]Johnson Controls, Inc. and Honeywell, Inc.

office buildings and shopping centers, to a Hewlett Packard 1000 computer at IECS' main office. IECS charges the user a monthly fee for the hook up to the central computer equipment. The monthly service charge is a fixed fee, determined by the type of system installed for the client and the rate of return on the investment.

*Leasing Through Energy Management
and Energy Service Companies*

Energy service companies do very little lease financing. The independent shared-savings financiers also do not assemble lease financing packages, with one or two exceptions. Although six energy service companies[2] offered to arrange lease financing, only one offered to participate in the lease transaction.[3] The energy service companies indicated that leasing was generally a small part of the energy service business because the energy service concept does not lend itself to lease financing.

Leasing is more prevalent among vendors and distributors of energy efficiency equipment. All the vendors we contacted utilized independent leasing companies, rather than participate directly in the lease transactions. Vendors and distributors do not assemble their own leasing packages because (1) they do not have or they do not want to spend the large front-end capital needed to purchase the equipment, and (2) they lack the expertise needed to operate a lease financing program. Engineering firms, distributors and energy service companies seeking to install shared-savings programs face similar problems. Vendors and distributors have turned to third-party financiers to assemble lease financing packages for their customers.

*Independent Leasing Companies*

Nine independent leasing companies were contacted regarding lease financing terms and transactions for energy efficiency equipment. We identified one company specifically focusing on leasing

---

[2]World Wide Energy Systems, Inc.; Diversified Energy Systems, Inc.; Energy Management, Inc.; International Energy Conservation Services; Northern Energy Corp.; and Technology Concepts, Inc.

[3]Diversified Energy Systems.

energy efficiency equipment.[4] Two other independent leasing companies anticipate an increase in the number of energy equipment lease transactions they will assemble in 1982.[5]

There was a great deal of similarity in the terms of the lease transactions arranged to finance energy efficiency equipment. Leasing companies utilizing financing leases,[6] where the tax benefits (energy tax credit, investment tax credit and depreciation) are passed through to the customer/lessee, usually charge one to three points above the prime interest rate.[7] Companies offering operating leases vary the financing rate according to the prime interest rate, the credit worthiness of the customer, and the allocation of tax benefits.

Where the customer receives the tax benefits of the transaction, the lease rate will vary from one point under prime to one or two points above prime.[8] If the tax benefits are retained by the lessor, the finance rate will be reduced significantly, often six to seven points below the prime interest rate.[9] Nearly all of the independent leasing companies contacted preferred a lease term of five years. Most stated they would consider a seven-year lease term.

Although the credit criteria varied among lease companies, none of the companies indicated that the energy efficiency equipment itself was sufficient collateral for the lease. Most leasing companies evaluated the lease transaction according to a standard credit criteria, which considered the value of the equipment, the soundness of the

---

[4] Energy Leasing Services, Inc.

[5] Equico Leasing Company and Barclay's American Leasing Company.

[6] Our criteria for classifying a lease as a financing lease included:
   A.  Eventual transfer of ownership of property from lessor to lessee by end of lease term.
   B.  Lease containing a bargain purchase option, and thus allowing lessee to acquire ownership at a bargain price.
   C.  Lease term spans 75% or more of the expected economic life of the property.
   D.  Present value of minimum lease payments, is 90% or more of excess of property's fair value over lessor's investment tax credit.

These criteria are necessary for a lessee to be deemed owner of the equipment during the lease term, for federal income tax purposes. See *Leveraged and Single Investor Leasing 1981*, Bruce Fritch (1981).

[7] See Table 14-2.

[8] See Table 14-2.

[9] See Table 14-2.

customer's company, profit and loss statements, and the lessee's debt and equity ratios.

Many of the companies contacted are not currently leasing energy efficiency equipment, but indicated they would if the proper opportunity arose.[10] Companies not yet involved in leasing energy equipment, as well as several banks,[11] mentioned the following problems with energy efficiency equipment leasing which had in some way influenced their decision not to enter the market:

1. The lack of a predictable resale value for energy efficiency equipment.

2. The energy equipment rarely represents adequate collateral for a lease transaction.

3. The cost of installation and/or removing the energy efficiency equipment is often as great as the cost of the equipment itself.

4. The total dollar value of the individual transactions is too small.[12]

5. Not all energy efficiency equipment is leasable; many basic retrofit improvements cannot be leased under current IRS regulations.

6. Not all leasable energy efficiency equipment qualifies for the energy tax credit. Where lease financing programs are assembled for investors, the lack of an energy tax credit limits the attractiveness of the package. Nearly all parties we spoke with, including leasing companies, energy service companies, syndicators and banks, considered the energy tax credit an important factor in assembling viable financial packages for energy efficiency equipment.

---

[10]See Table 14-1.

[11]Crocker Bank of San Francisco; Lloyds Bank, Leasing Division, Los Angeles; and Chemical Bank, New York.

[12]The smallest transaction one lessor would consider was $4 million. The fact that energy efficiency equipment is relatively inexpensive, compared to cogeneration facilities, windmills or coal plants, does not lessen the need for lease financing.

## Phase II—Model Contract Documents

Phase II of the Lane and Edson project includes a carefully developed Model Energy Service Agreement with an extensive commentary describing how, when and where such an agreement can be used and the rationale behind each provision.

It also includes two model Equipment Lease Agreements that can be used for energy equipment leasing transactions, along with a commentary discussing important tax and legal aspects of the documents.

These model documents are accompanied by an explanation of the key business and legal issues raised by leasing and shared-savings transactions. These documents will be available to be used, with proper modification and legal counsel, by entities interested in consummating energy efficiency transactions.

A brief description of these Model Documents follows.

In addition, an example of a Shared-Savings Program Management Service Agreement developed by Flack + Kurtz Energy Management Corporation is included in Appendix B.

### *Legal and Business Terms of Model Documents*

A shared-savings program represents a unique financing mechanism. Shared-savings programs combine a "one stop" energy service with 100% financing at no risk (financial or technical) to the energy user. However, shared-savings programs have a limited track record. Investors and building owners are understandably wary of a program which seems to offer "a free lunch" to all parties.

Energy users and financial institutions lack a basic understanding of shared-savings transactions. They do not know the extent of the ESC's undertakings or whether the energy service agreement can be terminated if the ESC does not achieve any energy savings. They are concerned about letting another company "control" their building's HVAC system. They do not believe "savings" can be fairly measured. They want to avoid providing the ESC with a "windfall" profit obtained by installing low-cost and fast-payback measures.

Energy users and investors raise similar questions regarding transactions involving leased energy efficiency equipment. The model

Energy Service Agreement, model Lease Agreements and related Commentaries answer these and many similar questions. The model Agreements will provide parties with a specific contract and a set of business terms that:

1. can be used by building owners, investors, and ESCs to compare and evaluate the relative benefits of other shared savings or leasing contracts;

2. can be used to structure the terms of programs to be offered by companies interested in starting shared savings or leasing transactions;

3. lower the costs of entry into the shared savings or leasing business by providing parties with a basic research regarding legal issues presented in a contract.

The Commentaries describe the step-by-step procedure that the ESC or lessor will follow in implementing the financing program. They identify the risks assumed by each party at each stage of the deal and the remedies available if one party defaults at any stage of the transaction.

The model Agreements must be modified to reflect the facts and circumstances of each transaction. They are complex legal documents that should be used after consultation with counsel to consider (1) the impact of the Agreements on the parties, (2) the impact of state and local law considerations and (3) tax aspects of the transaction.

Parties considering shared savings and leasing transactions should remember that the model contracts are designed to avoid future disputes among the parties by clearly defining each party's responsibilities. But a contract can only protect the integrity of the transaction up to a certain point. Honesty, good faith, cooperation, and financial and technical expertise must exist for the contract to produce a satisfactory deal.

## Reference

A detailed report outlining the advantages of leasing to both lessor and lessee is contained in the book *Innovative Financing for Energy*

*Efficiency Improvements: Phase I Report* by Martin Klepper. *Innovative Financing for Energy Efficiency Improvements* is available through Lane and Edson, P.C., Washington, D.C.

A second report by Lane and Edson—*Phase II, Model Contract Documents*—includes a model Energy Service Agreement and two model Equipment Lease Agreements.

# Chapter 15

# Energy Financing Tools for the '80s: Tax-Exempt Revenue Bond and IDB Financing

Alan Hills

Tax-exempt financing usually provides the lowest cost financing tool for local governments and/or private businesses who want to develop energy production or conservation facilities. Tax-exempt financing involves the issuance by a state, a local government, or an agency of tax-exempt bonds for its own use or for a loan of the bond proceeds to private businesses that agree to repay the borrowed funds through a long-term loan, lease or installment purchase agreement with the issuing government.

Tax-exempt financing can provide loans for a period in the range of up to 30 years at a lower interest rate than is available from local bank loans. Tax-exempt financing is governed by the provisions of Section 103 of the Internal Revenue Code of 1954 and interpretations of Section 103 by the IRS, courts and private legal counsels. However, additional state legislative authority and local government action will usually be needed, to implement a tax-exempt revenue bond program.

## Federal Law and Tax-Exempt Financing

Section 103 of the Internal Revenue Code (the Code) provides that the interest earned by a purchaser of a bond issued by a state or local governmental entity will be tax-exempt, provided the bond issuance complies with the requirements of Section 103 and regulations adopted thereunder. There are generally two types of tax-exempt bonds that could be used to finance energy production or conservation projects: industrial development bonds (IDBs) and municipal revenue bonds.

### I. Industrial Development Financing

#### A. IDB Financing Generally Prohibited

The Code generally prohibits the financing of privately-owned facilities through municipal borrowing by disallowing the exclusion from income taxation of interest income on such obligations, which are termed "industrial development bonds" (IDBs).

*1. Industrial development bond tests.* The Code provides that where more than 25 percent of bond proceeds are used directly or indirectly in the trade or business of any taxable entity, and debt service on the obligations is secured by an interest in property used in the taxable entity's trade or business, or payments made in respect of such property, these bonds meet the definition of an industrial development bond and the interest income tax exemption is disallowed.

*2. IDB tests interpreted.* Proceeds may be considered "used in a trade or business" where the private entity merely leases the financed property or manages it on a long-term contract: The Use Test does *not* require private ownership. The IDB tests are considered met where the present value of all payments received by the municipality from a private user of tax-exempt financed property are approximately equal to debt service on the obligations, even if the payments and the property do *not* directly secure the municipal bonds.

## B. *Certain Types of IDB Financing Permitted*

Under restrictive conditions relating to either the type of facility or its aggregate cost, certain tax-exempt industrial development financing is permitted.

*1. Exempt activity issues.* Tax-exempt bonds may be issued without restriction as to amount to finance certain facilities owned or leased by private entities. These certain facilities must be used in pursuit of one, or a combination of, exempt activities which are specified by the Code.

In the area of energy, private business may borrow unlimited amounts through the use of tax-exempt IDBs for solid waste disposal energy production facilities, facilities for the local furnishing of electricity within two contiguous counties and for hydroelectric generating facilities that meet certain specific requirements.

*2. Exempt "small issue" IDBs.* In addition, obligations may be issued in restricted aggregated amounts to finance any type of facility (subject to state law provisions) owned or leased by private entities.

a. Exempt $1,000,000 Issues
   Industrial Development Bonds of up to $1,000,000 principal amount may be issued to finance all or a portion of any privately owned or leased facility without regard to either its use (a state law concern) or its aggregate cost.

b. Exempt $10,000,000 Issues
   As an election in place of the $1,000,000 IDBs, an aggregate face amount of obligations not exceeding $10,000,000 can be issued to finance private facilities, provided that no less than 90 percent of the proceeds of the obligations are used to pay the capital costs of acquisition, construction, reconstruction, or improvement of land or property of a character subject to the allowance for depreciation. However, in the calculation of the $10,000,000 limitation, the Code requires the inclusion *not only* of the stated face amount of the issue, but *also all* (1) outstanding exempt small issues which finance facilities

located in the same political subdivision which have the same private user, (2) other capital expenditures made within the political subdivision by the private users of the facilities and (3) capital expenditures made by any person for property which will be used in connection with the facility; all within a six-year period commencing three years prior to and ending three years subsequent to the date of the bond issue. The amount of IDBs that can be issued then is equal to $10,000,-000 less the aggregate of items (1), (2), and (3), above.

However, the limitation on the total amount of capital expenditures and outstanding IDBs (but not the $10,000,000 limitation on the amount of IDBs issued) is increased to $20,000,000 for facilities financed in part with Urban Development Action Grant funds.

*3. General IDB issuance restrictions.* In addition to the restrictions related to a certain type of IDB exemption, certain other conditions attach to the issuance of any IDB, such as a requirement that the municipal issuer take some form of "official action" (e.g., an authorizing resolution) *prior* to the making of significant project expenditures, and a disallowance of the tax-exemption pertaining to any obligation held by a "substantial user" of the facility (who occupies at least 5 percent of project space or holds at least a 5 percent equity or profits interest in the project).

## II. Municipal Revenue Bond Financing

An alternative to private Industrial Development Bonds are Municipal Revenue Bonds. Municipal Revenue Bonds are *not* backed by the full faith and credit of the issuing municipality and are *not* limited by any state municipal debt ceilings or Federal Tax Code limitation on the amount of bonds issued. A revenue bond is simply a promise to repay the bondholders' principal and pay them interest out of the revenue derived from specific energy facilities or projects. For example, revenue bonds are often used to raise funds for the construction of electric generating facilities by individual municipal utilities or by a number of utilities through membership in "joint action" financing agencies. The issuing local government promises to pay the bondholders out of revenue derived or based upon the cost savings from the energy production or conservation facilities developed with the bond proceeds. The municipality will *not* be obligated to use other tax or revenue sources to repay the bondholders if the energy facilities do not derive sufficient revenues or savings. Municipal revenue bonds are issued by State or local governments or by certain non-profit public agencies or authorities for their own use as owners-developers of energy production and/or conservation facilities.

The energy production or conservation facilities must be owned and in some cases operated by the local government or public authority that issues the municipal revenue bonds. In addition, at least a significant portion of the benefits (energy cost savings) or service (energy production) from the energy facilities must be made available to the general public and no more than 25 percent of the benefits or service may be sold under long-term contracts to private business (excluding businesses individually using three percent or less of the benefits or production of the energy facilities).

## Legal Issues Related to Bond Issuance

A host of legal issues must be considered before proceeding with a tax-exempt municipal revenue or industrial development bond issuance. A local government must determine whether, under state and local law, bonds can be issued for the particular energy facilities being considered. The bonds must be used for a "public purpose" as defined by statute. An analysis of state and local law in each jurisdiction will be necessary in order to determine how the Federal tax law provisions can be utilized for the issuance of municipal revenue or industrial development bonds for the financing of energy production or conservation facilities.

## Tax-Exempt Financing and Tax Incentives— The Double-Dip Limitation

The Crude Oil Windfall Profits Tax Act of 1980 places a restriction on the use of tax-exempt industrial development bonds for energy production and conservation facilities in combination with use of the energy tax credit Congress provided that an energy production or conservation facility would *not* qualify for the energy tax credit if funds for the facility were obtained from the proceeds of a tax-exempt bond or other "subsidized government financing." The business energy tax credit must be reduced for the portion of the cost of the qualifying energy facility financed by a tax-exempt bond. In other words, tax-exempt bond proceeds used to pay for energy equipment or facilities cannot be included by the property owner as an expenditure that entitles the property owner to the energy tax credit.

Loss of the energy tax credit will reduce the benefits of tax-exempt financing, if the energy facilities otherwise qualify for the energy tax credit. *However, tax-exempt financing will continue to be attractive to most private firms even if they cannot claim the energy tax credit.* The savings from the low-interest, long-term financing is normally more valuable, on a discounted present value basis, than the loss of the energy tax credit. Moreover, the tax credit is not available for many energy production or conservation facilities.

Most importantly, the tax credits by themselves do *not* provide the capital required to develop the energy facilities, which tax-exempt financing *can* provide.

## Security for Tax-Exempt Municipal Revenue and Industrial Development Bonds

One of the most important considerations in structuring a tax-exempt energy financing is to identify (1) a secure revenue stream that will be used to repay the bonds and, (2) the security that will be provided to bondholders in the event the borrower defaults on repaying the loan.

### Basic Types of Security for Energy Project Financings

*A. Overall ("deep pocket") creditworthiness*—Projects for which the primary security for the debt financing is the cash flow and/or assets of the owner/developer of the project (utility, municipality or private developer) which are *not* related to the specific characteristics of the energy project being financed. In other words, the general financial strength of the developer or another participant in the project, not the assets and operating revenues of the project itself.

B. *Self-supported project financing*—Projects for which the security for the debt financing is the projected cash flow from operation of the project and the value of the facilities themselves, *not* the general financial strength or tax revenues of any participant or owner of the project.

Most energy production projects with more than marginal feasibility projections can be financed on a self-supporting basis, *without* relying upon the tax revenues or budget of the municipality developing the project or any other separate source of security.

For Industrial Development Bonds, the private business borrower will normally issue an unconditional guarantee to repay the borrowed funds based upon the general creditworthiness of the private borrower and/or a mortgage lien on the property being financed. Additional security for IDBs can be provided in certain instances through the use of a "third party" guarantee of debt repayment with insurance or a bank letter of credit, for a fee.

For publicly-owned energy production or conservation facilities, financed with municipal revenue bonds, the debt should be repaid from revenues earned from the sale of energy produced, other products and services provided or from the value of energy savings derived as a result of operating the energy facilities. To the extent possible, these revenue streams produced or the energy savings derived from the facilities should be assured by long-term contractual arrangements with creditworthy parties, who benefit from the savings or purchase the output of the energy facilities.

## Combined Financings—
## Tax-Exempt Bonds and Leasing

Until the mid-1970's, local governments normally issued tax-exempt bonds to finance facilities or equipment that would be directly owned and operated by these governments. More recently, however, ownership of certain types of public facilities has been placed in the hands of private investors in search of both tax benefits and operating income associated with ownership of enterprise projects. The resulting *municipal lease* can require the governmental entity to assume responsibility for operation, maintenance, insurance —all the normal responsibilities of the owner of a project. Alternatively, a private operator may assume responsibility for the facility as a direct owner or on behalf of a second private party, and may sell its services as operator to a municipality pursuant to a service contract.

One form of financing, called a *tax-leveraged lease* provides the maximum utilization of tax benefits associated with the construction of equipment or facilities, therefore lowering the overall financing cost, and it also shifts the risk of the financing away from the municipality in transactions where the private operator's credit will support the financing, along with the contractual purchasers of the energy production and/or beneficiaries of the energy savings of the project. The joint use of tax-exempt bonds and municipal leasing is called "combined" project financing.

### I.   Types of Financing Leases

A.   *"Guideline" true leases.* In 1975, the Internal Revenue Service issued guidelines in Revenue Procedure 75–21 to specify the leasing terms that would be treated as a "true lease" for tax purposes and would result in the owner-lessor having the right to claim the tax benefits associated with a facility or equipment, instead of treating the lease as a "sale" resulting in the lessee-user having the right to claim those tax benefits.

In a true lease, the owner-lessor has to supply at least 20 percent of the purchase price of a facility or equipment, and can borrow from a lender on a non-recourse basis the remaining 80 percent of the purchase price.

The lessee-user signs a lease agreement promising to pay the owner-lessor over the lease term enough money in rent to amortize the loan from the lender and to pay some cash rate of return to the owner-lessor. The lessee-user also agrees to act as if he owns the leased equipment or facility—operating it and maintaining it in a proper manner, insuring it, paying taxes and other costs related to it, and meeting other ownership responsibilities.

In addition, no "true lease" can be structured with a purchase option at a nominal price to the lessee-user at the end of the lease term; the lessee-user must be required to pay a fair market value price or renew the lease at a fair market rent.

Also, no "true lease" can be structured for what is called "limited use property." Limited use property, basically, is any equipment or facility which no third party, other than the lessee-user in the transaction in question, could use at the end of the lease term.

B. *"Safe harbor" leases.* The Economic Recovery Tax Act of 1981 provided certain new requirements for a lease transaction which, if met, will result in the financing being treated as a lease, instead of a sale. These rules for "safe harbor" leases do *not* replace the guidelines of "true" leases but are an alternative way of structuring a municipal lease financing.

"Safe harbor" lease requirements eliminate the requirements prohibiting bargain purchase options and the leasing of limited use property. As a result, "safe harbor" lease financings can be used to finance for private businesses a greater variety of facilities than under a true lease and on terms more attractive to private businesses functioning as lessee-users, since they can control the ownership at the end of the lease term of equipment and facilities vital to their business operations. However, "safe harbor" leasing can be utilized by local governments or agencies *only* in the area of mass transit vehicle financing.

The Tax Equity and Fiscal Responsibility Act of 1982 (TEFRA) added a number of new provisions regarding safe harbor leases which have the principal effect of reducing the value of the tax benefits derived from a safe harbor lease by approximately one-half. In addition, safe harbor leasing will not be allowed after December 31, 1983.

However, TEFRA did add a new type of lease, the so-called "Finance Lease," beginning on January 1, 1984. Under the provisions of TEFRA, finance leases must follow the requirements of traditional "guideline leases," with two exceptions:

1. The property lease may be "Limited Use Property."

2. At the end of the lease, the lessee may have a fixed-price purchase option of ten percent or more of the original cost of the leased property.

*C. Combined IDB financings and leases.* Under Federal law, Industrial Development Bonds will be denied tax-exempt status unless they are used to build various types of facilities of any size (including solid waste resource recovery facilities) or to build any type of facility utilizing small-issue IDBs. Each of these two types of bond transactions can be associated with leases which permit the combined utilization of tax benefits and tax-exempt interest rates. To some extent, the particular structure will be dictated by state law relating to industrial revenue bond financing, as well as the nature of the energy facilities being financed.

*D. Parallel bond and lease transactions.* Where the cost of financing a facility, plus associated capital expenditures, is close to the $10 million ceiling, a project may be financed in part by a tax-exempt bond issue of qualifying size and the balance by a tax-leveraged lease with taxable debt from third-party institutional investors. The Federal tax laws exempt a "true" lease transaction from the IDB capital expenditure tests, and so, the leased portion of the financing can be excluded when determining whether or not the financing meets the $10,000,000 or $20,000,000 (with UDAG funds) requirements of small-issue IDB financing.

*E. Municipal certificates of lease participation.* Certificates of Participation are obligations which evidence a direct proportionate interest in a stream of payments made by a municipal user under a lease financing agreement relating to the project financed with Certificate proceeds.

Under the laws of various states a municipality may enter into a capital lease obligation which, if terminable within each fiscal year, may *not* constitute a debt for certain state law purposes. Certificates of Participation may be issued to finance the purchase by a private entity of capital equipment which is leased to the municipality under a financing lease whose term is equal in length to that of the Certificates. The lease payments secure the Certificates and are made by the municipality to a trustee for the benefit of the Certificate holders, who have a security interest in the leased equipment.

A portion of each rental payment made under the Certificate financing agreement represents tax-exempt interest on the equipment purchase owed by the municipality to the private investor/lessor.

*F. Sale and leaseback arrangements.* One form of municipal lease financing, is the sale and leaseback, in which a private investor would acquire or construct facilities or equipment needed by a local government, often utilizing tax-exempt borrowing to finance the property. The private owner would then claim the available tax deductions or credits relating to the property and would lease the use of such facilities back to the local government on a long-term basis. The lease payments by the municipality would be in an amount sufficient to repay the debt borrowed by the private owner-lessor and provide a cash return to the private investor, in addition to the value of the tax deduction claimed as tax owner of the leased facilities. At the present time a large local government in the Southeast is utilizing such a sale-leaseback arrangement to finance a major cogeneration energy facility. Other local governments have also explored use of sale and leaseback financings for various types of energy production and/or conservation facilities.

### Necessary Elements of a Successful Energy Project Financing

I. Long-term energy supply contracts with creditworthy customers that will assure a sufficient revenue stream to meet all operating and maintenance costs of the project, and to pay the debt service costs on the financing of the project.

II. Receipt of all Federal, State, and local regulatory approvals, licenses and permits required for the construction and operation of the energy project, including:

A. All air-quality and other environmental impact approvals.

B. State public utility commission approval relating to ownership and operation of the project and regulation of the rates charged for service.

C. State and local zoning and project siting approvals and right-of-ways for construction of the energy facilities.

D. Local utility service franchise authority for the provision of energy services.

III. Long-term arrangements assuring adequate minimum amounts of fuel or other input to the project (i.e. solid waste) for production of energy to be supplied to customers.

IV. A strong construction contract for project development (preferably on a turnkey, firm cost basis) that will insure that the project will be completed on time and within budget or will provide appropriate penalty payments for time and cost overruns. The performance of the contractor under this contract should also be bonded with a reputable surety.

V. A well-qualified and experienced management to oversee the development and long-term operation and maintenance of the project. This is one of the most important aspects of a successful financing.

VI. A financing plan which is tailored to the specific characteristics of the energy project and which minimizes the overall cost of financing the project. The support and advice of a nationally-recognized investment banking firm, with expertise in all possible methods of financing can be critical to the successful financing of a public energy production or conservation project at the lowest possible cost.

## Determination of the Most Appropriate Financing Plan

Each municipal energy production or conservation project has unique technical, institutional and ownership characteristics requiring expertise in all forms of financing to develop the financing package which maximizes the project's feasibility by raising capital at the lowest possible cost.

Among the most important characteristics to be considered are:

I. Project revenue and expense projections and the annual net cash flows for the project.

II. The impact of the engineering characteristics of the project on the economics and financial feasibility projections.

III. The legal nature of the financial obligations of the customers of the system output under long-term energy sales or shared savings contracts:

    A. Take-or-Pay Requirements Contracts.

    B. Take-and-Pay Requirements Contracts.

    C. Fixed-Price Contracts.

    D. Initial Price Contracts with a price escalation index based upon future increases in the cost of alternative energy sources.

IV. The specific project ownership and operating policy goals or decisions made by the local government sponsoring the energy system development.

## The Role of a Local Government's Investment Banker

An investment banker can act as financial advisor to the local government by:

(1) discussing the benefits and drawbacks of various ownership and financing options and

(2) making recommendations regarding the most appropriate financing plans for any specific energy production or conservation project.

He should assume responsibility, along with the local government's project coordinator(s), to assure that the chosen ownership and financing plan is successfully developed and implemented and that all the other consultants and participants in the project, properly carry out their responsibilities in a timely manner.

By properly executing his responsibilities, an investment banker will maximize the chances that a local government's energy project will be successfully financed at the lowest possible interest cost.

# Chapter 16 ————————

# Risk Considerations for Bond Financing of Energy Projects

## James W. Benefiel

This chapter discusses risk planning considerations when bond financing is used to finance a portion of an energy project. Although it is written for a representative waste-to-energy project because these projects typically have used tax-exempt bonds, the concepts of risk management are applicable to other types of energy facilities.

It should be noted that under the 1982 tax act, several new constraints have been placed on tax-exempt bond financing. These constraints are not the subject of this paper. Suffice it to say that, properly structured, bonds still represent a viable source of funds for appropriate projects.

This chapter identifies the possible approaches to effective risk management that are crucial to the success of any bond financing. This section provides general background for the reader on the concept of risk. It raises and answers the questions:

- What do we mean by the term "risk," that is, how is it defined?
- How do risks arise in project planning?
- What are the principal effects of risks?
- Why do we concern ourselves with risks in energy resource recovery project planning?
- What is meant by the term "risk management"?

## Definition of Risk

As with any capital investment opportunity, waste-to-energy projects pose a variety of uncertainties about the future sufficiency of revenues to cover all costs and provide a fair return to the sponsor. In spite of these uncertainties, a single "baseline" estimate of future costs and revenues typically is developed during the feasibility study stage and is updated in subsequent planning stages.

Risks arise when outcomes have the potential to vary substantially from these baseline estimates. Risks, then, are a measure of the variability of project results around a baseline. The variability, rather than the absolute value, of a parameter is the key. For example, an individual might have purchased as an investment a U.S. Treasury bill priced to achieve a yield to maturity 12 percent per year. Although the return might seem high by historical standards, the risk is essentially zero if the security is held to maturity because the return is fixed. (While it is true that there is some risk of failure to pay principal and interest, this is considered exceedingly slight for domestic investors of U.S. Government securities.)

## Sources of Risk

Risks can arise from a variety of sources because the project planner is forecasting uncertain future events. These risks can be caused by the project participants (e.g., inadequate management control leading to delays and cost overruns), by entities such as suppliers or customers who are involved with but are not parties to the project (e.g., by ultimately raising material prices or refusing to accept delivery of product) or by external events. These external events can be further broken down as (1) related to developments in the industry or (2) arising from the general economy. An example of industry-related risks would be a regulation issued after the project starts operating that requires costly control measures to guard against hazardous wastes. An example of a general economic risk would be an unanticipated rise in interest rates.

## Effects of Risks

The major effects of risks are to vary actual results from those projected. Although variability could either positively or negatively affect results, the term "risk" usually implies adverse impacts from the point of view of the sponsor. These adverse impacts for waste-to-energy projects can be measured in terms of either low returns to equity or high tipping fees relative to projected baseline values.

## Reasons for Concern

There are two major reasons to perform risk analyses for each waste-to-energy project. The first reason is the obvious need of the project participants to identify and evaluate project risks so as to minimize the possibility and/or impact of future adverse events. The second relates to financing. Waste-to-energy projects typically seek large amounts of debt financing in the form of long-term, tax-exempt bonds. These bonds are usually a part of resource recovery financing because of their low cost relative to other sources of funds. Further, because waste-to-energy projects generate revenue streams, these projects are often project-financed with little or no recourse to the sponsor. Properly structured, a project financing may not need to be reflected on the balance sheet or as a direct liability of the sponsor.

Problems arise because lenders—creditors of a waste-to-energy project—are not risk takers. They are generally large financial institutions (for example, insurance companies and commercial banks) or wealthy individuals seeking relatively secure fixed income. These creditors demand protection against nearly all risks, sometimes including changing bond market conditions. Financing any project rests on the sponsor's ability to entice investors and to allay creditor concerns by demonstrating a sufficient level of security.

The prime source of repayment is the project itself. It follows that the sponsor must demonstrate to the creditor's satisfaction that the project is feasible. This is accomplished by projecting, from disposal fees as well as from energy and materials products, revenues at least sufficient to cover debt service after operating and maintenance costs.

Even in a revenue bond financing, creditors typically require assurance of repayment by the project sponsor or by some other interested party (for example, a full-service contractor or major customer). Creditors look to the project sponsor's ability and willingness to guarantee debt service. Ability is gauged through such measures as financial ratios and credit rating. Willingness is more subjective: prospective creditors approximate the sponsor's determination to honor its debt based on past performance and discussions with management.

A sponsor may be unwilling or unable to guarantee payment. For example, a municipal sponsor would be unwilling to guarantee payment if such a guarantee required the levying of taxes in a jurisdiction limited in additional borrowings or if unable to pass a referendum. A municipal or private sponsor would be unable to guarantee payment if it had not established a track record with similar borrowings, or if the size of the borrowing were disproportionate to the sponsor's current financial structure. In either of these situations, a third party may be called upon to provide the required guarantees. If another party provides guarantees, creditors will evaluate the party's capability to pay principal and interest. Willingness to pay is again a key to obtaining financing. Often the third party guarantor must have sufficient economic interest in the project that it will benefit him to "make it work."

### Risk Management

Whatever the makeup of parties to a project, planners should ensure that each risk is borne by the party who is most capable of incurring or assuming that risk. This point brings up the concept of risk management. Risk management means the containment of risks where possible and the allocation of remaining risks to the parties most responsible for or most able to shoulder them.

Risk management involves:

- identifying each risk;
- assessing its potential impact on the project;
- implementing cost effective measures to reduce adverse impacts; and

- allocating remaining risks to appropriate parties.

The following section identifies typical risks that can arise from representative waste-to-energy projects. Subsequent sections of this paper assess the impacts of postulated risks, then identify potential measures to mitigate and allocate major risks.

## Classifications of Risks

Nearly every potential participant in a waste-to-energy project has a measure of some typical risks. Many have only a partial picture, however. To ensure a successful financing, it is necessary to develop a thorough classification system for risk. Such a system project allows participants to:

- characterize their own risk posture;
- uncover risks that might otherwise be overlooked until later project planning; and
- provide a systematic method to assess risk impacts.

One system we have developed classifies the various risks according to the components of the income statement they would most likely affect. For waste-to-energy projects, the system was derived from the basic income statement equation:

MSW Disposal Revenues + Energy and Materials Revenues
= Operating and Maintenance Costs + Capital Recovery

The components on the left side of the equation are elements of project revenue. The components on the right side of the equation are labeled the variable and fixed costs of production. For a public sector project, "capital recovery" means the ability to repay all debt incurred for the project. For a private sector project, capital recovery includes a profit to the owners after all expenses, including taxes, are paid. Items that may be included under each of these components are shown in Figure 16-1. This figure also shows the degree of control that project participants might be expected to exert over each income statement component.

This risk classification scheme is not specific to a particular project. Rather it has been developed to provide widespread utility for

| Component | Item | *Degree of Control by Project Participants* |
|---|---|---|
| Waste Disposal Revenue | Waste Input | Medium |
| | Tipping Fee | Medium |
| Energy & Materials Revenue | Production | High-Medium |
| | Energy Price | Medium-Low |
| | Materials Production | High-Medium |
| | Materials Price | Medium-Low |
| Operating & Maintenance Costs | Operating & Maintenance Labor | High-Medium |
| | Power & Other Utilities | Medium-Low |
| | Vehicle Fuel & Maintenance | Medium-Low |
| | Tailings Disposal | Medium-Low |
| | Overhead | Medium |
| | Leases | High |
| | Material & Supplies | Medium |
| | Contract Maintenance | High-Medium |
| | Other Maintenance Expenses | Medium-Low |
| | Contingency Landfill Disposal | Medium-Low |
| Capital Costs & Capital Recovery | Land & Site Preparation | High |
| | Buildings | High-Medium |
| | Process Equipment | High-Medium |
| | Off-Sites | Medium-Low |
| | Plant Betterment/Placement | Medium-Low |
| | Construction | Medium |
| | Startup Costs | Medium-Low |
| | Reserve Funds | Medium-Low |
| | Contingencies | Low |
| | Capitalized Interest | Medium-Low |
| | Financing Costs | Medium-Low |
| | Insurance | Medium-Low |
| | Depreciation | High-Medium |
| | Taxes | Low |

**Figure 16-1.  Items included in resource recovery project income statement components**

any project. Because there are numerous potential ownership structures and a variety of participations in any waste-to-energy project, we find that explicit consideration of the various categories of risk often results in identifying risks that were previously unrecognized. Each time project participants consider significant changes—for example, substituting a new customer, seeking third-party financing, or encouraging additional communities to supply waste—it is useful to review potential changes in project risks. In this way, one can continuously monitor for unacceptable risks and take appropriate measures to address them.

The equation cited at the beginning of this section holds for all waste-to-energy projects. The challenge to the project sponsor is to demonstrate to the satisfaction of prospective creditors (and perhaps equity participants as well) that revenues are adequate to meet all costs including both debt service and a fair return on any equity capital. A municipal participant is also concerned that disposal fees to residents and businesses be kept as low as possible.

Major elements of risk that might be expected to influence the components include:

1. *For Waste Disposal Revenues*

   • inadequate solid waste quality or quantity, caused by overly optimistic estimates, inability to secure waste supply, physical changes in the waste supply or losses to competing disposal options; and

   • low throughput, caused by technical problems in the process plant.

2. *For Energy and Materials Product Revenues*

   • inadequate solid waste quality or quantity;

   • declining price caused by declines in prices of competing fuels, inability to meet customer specifications, or changes in regulations;

   • changes in customer characteristics; such as customer process obsolescence, breach of contract, or business failure; and

   • low throughput.

3. *For Operating and Maintenance Costs*

- reduced efficiencies, which may be due to an overestimation, poor management, or technical problems (that is, low throughput); and

- subsequent increase in component costs through either general inflation or specific legislation and/or regulation.

4. *For Capital Recovery*

- project-related cost increases, such as time delays, cost overruns, or additional costs to achieve specified performance;

- industry-related cost increases caused by poor performance of previous waste-to-energy plants. Creditors may thus require high contingency funds or high debt service coverage factors;

- cost increases related to the general economy, such as high interest rates and short bond lives; and

- cost increases caused by subsequent events, mainly legislative or regulatory.

The following section provides examples of risks for the first classification cited above: those relating to waste disposal.

*Waste Disposal Revenue Risks*

Refuse is the raw material for energy-resource recovery projects, and, like other raw materials, its supply can be uncertain. Risks associated with the waste stream include:

*Overestimation.* The processing facility is sized based on review of records available and limited sampling. Both the records and the sample are subject to some error.

*Examples:*

- A landfill without a scale records waste in units of cubic yards. Each trip of a commercial truck is recorded at the truck capacity whether or not the truck is full;

- A limited sample shows significant aluminum composition. However, the sample is mostly hotel waste which includes many soft drink cans.

*Inability to secure supply.* Haulers may choose not to support the waste-to-energy project because of the costs of doing so. The facility size may be based on the total available waste generated in a community, rather than on the amount ultimately contracted for. This would result in capital costs being spread over lower-than-designed-capacity throughput.

*Example:*

- A major private hauler operating its own landfill declines to supply waste to the project because of the revenue it achieves on disposal. This results in 30 percent less waste than design capacity.

*Waste composition.* Changes in waste composition can reduce the combustible or recoverable material content, which can reduce revenue realized per ton of waste. Similarly, the unprocessable fraction could increase, which can increase costs for disposal of residues. Changes in composition can occur from regulations ("bottle bills"), from source separation activities, from changes in consumer behavior, from packaging industry trends, and from others.

*Examples:*

- A shift of packaging materials from paper to plastic causes the energy content and combustion characteristics of the waste stream to change. Energy yield from combustion declines, thereby reducing revenues.
- Mandatory deposit legislation for glass bottles and a recycling program for cans reduce the recoverable glass and metal fraction of the waste stream, reducing revenues from recovered materials.

*Declining waste quantity.* Reductions in waste stream tonnage subsequent to plant startup can result from regulatory, consumer, or industry actions such as those described above. In addition, haulers may withdraw from the project reducing the waste input to the plant.

*Examples:*

- A local paper, bottle and can recycling center opens, reducing the annual tonnage of waste shipped by the principal municipal supplier. Revenue from tipping fees, energy sales, and recovered materials declines.

- Private haulers challenge a municipal ordinance that requires them to dump at the facility. If the suit is successful, tonnage may be reduced by 50 percent.

*Competing uses.* Other projects may compete for the same waste stream. These competing uses can reduce the quantity of waste or force the operator to reduce tipping fees to retain the needed share of the waste stream.

*Examples:*

- Another project, designed to produce refuse-derived fuel (RDF), opens in an adjoining county. Competing with the sponsor's plant, its advanced technology allows it to offer a tipping fee 25 percent lower than the existing facility's fees. Two municipalities attempt to renegotiate their disposal contracts for parity in tipping fees. One municipality, on a five-year renewable contract, plans not to renew.

- A member municipality of a regional authority, dissatisfied with high tipping fees, successfully develops its own landfill and withdraws from the project, resulting in a loss of a large fraction of the project's waste stream and accompanying revenues.

In a manner similar to the preceeding risks associated with product revenues, operating costs, and capital recovery would also be developed for each actual waste-to-energy project.

The examples of this section have served to identify risks under the classification system developed. The following section notes how the impact of each risk can be estimated to allow planners to take appropriate measures to manage risk.

## Quantitative Assessment of Risk Impacts

This section quantifies the potential impacts of the risks identified in the previous section on a typical municipal solid waste-to-energy project. The measure chosen for presentation includes the increase in tipping fee required to cover expenses or the reduction in equity rate of return if additional expenses are not passed through. This is because the material was taken from a study performed for a municipal project sponsor. For a private sector sponsor, the reduction in return on equity is also a relevant measure. The reference against which each of the risks are evaluated is a baseline case developed in concert with the sponsor and its engineers. The baseline case projected a first year tipping fee of $23/T declining to $2/T by year 20.

### *Assessment Methodology*

Quantification of risks involves the following steps:

- Determine when an event might occur (e.g., during construction, first year of operation, or subsequent years);
- Establish a range of the parameter affected (e.g., 20 percent cost overrun);
- Calculate additional costs; and
- Derive the impact on tipping fee or equity return.

Figure 16-2 shows when the various contingent events that comprise the project risks might occur. This exhibit is rather arbitrarily cut off at the 10-year point for three reasons. First, events that occur in the early years of the project will likely have greater economic impacts because the project's cash flow is small in early years. Second, early cash flows are much more "valuable" to the project because of the time value of money. And third, the ability to project or forecast events in distant years is subject to decreasing accuracy.

It is assumed in Figure 16-2, the time that an event might occur is divided into three periods: construction, early operation, and subsequent operation. These classifications were developed to highlight the differing impacts that can occur based on the time dimension. The exhibit shows the earliest period (since this will probably have

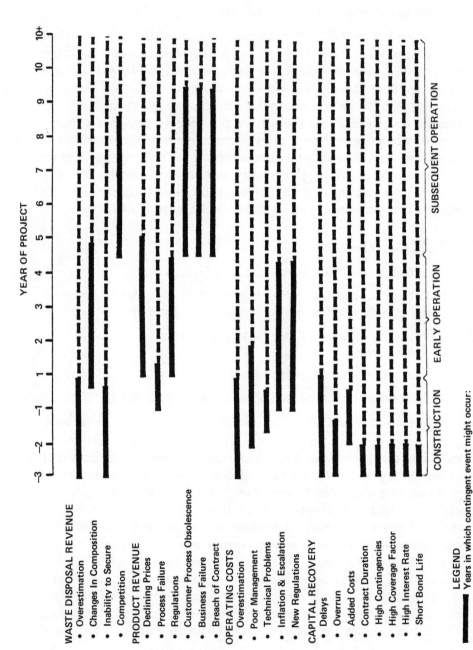

Figure 16-2.   Representative schedule of contingent events

the greatest impact) that an event might occur. Selected risks such as technical problems or additional capital costs may bridge the two periods of construction and initial operation. And, of course, contingent events can always occur later in the project life than show in the exhibit.

## Assessments

In order to assess the impact of risks upon a particular project, it is necessary to estimate the magnitude of variations that may occur, and then input these into a financial analysis model. Figure 16-3 provides one example of how risks may be quantified. Note that they are arranged in terms of the classification system developed previously. The postulated variations were based upon the previous experience of the consultants and the level of effort that went into developing the baseline estimate. As a project moves through various stages, subsequent estimates should show greater accuracies.

Figure 16-4 shows how risk impacts can be displayed graphically, in this case for variations from the base case due to capital recovery risks.

For actual projects, each of the risks identified previously would be evaluated in a similar manner in "sensitivity analyses." Systematic evaluation of potential risk elements allows project sponsors to explore the sensitivity of baseline results to changes in input parameters. Contingencies that would have unacceptably adverse consequences on the project can be identified. Risk management strategies (the subject of the next section) may then be pursued for selected risks.

## Risk Management

Risk management is the structured process of containing the risks that have been identified and evaluated. The major elements of risk management are to:

1. Contain controllable risks where such can be done cost effectively;

2. Allocate risks to the party most able to control them; and

3. Contain other risks by obtaining insurance.

| Parameter | Risk Category | Component | Variation |
|---|---|---|---|
| Waste Disposal | Overestimation | MSW Quantity | −20% |
| | Changes in Composition | Processible Fraction | −5% |
| | Inability to Secure | MSW Quantity | −20% |
| | Competitive Losses | MSW Quantity | −20% |
| Product Revenue | Declining Prices | Energy Price | 2% year Inflation |
| | Inability to Meet Specification | Product Yield or Product Price | −10% |
| | Changes in Regulations | Product Prices | −20% |
| | Customer Process Obsolescence | Project Life | no change |
| | Business Failure | Project Life (inspection) | −15 years |
| | Breach of Contract | Project Life | −15 years |
| Operating & Maintenance Costs | Overestimation | Total O&M Costs | +20% |
| | Poor Management | Total O&M Costs | +20% |
| | Technical Problems | Product Yield | −20% |
| | Subsequent Increases | Labor | +20% (1 yr change) |
| | Legislation & Regulations | Total O&M Costs | +20% |
| Capital Recovery | Delays | Construction Period | +½ year |
| | Cost Overruns | Construction Cost | +20% |
| | Additional Costs | Construction Cost | +20% |
| | High Contingency Fund Requirements | Fund Requirements in Bond Buildup | +20% |
| | High Debt Service Coverage Factor | Minimum Coverage Factor | +20% |
| | High Interest Rates | Interest Rate | +2 percentage points |
| | Short Bond Life | Bond Life | −15 years |

**Figure 16-3. Variations of input parameters used for risk assessment**

## Risk Mitigation

One can develop a set of strategies for risk mitigation as in Figure 16-5. These strategies evolve from a systematic evaluation of the various causes of identifiable risks. Thus, if the probability of a certain event is large, project participants should take measures to reduce that probability. Likewise, if the likely impact of a contingent event is large, project participants should take measures to reduce the

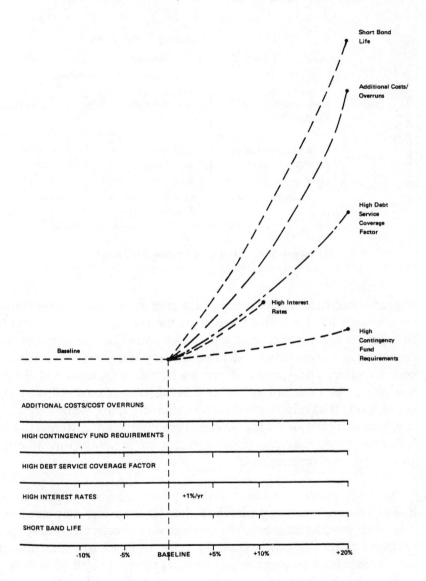

**Figure 16-4. Variation of project results around baseline
(Capital Recovery Risks)**

Probability of Occurrence

| | | High | Medium | Low |
|---|---|---|---|---|
| *Likely Economic Impact* | **High** | Reduce both probability and impact | Reduce impact then probability | Reduce impact |
| | **Medium** | Reduce probability then impact | Reduce probability and/or impact | Reduce impact if desired |
| | **Low** | Reduce probability | Reduce probability if desired | Ignore |

**Figure 16-5. Strategies for risk mitigation**

impact should the event occur. Each risk mitigation measure may require additional cost on the part of the sponsor. The challenge is to compare the expected cost with the expected benefits (that is, the reduction in uncertainty) and to select only those measures that are cost effective. The structured process of risk mitigation and allocation should be reviewed and refined as subsequent stages of the project warrant. Risk mitigation measures often are implemented through contractual provisions with vendors, suppliers, and customers. The following paragraphs cite possible mitigation measures for the category of product revenue risks.

*Declining product prices.* Contract prices are often pegged to an index. To minimize the probability that future prices may not keep pace with production costs, the sponsor should select an index that is closely related to production. To tailor an index to the facility, it may be necessary to combine in a formula several published indices.

As a second measure, the sponsor may wish to allow for passing through documented cost increases to the plant's customers. Also, the sponsor should monitor prices of competitive fuels and energy with a view towards renegotiating the contracts if wide gaps in prices develop.

Other parties to the project, such as waste suppliers or energy customers, will naturally seek a cap on disposal charges or a specified price discount from displaced fuels to ensure that their continued participation is economically advantageous. Further, municipalities may wish the right to commission operational audits periodically to assure themselves that the plant continues to operate efficiently.

*Example:*

- As a precaution against declining prices, a waste-to-energy sponsor negotiates steam sales agreements with major customers that provide that the purchase price shall be adjusted by an index that is composed 70% of a local labor index, 20% by a federal fuel index, and 10% by the ratio of short-term interest rates to the baseline interest rate. The agreement further provides that the price discount of steam from waste when compared to the price of natural gas-fired steam to the customer shall be a minimum 25% but shall not exceed 40%.

*Inability to meet user specification.* The primary reason a facility may not be able to meet user specifications is process failure. A secondary reason could be unreliable delivery schedules of a particular transportation mode. For the first case, risks may be reduced by using only proven equipment and processes. Engage only those professional service firms who have a demonstrated track record and a commitment to making the plant work. To combat the second risk, the sponsor should consider alternate transportation modes or carriers.

*Example:*

- As a precaution against process failure, a municipality issuing a full scope RFP requires that the technology to be offered be proven through at least one year of commercial operation at full scale. The potential operator must also have completed a project through design, construction, and one year of operation.

*Regulations.* An individual process plant is likely to have little influence on new regulations. However, it is not necessary that a sponsor be surprised to learn of new regulations. A project sponsor can monitor regulatory developments, through industry associations at the state and federal levels, and can initiate early discussions with regulators when potentially adverse developments are identified. The discussions can cover a range of topics, such as costs and benefits, need for more research, and alternate control technologies.

*Example:*

- A municipal incinerator operator learns that the state is considering a bill that would classify flyash as hazardous waste, resulting in substantially increased disposal costs. The municipality introduces evidence concerning the relative health hazards of flyash and raw municipal solid waste (MSW). Based on acceptable practices for handling the latter waste, the legislature exempts MSW ash from major portions of the bill.

*Customer process obsolescence.* In an era of rapidly rising energy prices, equipment manufacturers are continually seeking process improvements that will reduce energy usage without sacrificing productivity. Also, new production processes are undergoing rapid change, while more established technologies are not. The sponsor can decrease the risk that process obsolescence will substantially reduce the needed energy by:

- supplying only a part of the customer's current energy needs (this allows for future energy conservation);
- avoiding short-process-life customers (such as computers) and instead concentrating on long-process-lived industries (such as metals, chemicals, etc.); and
- negotiating take-or-pay contracts whose durations approximate the anticipated lifetime of the process plant.

*Example:*

- In surveying potential customers for energy from municipal waste, a municipality limits its search to those companies that have a year-round need for at least twice the energy to be produced by the plant and that currently use long-term contracts for their essential materials (the latter being an approximation for long-lived processes).

*Breach of contract.* Contract breaches may be deterred by large penalties for any material breach. The project sponsor may have difficulty negotiating such penalties, however. A bit of prescriptive medicine would be to initiate and maintain open communications with parties to the project to resolve differences as they occur.

*Example:*

- A ferrous scrap dealer agrees to a long-term contract with price index and floor. To minimize the possibility that the dealer would seek cheaper sources of scrap, the project sponsor successfully negotiates a provision requiring double payment for failure to accept scrap delivery at the floor price.

*Business failure.* The risk of business failure can be minimized by contracting only with reputable firms in healthy industries. However, recent combinations of high interest rates, tight credit, depressed demand and high inflation have shown how even established companies can incur financial difficulties. The best prescription is to monitor the customer's financial condition and commence early discussions with potential backup customers when this seems warranted. This monitoring can be informal (e.g., through newspaper accounts, annual reports, and periodic meetings) but should be routine to prevent surprises.

## Risk Allocation

If risks cannot be reduced to a point at which they have little impact they must be allocated among the appropriate parties. Risk policy can strongly influence the choice of procurement methods, contract terms, and financing mechanisms. However, even extremely risk-averse sponsors must expect to share the burden of some risk if they seek to ensure that the project goes forward to completion and operates successfully. This is because other parties will likely demand all the benefits of the project as incentives, if a sponsor allocates all risks to these parties. That is, if the sponsor is unwilling to accept any risk, it should not anticipate receiving any rewards from a successful project.

There may be many opportunities for alternate allocations of risk among the participants. It is even possible to assign a risk to several parties as long as each party understands the nature of the risk he is absorbing. The following material proposes allocation measures for the capital recovery category of risks.

*Capital recovery risk allocations.* Capital recovery includes the fixed cost of construction plus financing costs and other costs such as insurance and taxes. Risks that are directly related to the project such as delays and construction cost overruns are properly allocated to the responsible parties. Risks that are external to the project are usually absorbed by the sponsor/host community because other participants are usually unwilling to incur a risk over which they have no control.

*Project-related risks.* These risks include (1) delays of equipment, engineering services, and construction/erection and (2) cost overruns. They are most often allocated to the parties most able to control them through posting of performance and/or payment bonds and minimum specified levels of insurance. Fixed-price bids effectively transfer the risk of overruns to the contractor, whereas firm schedule deadlines and penalties transfer the risk of delays to them.

*Examples:*

- A supplier quotes a fixed price to deliver and install a turbine generator by a certain date. As a condition of the sale, the supplier agrees to a daily penalty for each day the generator is late.

- An architecture-engineering firm quotes a fixed price for turn-key construction of a process plant to be delivered to the sponsor 30 months from date of contract. The firm agrees to a penalty fee plus the cost of transportation/disposal of all solid waste received at the facility beyond a selected date.

*Other capital recovery risks.* Other risks of capital recovery that are external to the project include (1) those related to the industry, such as high contingency funds or high specified debt service coverage factor, and (2) those related to the general economy, such as high interest rates or short bond lives. Since these are beyond the control of any project participant, they usually devolve to the ultimate sponsor. It was noted in this chapter's section on risk mitigation that these risks are difficult to reduce. Industry-related risks can potentially be allocated to creditworthy parties such as a private customer or full-service contractor by requiring unconditional guarantees of them. However, if the industry-wide problems relate to technology, either (1) the parties may be unwilling to put forth guarantees or (2) these guarantees may be of little value to creditors.

It is precisely the inability to reduce or sufficiently allocate these risks during the unsettled capital markets of recent years that has led to the postponement of many waste-to-energy projects. If more projects are to proceed, planners need to become more sensitive to capital market trends while lenders and investors may need to be willing to pursue new financial approaches such as balloon payments (less than full amortization), early call provisions, or convertible securities. In this manner, investors and sponsors may share some of the risk of future capital market conditions.

A more fundamental problem may arise from the failure of project participants to give adequate consideration to risks at all phases of the project. To prevent major roadblocks, it is necessary for all parties to obtain agreement on:

- risks arising from the project;
- potential risk impacts; and
- risk mitigation measures and allocation.

In this manner, appropriate agreements can be fashioned that will either satisfy all parties or lead to the search for substitute parties willing to absorb a share of the risks.

Figure 16-6 provides a simplified format for keeping track of risks and responsibilities among the various participants. It is recommended that sponsors use the methodology described here at each critical point in the proposed project's development.

Continued attention to risks and risk implications should lead to more bond financings of feasible waste-to-energy projects. Moreover, as noted previously, the concept of risk management described here, is applicable to a wide variety of energy projects when bond financing is a consideration.

PARTY ASSIGNED (check appropriate box)

| RISK CATEGORIES | Sponsor | Designer | Constructor | Operator | Supplier | Customer |
|---|---|---|---|---|---|---|
| **I. Waste Supply** | | | | | | |
| 1. Overestimation | | | | | | |
| 2. Inability to Secure Supply | | | | | | |
| 3. Changes in Waste Composition | | | | | | |
| 4. Decline in Waste Quantity | | | | | | |
| 5. Losses to Competition | | | | | | |
| **II. Product Revenue** | | | | | | |
| 1. Product Prices | | | | | | |
| 2. Customer Characteristics | | | | | | |
| **III. Operation & Maintenance** | | | | | | |
| 1. Inefficiencies | | | | | | |
| 2. Subsequent Cost Increases | | | | | | |
| **IV. Capital Recovery** | | | | | | |
| 1. Project Related | | | | | | |
| 2. Industry Related | | | | | | |
| 3. General Economy | | | | | | |

**Figure 16-6. Risk allocation matrix**

# Chapter 17

# Federal Regulations and Energy Tax Credits— How Do They Affect Energy Project Financing?*

George M. Greider

An article in the *Wall Street Journal*[1] in late 1982 was headlined "Despite the Glut of Heating Oil and Natural Gas, Prices Aren't Expected to Drop This Winter." It quoted an official of the Massachusetts Energy Office who said if he was sitting in Economics 101 and talking about supply and demand, home heating prices would be assumed to drop.

He then went on to add, somewhat unnecessarily, that this is not Economics 101. The reason why simple economic models or theoretical relationships don't hold in the real world is that we have a pattern in this country, that has developed over time, of a great deal of government intervention in many different aspects of our economy. These interventions are most dramatic in our domestic energy markets.

Federal government assistance to business, that is, tax preferences, loans, guarantees, research and development, grants, etc. currently amount to 13.9% of our total gross national product.[2] The federal

---

*Presented at The Energy Roundtable held at Hartford, Connecticut, October 21, 1982.

government is not only deeply involved in competition in the capital markets, it is directly invested in domestic economic activity to the point of about 14%.

Robert Reich, a Harvard economist, was quoted as saying that we have produced "a hodgepodge of public policies bearing no direct relationship to overall industrial health."[3] And when we look at the interventions in the energy market, this situation becomes even more dramatic.

Even though there is an abundance (apparently) of domestic natural gas supplies in this country, we're seeing price rises that may go as high as 22-23%.[4] The reason is because natural gas's prices have been regulated for many years. We are currently moving towards a deregulation target date of 1986 when the price of natural gas will rise to something more appropriate and approximate to the cost of production.

It is interesting to note that, while the U.S. energy prices have been held below world prices as a result of both oil and gas regulation, the allowances for depletion and the expensing of intangible drilling costs, that represented as much as a 25% reduction in the cost of oil and gas between 1950 and 1977,[5] were initiated by our government in an attempt to maintain a domestic energy production capacity in the face of very inexpensive foreign oil and gas.

The government got into the market originally to maintain a secure supply, back in the fifties and early sixties. However, as a result of our political leadership's unwillingness to adjust prices realistically upwards during the late sixties, U.S. energy prices fell behind those in other developed countries.

The consumers' lower price was purchased at a fairly high price to the federal government. Battelle Northwest did a study[6] in 1979-80 which totalled the direct interventions, the tax incentives, regulatory relief, etc. It did not look at such difficult to quantify things as the Price-Anderson Act, which places limits to private liability for catastrophies resulting from nuclear generation. Battelle's conclusion (Table 17-1) was that the federal government had spent $217 billion (1977 dollars) in supporting, in one fashion or another, the development of a number of energy streams.

The big winner was oil—which received $100 billion or approximately half the incentives (Table 17-2). Approximately $43 billion in supports went to the nuclear generation of electricity and to hydropower development through the Bonneville Power Authority and the Tennessee Valley Authority. About $15 billion was provided to subsidize natural gas development; and coal did not make it into double figures.

This is a very dramatic indication of the amount of federal intervention. It is clear that we are not starting off even at the starting line when we look at the actual costs of any one energy technology versus another. Because these subsidies and encouragements have been a major part of our economic history, we have artificially and politically structured the relationships among competing types of fuel.

If this were a stable picture we could, perhaps, account for the differences and be able to figure out what the next cost is going to be. However, energy market pricing comparisons, which are absolutely critical for any kind of project financing package, are based upon volatile government interventions which change annually, or at least biannually, as the Congress changes.

**The best thing at this point that the federal government could do relative to energy project financing would be to stop passing laws.**

From 1978 through the recess of the current congress, there has been major legislation affecting the economics of every kind of energy project finance introduced and passed in every session. Just as we have had to take into account the steep rise in prices over the last 10 years, we also have had to adjust annually to a very rapidly shifting set of new rules and subsidies.

Here's an example of the problems that have been created for energy planners. Suppose we were asked to decide the type of fuel to be used in a new industrial process. Should we use oil? Oil has a nice, fairly flat inflation rate right now. It's soft; we hear about oil gluts. Yet we know that by trend oil prices are rising precipitously.

Figure 17-1 shows not only the obvious fact that oil prices have risen almost exponentially in the last ten years, but that at the same time, the tax incentives mentioned earlier have increased at about the same rate.

On the other hand, even though we think that natural gas prices

Table 17-1. An Estimate of the Cost of Incentives Used to Stimulate Energy Production[7]
(in Billions of 1977 $)
(reprinted from Cone et al. December 1978, p. 276)

| | Nuclear | Hydro | Coal | Oil | Gas | Electricity | Total | % of Total Incentives |
|---|---|---|---|---|---|---|---|---|
| Taxation | | 1.8 | 4.03 | 50.4 | 16.04 | 31.37 | 103.64 | 47.7 |
| Disbursements | | | 0.67 | 1.1 | 0.06 | | 1.10 | 0.5 |
| Requirements | 1.1 | 0.03 | 2.31 | 41.9 | | | 43.76 | 20.1 |
| Traditional Services | | | 2.68 | 6.0 | 0.3 | 0.48 | 8.79 | 4.0 |
| Nontraditional Services | 15.1 | | | 1.5 | | | 19.58 | 9.0 |
| Market Activity | 1.8 | 13.5 | 0.02 | 0.4 | 0.1 | 24.73 | 40.55 | 18.7 |
| Totals | 18.0 | 15.33 | 9.71 | 101.3 | 16.50 | 56.58 | 217.42 | 100.0 |
| % of Total Incentives | 8.3 | 7.0 | 4.5 | 46.6 | 7.6 | 26.0 | 100 | |

## Table 17-2. Summary of Oil Incentives by Type[8]
### *(in millions of 1977 $)*
### (Cone *et al.* December 1978, p. 226)

| Incentive Area | Taxation | Disbursement | Requirements | Traditional Services | Nontraditional Services | Market Activity | Total |
|---|---|---|---|---|---|---|---|
| Research & Development | | | | | 1,022 | | |
| Oil Exploration & Production | | | | | | | |
|   Geological Survey—Data | | | | | 491 | | |
|   Bureau of Land Management—Leasing | | | | | | 433 | |
|   Bureau of Mines—Data | | | | | 16* | | |
|   Stripper Well Price Incentives | | | 12,140 | | | | |
|   Incentives for New Oil | | | 23,940 | | | | |
|   Federal Energy Administration | | | 660 | | | | |
|   Intangible Drilling Expensing | 14,160 | | | | | | |
|   % Depletion Allowance | 36,230 | | | | | | |
| Petroleum Refining & Transportation | | | | | | | |
|   High Yield on Pipelines | | | 5,200 | | | | |
|   Maintenance of Ports & Waterways | | | | 5,985 | | | |
|   Subsidies for Tankers | | 1,120 | | | | | |
| TOTAL | 50,390 | 1,120 | 41,940 | 5,985 | 1,529 | 433 | 101,397 |

*1964 to 1977 only

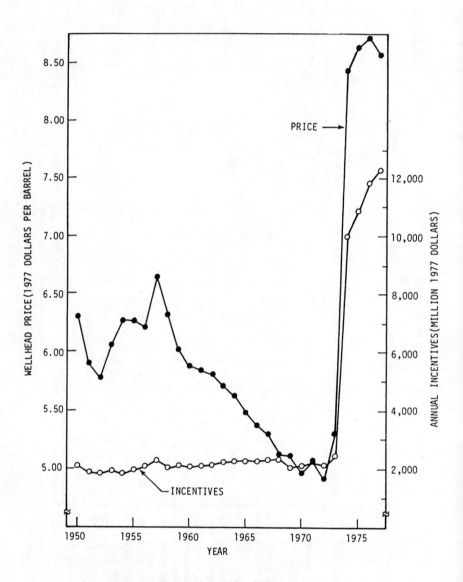

**Figure 17-1.  Oil prices and annual incentives**[9]

have been fairly flat by trend, we know for certain that they are going to be rising very rapidly, by 20–30%, just this heating season Winter 1982–83), according to the *Wall Street Journal*.[10] We know that this trend may be accelerated precipitously by federal deregulation in 1986; or it may not. If our politicians seek further to protect us from the consequences of our years of evading economic reality in this area, natural gas prices could take another downturn.

The price of electricity can be readily expected to rise. As was indicated in the *New York Times*,[11] when the current electrical generating capacity of Millstone One (a nuclear plant in Connecticut) at 1½ to 2 cents a kilowatt hour and Millstone Two at 2½ to 4 cents a kilowatt hour, is joined by Millstone Three, the construction cost will be approximately 21 cents a kilowatt hour. The Department of Public Utility Control in Connecticut could elect to phase in the recapture of these costs sooner, so that instead of having a big rate increase later there may be small gradual increases earlier on.

What fuel do we choose? The preference would be, by any rational analysis, none of the above. We would prefer something else; something we can get a fix on, something that will have a stable cost. We need to find some kind of energy stream that we can guarantee on a fixed-cost basis. Energy, of course, that we can purchase for less than we would have to spend for some other form of energy, like oil, gas, or whatever. However, until we know what the projected price is going to be of oil, gas, electricity, or whatever, we can't know what makes economic sense as either an ultimate fuel source or an energy conservation investment.

Professor Dechesnau of Harvard says, "the government-improvised restrictions on free market activity are responsible for many of the energy problems facing the United States."[12] As a result of this patchwork of interventions and the hodgepodge of subsidies, regulations and encouragements, it's no wonder we have a national energy policy, as someone said recently, "created by Curly, Moe and Larry."

The question of whether or not natural gas is decontrolled in 1986 as is prescribed in the Natural Gas Policy Act, or by some other schedule, is a decision upon which the producers and distributors disagree. The people within the industry disagree, because deep well drillers, new gas suppliers and others are better off with the current regulations than with a deregulated market. This decision on the deregulation schedule will have to be made by Congress and the Federal Energy Regulatory Commission. Again, it is a political decision, the nature and logic of which is ". . . well concealed from all but the politicians making them."[13]

When we try to make some kind of sense about what the wild cards are in the deck, we almost have to conclude that we don't know. One investment bank analyst told me of trying to finance a cogeneration project based upon the purchase of electricity by a utility. Based upon avoided cost available under existing federal regulation, and likely future fuel and demand scenarios, the analyst had to compute the avoided cost figure as falling someplace between zero and seven cents a kilowatt hour. How do you base financing on that kind of revenue stream?

When we look at electricity, political decision-making is even more obvious. There is not, in any real sense, any market for electricity. Again quoting Mr. Greenert,[14] "the problem with electricity is that there is no free market or alternative (since one can usually only buy electricity from one supplier; i.e., the regulated utility which serves the area,—Ed). And thus the job of seeking equilibrium between producers and consumers is totally political."

The Public Utility Regulatory Policy Act, also known affectionately or unaffectionately as PURPA, has created a new industry of nonutility small power producers.[15] This sounds like a fairly good idea. If the preferred choice was none of the above conventional sources, these small power producers might be a way to get a more reliable supply and price for energy.

However, their (typically renewable energy) technology relies upon difficult-to-predict energy streams: for example, hydro—whether it rains or it's dry; wind—whether it blows or whether it doesn't. This greatly complicates the problem of supply projection for a business purchasing power from a small power producer. It complicates even further the problem faced by a centralized utility, required by PURPA to purchase electricity produced by small power producers, in figuring out the future of their energy supply network; and thus projecting their own needs for growth.

We can clearly make the case that there has been a very large amount of government intervention in energy markets. The historical support that has been given to subsidize the Tennessee Valley Authority, the Bonneville Power Administration, oil and gas development, etc., means the current cost of energy (not only as a result of these subsidies but also due to cost increases generally) is much less than the marginal cost, or the true replacement cost of new energy.[16]

It is also important to note that the market mechanism by which we would hope that the cost to produce energy would inform decisions to consume is actually lagged a great deal by the phase-in of marginal costs into average cost. Recall the example of Millstone 1, 2 and 3 nuclear plants.

Currently, the major market interventions that the government interposes in the energy area are: utility rate regulation; gas and oil depletion allowances; the expensing of intangible drilling cost; and natural gas price regulation and its impending deregulation. In addition, we still have the remnants of the scatter-gun special encouragements for energy development (such as the $17.5 billion Synfuels Corporation) enacted through the Carter years.

Beyond that, the changes in the general economic climate and energy prices produced by downturns in the market and attempts by the current administration to stimulate new investments has had important effects for some energy projects' economic viability (such as synthetic fuels) and the means by which they may be financed (for example, safe harbor leasing of equipment).

There are other nonrational and nonquantifiable factors which we also must take into account. Energy price, demand and supply make a nice intellectual triad, but we really must introduce more factors into the relationship. In addition to the tax and regulatory factors, there are geopolitical and cultural and personal influences.

First of all, the pricing by the Organization of Petroleum Exporting Countries is not tied directly to any quantifiable element. It may not, in fact, be predictable by any but the most voodoo of economic projections. The international politics of energy production are clearly very volatile. We need also to take into account the cost to our national security for having an uncertain supply providing 25% of the oil we consume.

What has been the market effect of all this?

Oil distillants are still cheaper in the U.S. than they are in other energy-importing countries. Gas prices are likely to escalate in the next three to four years. Electric generation costs, because of changes in safety and environmental laws, as well as recent economic events, are much higher at the margins than they are on the average.

Any attempt to reduce oil reliance will require significant capital investment. But the return on those investments must be considered likely to fluctuate wildly and in often unpredictable ways. Energy projects almost have to be economically rational—independent of the cost of oil—or at zero cents a kilowatt hour. Or their rationality and economics must be computed and evaluated under a vast array of scenarios, the conditions of which are updated quarterly at the very least.

A major national credit corporation has just backed off from a $67 million cogeneration facility in California, which made lovely economic sense when the project was planned at 7¢ a kilowatt hour for avoided cost, but which makes no economic sense at 5¢ a kilowatt hour, which is what they can get now.

As a result of these myriad rate and subsidy interventions and their obviously uncertain future, energy prices seem to have a life of their own independent of supply and demand. While this is hard on the consumer, it is also, as noted earlier, a hardship for the producer. Nowhere is this uncertainty more obvious (nor the controversy more broadly debated) than in the case of energy tax credits.

### Energy Tax Credits: Help or Hindrance?

There have been at least 13 recent studies regarding the effectiveness of various energy tax incentives on investments in either energy conservation or nonfossil, nonnuclear fuel.[16-28]

In addition, there was a study comparing *all* the studies. The study of studies was done by Brookhaven National Laboratories,[29] and I would like to quote just a couple of things from their conclusions:

First: "It is difficult to determine precisely what impact energy tax incentives have [on energy conservation and energy production]."[30] Second, it is likely that tax credits have not had ". . . a substantial effect in altering behavior unless it [tax credit] is relatively large."[31] (By relatively large, they mean 40% of capital costs.) "Perceived savings in fuel bills appear to be much more important than the initial capital cost in . . . energy conservation investments."[32] To the extent that our energy costs are stable or going down, it is not economically rational in almost every case to engage in any kind of alternative energy production or conservation project.

That is exactly what we are seeing. Those of us who consult on energy project development don't have a lot of people beating down our doors. Those of us who have been advocating energy conservation or alternative fuel development are finding our advice falling on very deaf ears.

People have pointed to the late unlamented safe-harbor leasing provisions, and the great new opportunities for energy tax credits under ERTA,[33] but in point of fact, those tax credits, etc. really don't seem to have much effect. In hearings on the repeal of the energy tax credits in Washington in 1982, advocates for the continuation of the whole panoply of Carter initiatives claimed energy tax credits brought a 7–8% addition to internal rate of return/return of equity figures.[34] So if there was a project which without the tax credit would yield 17% rate of return, with the tax credit the yield was 24% or 25%. That is not really a large increment when businesses prefer productivity to cost-cutting investments. It is nearly impossible for tax credits to overcome that preference.[35]

There are a number of difficulties associated with taking some of those tax credits (not the least of which is the almost certain trip to tax court and audit procedures for leveraged tax shelters and other third-party investment vehicles).[36] My experience and that of most other professionals has been that the energy tax credits have had little effect upon the production of alternative fuels.

For example: Cogeneration tax credits at a revenue loss of $380 million, will result in 1.8% more of the technically-feasible electrical generating capacity being developed.[37] A study done by Arthur D. Little[38] investigated the effects of tax credits at 10-25-40-55 and 70% of capital cost. Their econometric model predicts no net increase in investment in a favored energy project.

Rather, the effect is to shift the time of investment forward one to two and one-half years from when the investment was going to be made anyway. Instead of a curve that was convex, you would see something a little bit more concave. But you get to the same place that you would have gotten anyway; you're just moving it up a couple of years.

The problem, when people go to Congress and try to argue the case for more energy tax credits, is ". . . not so much that these effects are so small, but that they are small enough to strain the policymakers' willingness to use them."[39] Today, when there is strong pressure to cut the federal budget, and strong pressure to reduce expenditures, and to reduce revenue losses, an energy production credit or energy conservation credit or business energy tax credit or residential energy tax credit has little chance of survival.

A recent study done by the Northeast Midwest Institute (and there have been many others reported in such publications as *Wall Street Journal*) stipulated that the reason for the current oil glut is that everyone is doing an excellent job of conserving energy.

However, look at where this energy conservation is taking place: residential and commercial sector—reduced energy use by about 7%; transportation sector—reduced consumption about 24% (closer to 10% or 15% if we exclude business-related transportation).

The major reduction in energy conservation has come from the industrial sector, which has reduced consumption by 69%.[40] Oakridge National Laboratory[41] investigated the factors causing energy conservation. They concluded that about half of the reduction of energy use in this country was due to price-induced energy conservation activities, setbacks, insulation, and so on. About half was due to decreases in economic activity, i.e., the downturn in the gross national product. And a small, but nontrivial, percent was due to government interventions.

Energy consumption will continue to be flat pending our long-awaited economic recovery. Prices of oil will remain soft. Gas and electric costs will go up: gas costs, nationally; and electric costs, dramatically in scattered localities.

Special energy tax credits are phasing out. A very few people are making a great deal of money taking advantage of some of the existing tax credits under some of the most flexible financing options available. (John DeLorean would have been better advised to look into some of those investment opportunities than those he chose. Nonetheless, there remains the downside risk, perhaps not as great as those he's facing, but still very real, of economic and civil penalties.)

The Economic Recovery Tax Act, passed last year, provides incentives and opportunities for all types of investments, but reduced some of the advantages that cogeneration and alternative fuels have had by placing renewable energy equipment in the same category of depreciation as conventional fuels equipment; that is, moving conventional fuel equipment from the 15-year depreciation or longer up into a 5-year depreciation schedule.[42] Some of the advantages of ACRS were lost.

That is important, because depreciation allowances, according to the Senate Finance Committee, account for 50% of the funds available for industrial investment.[43] So the long-term trends are going to put renewable energy and conservation investments pretty much in the same economic arena with conventional fuels (which already have a very high historical advantage as a result of subsidies and regulations).

Corporate planning of energy projects was given a new set of rules by the Economic Recovery Tax Act, which increased the flexibility of their options. But these options were confounded by the Tax Equity and Fiscal Responsibility Act. Under TEFRA, there have been some losses for the equipment and lease-financing businesses.[44] There have been gains for resource recovery projects.[45] There have been some new incentives for hospitals to engage in energy conservation financing.[46]

Today U.S. and world prices are down (at least from 1980–81 highs) and supplies are up (at least relative to the demands of a recessionary world economy). A renewed war in the Middle East and revival of the economy are both likely events. Sooner or later, energy supply and price will leap back into the public agenda. Public debate and public figures will focus on new interventions. Another set of rules will be written—to the glee and profit of some lawyers and bankers, to the confusion of the rest of us.

In the meantime we may have a brief period in which energy planners and financial analysts will be able to work undistracted for a few years, completing our economic adaptation to the era of expensive energy. Far more likely, however, is continued economic tinkering from Washington. The only recourse for planners and analysts is continued vigorous self-education and the immediate acquisition of a reliable crystal ball.

## References

1.  Shao, Marcia; "Despite Glut of Heating Oil and Natural Gas, Prices Aren't Expected to Drop This Winter"; *Wall Street Journal;* New York City; September 1, 1982.
2.  Reich, Robert; quoted in "Debate Heats Up Again on Industrial Policy"; *Wall Street Journal;* New York City; October 11, 1982.
3.  *Ibid.*
4.  Shao, M.; *op. cit.*
5.  _____; "Studies On Effectiveness Of Energy Tax Incentives Are Inconclusive"; U.S. General Accounting Office; Washington, D.C.; March 11, 1982 (EMD 82–20).
6.  _____; "An Analysis of the Results of Federal Incentives Used to Stimulate Energy Production"; Battelle Pacific Northwest Laboratory for the U.S. Department of Energy; Washington, D.C.; June 1980 (PNL–3422, UC–59) (Contract DE–AC06–76RLO 1830).
7.  *Ibid.*
8.  *Ibid.*
9.  *Ibid.*
10. Shao, M.; *op. cit.*
11. Wald, Matthew L.; "How Atomic Power Cost Just Grew"; *New York Times;* New York City; October 17, 1982.
12. Dechesnau, T. D.; *Competition in United States Energy Industry;* Ballinger; Cambridge, Massachusetts; 1975.
13. Greenert, Clyde; Energy Policy Manager of Union Carbide; speech to International Energy Conservation Conference; Houston, Texas; April 6, 1982.
14. *Ibid.*
15. Lotker, Michael; "Community Ownership of Solar-Electric Systems: Legal and Financial Issues"; presented at Second Annual Conference of Community Renewable Energy Systems; Seattle, Washington; September 5, 1980.
16. Brown, S.P.A. and Anandalingam, G.; "Economic Analysis of Tax Credit Incentives for Business Investment in Energy Conservation and Production"; Brookhaven National Laboratory; Upton, Long Island, New York;

December 1981; for the U.S. Department of Energy (BNL 51526) (Contract DE–AC02–76CH00016).

17. Little, Arthur D.; "The Cost of Federal Tax Programs to Develop the Market for Industrial Solar and Wind Energy Techniques"; prepared for the Lawrence Livermore Laboratory; University of California; November 1981; Cambridge, Massachusetts.

18. Urban Systems Research and Engineering, Inc.; "Analysis of the Impact of Federal Tax Incentives on the Market Diffusion for Solar Thermal/WECS Technologies"; prepared for the Lawrence Livermore Laboratory; University of California; October 1981; Washington, D.C.

19. ICF, Inc. and Mathematica Policy Research; "Analysis of Conservation Improvements and Retrofit Changes in the Residential Sector"; prepared for the Office of Policy, Planning and Analysis and the Energy Information Administration; U.S. Department of Energy; June 1981; Washington, D.C.

20. Charles River Associates, Inc.; "An Analysis of the Residential Energy Conservation Tax Credits: Concepts and Numerical Estimates"; prepared for the Office of Planning, Analysis and Evaluation; U.S. Department of Energy, June 1981; Boston, Massachusetts.

21. Rodberg, Leonard and Schachter, Meg; "State Conservation and Solar Energy Tax Programs: Incentives or Windfalls?" The Council of State Planning Agencies; Washington, D.C.; 1978.

22. Oak Ridge National Laboratory; "A Simulation Analysis of Alternate Policies to Stimulate Energy Conservation in Commercial Buildings"; prepared for the Conservation and Solar Energy Office and the Energy Information Administration; U.S. Department of Energy; November 1980.

23. Energy Information Administration; U.S. Department of Energy; "An Evaluation of Energy Related Tax and Tax Credit Programs"; July 17, 1978.

24. Charles River Associates (follow-up work to their June 1981 report); draft final report, February 15, 1982.

25. Brookhaven National Laboratories; "Economic Analysis of Selected Provisions of the 1978 Energy Tax Act"; prepared for the Office of Policy, Planning and Analysis; U.S. Department of Energy; draft final report; 1982.

26. Oak Ridge National Laboratory; "Analysis of the Correlation Between Energy Tax Credits and Various Factors"; prepared for the Office of Policy, Planning and Analysis and the Conservation and Renewables Office; U.S. Department of Energy; 1982.

27. Solar Energy Research Institute; "Analysis of Tax Credits for Residential Solar Water Heaters"; 1982.

28. Congressional Research Service; "Economic Evaluation of Federal Tax Credits for Residential Conservation"; 1982.

29. _____; "Studies on Effectiveness of Energy Tax Incentives Are Inconclusive"; USGAO; EMD 82–20.

30. *Ibid.*, p. 3.

31. *Ibid.*, p. 4.

32. *Ibid.*, p. 5.

33. Klepper, Sherman, and Carroll; *Innovative Financing for Energy Efficiency Improvements;* Lane & Edson, P.C.; Washington, D.C.; 1982.

34. Blum, Edward R., Ph.D.; Vice President and Executive Director; Merril Lynch White Weld Capital Markets Group; testimony to U.S. House of Representatives, Committee on Science and Technology; July 13, 1982.

35. Gwin, Holly; "Industrial Energy Conservation: Potential and Costs"; Environmental Policy Institute; Washington, D.C.; 1982.

36. Eggers, Robert W.; U.S. Internal Revenue Service; quoted in *Wall Street Journal;* New York City; October 5, 1982.

37. Brown and Anandalingham; *op. cit.;* p. xviii.

38. Little, Arthur D.; *op. cit.*

39. Friedman, Benjamin; "Discussion of Effects of Tax Policy on Capital Formation"; *Journal of Finance;* May 1976.

40. DeVaul, Diane; "Balance or Bias: Building an Equitable Energy Budget"; Northeast–Midwest Institute; September 1982; p. 2.

41. Hirst, E., et al.; "Energy Use from 1973 to 1980: the Role of Improved Energy Efficiency"; Oak Ridge National Laboratory; Oak Ridge, Tennessee; December 1981; for the U.S. Department of Energy under contract W–7405–eng–26.

42. _____; "The Impact of the Economic Recovery Tax Act of 1981 on the Renewable Energy Industry"; Renewable Energy Institute; Washington, D.C.; July 1982.

43. The Tax Council; testimony to U.S. Senate Committee on finance hearings on tax cut proposals; July 1980.

44. _____; "Tax Law Will Slice Energy Credits, End Safe Harbor"; *Energy User News;* New York City; August 23, 1982.

45. Proceeding "Resource Recovery Financing Conference"; U.S. Conference of Mayors; Washington, D.C.; March 29–30, 1982; Appendix B.

46. Tax Equity and Fiscal Responsibility Act of 1982; Title 1, Part 1, Section 101; August 17, 1982 (ref: Report No. 97–530).

47. Stanger, Robert A.; *Tax Shelters: The Bottom Line;* Robert A. Stanger and Company; Fair Haven, New Jersey; 1982.

48. Lotker, Michael and Rosenblatt, Joel; "Tax Advantaged Financing Opportunities in Renewable Energy Development"; *Solar Sciences;* Washington, D.C.; Spring 1982.

49. Danaher, Francis; "Heating Plant Improvement Loan Program"; The Energy Roundtable; Hartford, Connecticut; 1982.

50. Morgan, Steven; "Innovative Approaches to Multi Family Energy Conservation"; The Energy Roundtable; Hartford, Connecticut; 1982.

# Appendix A ─────────────

# A Checklist of Long-Range Planning Considerations in Energy Project Financings

Robert T. DePree

Project financings raise important long-range planning considerations. For the project's beneficial user to achieve his objectives, particular attention should be addressed to each of the following:

1. The characteristics of a project financing.

2. The tradeoffs by the beneficial user among the ingredients of economic benefit, and financial, business, and technological risk.

3. The appropriate financing structure.

Each of these areas is summarized below.

1. *The characteristics of a project financing:*

   a. Large capital requirements.

   b. Long lead times to completions.

   c. Assets controlled by the beneficial user which he cannot afford or prefers not to finance using conventional methods.

   d. Contract letting and financial commitment by the beneficial user prior to securing third-party financing commitments.

e. Large amounts at stake for the beneficial user in the final features of the third-party financial placements and contractual commitments.

2. *The tradeoffs by the beneficial user among the ingredients of economic benefit, and financial, business, and technological risk:*

a. The total economic benefits associated with a particular project will usually be allocated among the participants in proportions which recognize the level of their capital commitments and the magnitude and nature of the risks assumed.

b. The primary uninsurable business risks can be concentrated in one party or diffused among various participants. These risks can include:

    i)   market risk (who will purchase project output and at what price);

    ii)  operating risk (who will manage operations and at what cost);

    iii) supply risks (who will risk the availability of crucial supplies and at what cost);

    iv)  technological risks (who will risk technological failure and obsolescence);

    v)   legal risk (who will bear the risk of any legal or government constraint on efficient operations); and

    vi)  Force Majeure risk (who will bear all other uninsurable risks).

3. *The appropriate financing structure:*

Project finance structuring and placement can range from a single private debt or lease placement to a multiple party venture capital placement involving equipment and supplies vendors, multiple beneficial users, third-party operators, interim and permanent lenders, and TBT or conventional lessors. Exhibits I and II are diagrammatic representations of simple

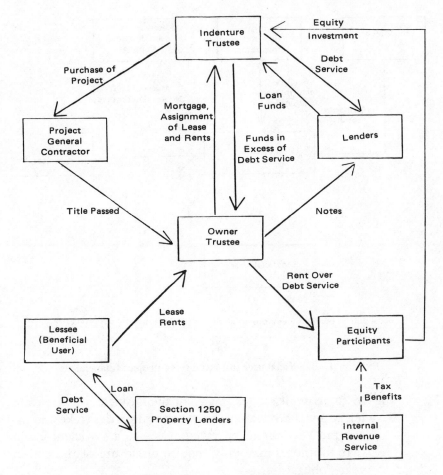

**Exhibit I. Beneficial user assumes project financial risk**

and complex, respectively, project-financing structures that may be appropriate in a specific case.

a. In the simplest cases, the beneficial user consents to the execution of a binding financial obligation (purchase contract, hell or high water lease) which will usually require footnote disclosure of the beneficial user's entire future financial liability undertaken to fund the project under FAS 5 or FAS 13.

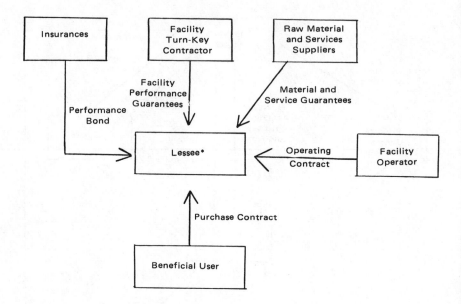

*Lessee will be owned by any one or all of the parties assuming operating risk.

**Exhibit II.  Beneficial user insulated from project financial risk**

    b.  In the complex cases, many of the business risks are trans-
ferred by the beneficial user to third parties (take and pay
contract, economic operating lease) to a sufficient extent
that footnotes may only require disclosure of the current
year's obligations.

* * * * * *

In all cases the beneficial user should be best served by careful
planning of and control over key aspects of the project financing
process. Some elements of a planned approach are:

A.  Define corporate priorities in areas where tradeoffs can occur.

    a.  Establish maximum economic and financial risk levels to
be assumed, including accounting objectives.

     b. Identify business risks to be retained and to be transferred to third parties.

     c. Identify rights, services, material supplies and technical expertise on which any third-party risk takers will require comfort. Determine what comfort can be provided.

     d. Assess project logistics, engineering features, and economic efficiency from the perspective of each third-party risk taker.

B. Assess structural alternatives with accountants, attorneys, prospective financial intermediaries, and selected third-party principals, if desirable. Focus on the risk/return profile of each proposed participant's position to assess its basic economic sense.

C. Establish financing objectives.

     a. optimal structure

     b. minimum acceptable structure.

D. Solicit substantive proposals from financial intermediaries.

     a. structural contributions

     b. market breadth

     c. individuals assigned.

E. Form the financing team and structure roles.

     a. co-management may be appropriate for complex financings

     b. internal control is crucial to achieving financing objectives.

F. Finalize offering terms.

     a. review entire project

     b. finalize structure of offer.

G. Market offering to appropriate prospects.

     a. get early feedback

     b. adjust structural shortcomings

     c. circle with terms letter.

H. Close.

# Appendix B

# Firms Which Provide Energy System Retrofit Services

This listing has been abstracted from the GPU *Catalog of Innovative Conservation Financing Companies,* prepared by General Public Utilities Corporation and its System Companies: Jersey Central Power and Light Company, Metropolitan Edison Company, and Pennsylvania Electric Company.

A complete catalog is available by requesting one on company letterhead stationery and including the specific project in which the company is involved. Address the letter to Manager of Conservation, General Public Utilities Corporation, 100 Interpace Parkway, Parsippany, New Jersey 07054.

Advanced Roof-Energy Systems, Inc., Champion Tower, 400 E. Anderson Lane, Suite 460, Austin, TX 75752, (512) 835-9000.

Aegis Energy Associates, 607 Airport Blvd., Doylestown, PA, (215) 348-7662.

American Energy Savings, Inc., 8956 Tampa Ave., Northridge, CA 91324, (213) 886-2996.

Associated Energy Consultants of PA, Box 461, Dubois, PA 25801, (814) 371-0770.

BBC Energy Management, Inc., 316 Park Crest Drive, Freeport, IL 61032, (815) 235-6014.

Barber-Colman Company, Environmental Controls Division, 1300 Rock Street, Rockford, IL 61101, (815) 877-0241.

CSL Energy Controls, CSL Industries, 2029 Century Park East, Suite 110, Los Angeles, CA 90067, (213) 553-8141.

Computerized Energy Management, Inc., Div. of Erin Mechanical Inc., 5209 Detroit Ave., Cleveland, OH 44102, (216) 281-4600.

Corporate Energy Management, Inc., 20 Nassau Street, Suite 242, Princeton, NJ 08540, (609) 921-1182.

DeBar Business Services, Inc., 530 South Federal Highway, Deerfield Beach, FL 33441, (305) 428-9178. Other office: 25 Edinburgh Road, Middletown, NY 20940.

DiClemente-Siegal Engineering, Inc., 22255 Greenfield Road, Suite 500, Southfield, MI 48075, (313) 569-1430. Branch office: 3734 Fortune Blvd., Saginaw, MI 48603.

Diversified Energy Systems, Inc., DES/CE, 1017 W. 9th Ave., Suite D, King of Prussia, PA 19406, (215) 337-0587.

Econergy, Inc., 2466 West 2nd St., Denver, CO.

Economy Systems Ltd., P.O. Box 2136, Ann Arbor, MI 48106, (313) 688-7065.

Electro Power Controls, Inc., P.O. Box 746, Edison, NJ 08818, (201) 548-9800.

Energistics, Inc., P.O. Box 943, Neptune, NJ 07753, (201) 775-4024.

Energy Applications Inc., Suite 227, Long Beach Village Center, Columbia, MD 21045, (301) 730-0663.

Energy Conservation Technicians, Div. of Worcester Air Conditioning Co. Inc., 148 Pleasant St., P.O. Box 100, Ashland, MA 01721, (617) 235-7400.

Energy Control Systems Inc., 828 E. Lewelling Blvd., Hayward, CA 94541, (415) 481-1701. Branch office: 1325 Airmotive Way No. 175, Reno, NV 89502.

Energy Leasing Services, Inc., 45 Newbury St., Boston, MA 02116, (617) 266-4700.

Energy Management & Generation, Inc., 2190 Hamburg Turnpike, Wayne, NJ 07420, (201) 839-7970.

Energy Management Controls, 3521 Florida Ave., Kenner, LA 70062, (504) 467-6758. Branch office: 2200 S. Post Oak Road, Houston, TX 77056, (713) 738-4396.

Energy Management Controls, 276 S. Logan St., Elyria, OH 44036, (216) 365-0485.

Energy Management Engineering, Inc., 7957 California Ave., Fair Oaks, CA 95628, (916) 967-2951.

Energy Management Services, 2933 E. 3300 So., Salt Lake City, UT 84109.

Energy Management, Inc., 200 Boylston St., Newton, MA 02167.

Energy Master of Maryland, Inc., 12021 Old Gunpowder Road, Beltsville, MD 20705, (301) 937-0307. Branch office: 6617 Bowie Drive, Springfield, VA 22150.

Energy Recovery for Industry & Commerce, Inc., (ERIC), 3810 First Ave. North, Birmingham, AL 35222, (205) 591-3051.

Energy Services and Management Corp., 125 High St., Suite 903, Boston, MA 02110, (617) 482-8855.

Energy Services, Inc., 510 Fairgrounds Court, Nashville, TN 37211, (615) 242-4355.

Energy Solutions, Inc., P.O. Box 1062, Freehold, NJ 07728, (201) 431-9200.

Entech Engineering Associates, 828 Penn St., P.O. Box 32, Reading, PA 19603, (215) 373-6667.

Environmental Interfaces, Inc., 2795 Randi Lane, Salem, OR 97303, (503) 363-3313.

French-Reneker-Associates, Inc., 1501 S. Main St., Box 135, Fairfield, IA 52556, (515) 472-5145.

General Energy Services, 104 Lexington Ave., Buffalo, NY 14222, (716) 885-1653.

General Systems, Inc., 1360 W. 9th St., Cleveland, OH 44113, (216) 574-9222.

Harley Ellington Pierce Yee Associates, 26111 Evergreen Road, Southfield, MI 48076, (313) 354-0300.

Heaton-Levine Energy Management Engineers, 1145-A Mission St., San Francisco, CA 94103, (415) 864-0436.

Herzog-Hart Corp., Hart Corp., 462 Boylston St., Boston, MA 02116, (617) 247-2500. Other offices: 32 Barton Ave., Barrington, RI 02806, (401) 245-0450; 951 Government St., Suite 320, Mobile, AL 36604, (205) 438-3616.

Hillsboro Electric, Energy Management Div., 3914 Hillsboro Circle, Nashville, TN 37215, (615) 297-1419.

Honeywell Corporation Commercial Buildings Group, Honeywell Plaza, Minneapolis, MN 55408, (612) 830-3842.

International Energy Conservation Services, 5600 Roswell Rd. NE, Suite 100, Prado West, Atlanta, GA 30342.

Jazco Corp., P.O. Box 200, Massapequa Park, NY 11762, (516) 795-4323.

Johnson Controls, Inc., 507 E. Michigan St., P.O. Box 423, Milwaukee, WI 53201, (414) 274-4881.

Lighting Technology, Inc., 2115 112th Ave. N.E., P.O. Box 3532, Bellevue, WA 98009, (206) 455-4041.

M. Garetano Associates, Inc., 1324 Motor Pkwy., Hauppauge, NY 11788, (516) 348-0390.

Natkin Energy Management, Natkin & Co. (Fischback Corp.), 2775 So. Vallego, P.O. Box 1598, Englewood, CO 80150, (303) 762-1610.

New Energy West, Inc., 3020 Bridgeway, Suite 215, Sausalito, CA 94965, (415) 331-1298.

New York Energyworks, Inc., 11 Phoenix St., Hempstead, NY 11550, (212) 591-1999.

Northeast Energy Associates, P.O. Box 456, Concord, MA 01742.

Northeast Energy Auditing Team, Inc., 7453 Morgan Road, Liverpool, NY 13088, (315) 451-7954.

Northeastern Solar Management, 15 Bond St., Great Neck, NY 11021, (516) 829-5373.

Pacific Energy Spectrum, 11941 Wilshire Blvd., Los Angeles, CA 90025, (213) 477-1461.

Parsons Brinkerhoff, Inc., 1 Penn Plaza, New York, NY 10019, (212) 239-7900.

OLA, Inc., 2036 Pierce Mill Road N.W., Washington, DC 20010, (202) 462-6234.

R. D. Goss, Inc., R. 519 Williams St., Clearfield, PA 16830, (814) 765-9606. Other offices: Altoona, PA, (814) 946-1246; State College, PA, (814) 238-3756; Indiana, PA, (412) 349-9760; and Lewistown, PA, (717) 248-6920.

Rosenfield, Steinberg and Associates, 2102 6th St., Santa Monica, CA 90405, (213) 396-6663.

Rupper Associates, Ltd., 910 Merrick Road, Suite 5, Copiague, NY 11726, (516) 789-1931.

SUN LAW Energy Corp., 14651 Ventura Blvd., Sherman Oaks, CA 94013, (213) 990-6020.

Scallop Thermal Management, Inc., a Royal Dutch/Shell Group Co., 80 Fifth Ave., New York, NY 10011, (212) 929-5530.

Servidyne Inc., 2120 Marietta Blvd. N.W., Atlanta, GA 30377, (404) 352-2050. Other offices: 6712 Whitestone Road, Baltimore, MD 21207, (301) 944-8332; 2805 Butterfield Road, Suite 150, Oak Brook, IL 60521, (312) 325-7013; 210 W. Stone Ave., Greenville, SC 29609, (803) 242-3505; 909 Crosstimbers, Houston, TX 77022, (713) 692-6138; 10848 Ventura Blvd., Suite D, Studio City, CA 91604, (213) 985-5600; 7255 N.W. 44th St., Miami, FL 33166, (305) 592-6670; 1421 N. Causeway Blvd., Metairie, LA 70001, (504) 835-7917; 48-01 28th Ave., Long Island City, NY 11103, (212) 932-4621; 6400 Hamilton Ave., Pittsburgh, PA 15206, (412) 361-1675; 11744 Parklawn Drive, Rockville, MD 20852, (301) 770-5191; and 12 Alfred St., Woburn, MA 01801, (617) 938-9215.

Standard Utilities Research Engineers, Inc. (SURE), 250 E. 17th St. G., P.O. Box 2062, Costa Mesa, CA 92627, (714) 645-7733, David Farrell, Managing Director.

Superior Energy Management Div. of Superior Supply Co., Inc., 215 Laura, Wichita, KS 67211, (316) 263-6212. Branch office: 225 North Fifth St., Salina, KS 67401, (913) 825-2171.

Sure Air, Ltd., 291 Broadway, New York, NY 10007, (212) 962-3500.

Synergic Resources Corp., One Bala Plaza, Suite 630, Bala Cynwyd, PA 19004, (215) 667-2160.

T.E.M.P. (Total Energy Management Planning) Associates, P.O. Box 12634, Jackson, MS 39211, (601) 956-5711.

The Benham Group, 1200 N.W. 63rd St., P.O. Box 20400, Oklahoma City, OK 73156, (405) 848-6631.

The Montgomery Wells Co., Starks Bldg., Louisville, KY 40202, (502) 589-9924.

Time Energy Systems, Inc., 10635 Richmond Ave., Houston, TX 77042.

Total Energy Management Consultants (TEMCON), 2350 Station St., Indianapolis, IN 46218, (317) 547-5211.

W. S. Fleming and Associates, Inc., 840 James St., Syracuse, NY 13203, (315) 472-4405. Other offices: 3 Computer Drive, Albany, NY 12205, (518) 458-2249; 2 Metro Plaza, 8240 Professional Place, Landover, MD 20785, (301) 459-3565.

Western Pacific International, 880 So. Palm Ave., Suite 11, Alhambra, CA 91803, (213) 289-5928. Other offices: Sacramento, CA; San Francisco, CA; Santa Barbara, CA; Fresno, CA; Bakersfield, CA; and San Diego, CA.

# Appendix C

## Shared Savings Program Management Service Agreement

# Flack+Kurtz Energy Management Corporation

475 Fifth Avenue, New York, NY 10017                    (212) 532-9600

**EMC**

TO:

RE:

DATE:

---------------------------------------------------------------------------------

SHARED SAVINGS PROGRAM
MANAGEMENT SERVICE AGREEMENT

A.  PARTIES TO THIS AGREEMENT

    1)  FLACK + KURTZ ENERGY MANAGEMENT CORP.
       475 5th Avenue
       New York, NY   10017
       (Hereafter "the MANAGER")

    2)

       (Hereafter 'the USER")

B.  GENERAL SCOPE OF THIS AGREEMENTS:

Under this agreement, Manager, an independent contractor, intends to use its best efforts to secure the rights to install, operate and manage on User's premises an energy management system as described in Exhibit A, the "System" and to provide management services to the USER.  The services will include:
    a)  study of the USER'S energy use on the premises as specified in
       Exhibit B (the "Premises");
    b)  submit recommendations as a result of this study for USER'S
       approval prior to installation,
    c)  installation and service of the System designed to reduce
       energy use of the USER'S energy consuming equipment, and
    d)  periodic update of energy control operations to ensure efficient
       use of the installed System.

USER and MANAGER agree that the MANAGER shall have ninety (90) days to secure the rights to provide such System.  Should MANAGER be successful in securing such rights, USER agrees to acknowledge OWNER as having title to the System to be installed and operated on USER'S premises.  Prior to installation of the System, MANAGER agrees to disclose the name of the OWNER and provide USER with copy of its Management Agreement with OWNER.

In return for these services, the USER will pay to the MANAGER (note #1) % of the savings resulting from reduced energy use following installation of systems.

---

Denver    Washington, D.C.    Philadelphia

**EMC**

C.  SPECIFIC TERMS OF THIS AGREEMENT:

1.  MANAGEMENT SERVICES TO BE PROVIDED BY MANAGER

a.  MANAGER will conduct a study at its sole cost, of the USER'S current energy usage, on the specified premises and provide the USER with a report describing the results of its study and explaining recommendations for installation and service of the System.

b.  MANAGER will install, and service the SYSTEM at no cost to User to control energy use on the USER'S premises.

c.  The MANAGER shall service and make necessary repairs to the System and keep the System in good operational condition for the term of this agreement.  The MANAGER shall service the System promptly upon notification that service is required.  In the event MANAGER fails to service the System with forty-eight (48) hours of notice, USER shall have the right to independently contract for repairs or service, with all expenses therefore, to be borne by MANAGER.

d.  The MANAGER shall repair or replace any of the systems or USER'S existing equipment damaged as a result of actions by the MANAGER.

e.  In the event that MANAGER determines that it would be cost beneficial to update or modify the System so savings may continue or be enhanced MANAGER shall provide notice in writing to USER for USER'S aprroval prior to proceeding.  Such updating or modification shall be at no cost to User.  In the event of any such modification, Exhibit A shall be amended accordingly.

f.  This agreement shall terminate (note #2) years from the date hereof unless extended upon written mutual agreement of the parties, such mutual agreement to be reached at least three (3) months prior to termination date.  Extensions will be for (note #2) year periods with a maximum of three such extensions.

2.  USER OBLIGATIONS

In return for these services, the USER agrees to:

a.  Give the MANAGER exclusive rights to install and service the System on the specified premises for the term of this Agreement.

b.  Provide access to the specified premises for MANAGER or subcontractors or OWNER'S designee during regular working hours to survey the premises or to install, adjust inspect, or service the SYSTEMS.

(2)

**EMC**

c. Furnish MANAGER all data reasonably requested concerning energy consumption, both prior to and after SYSTEM installation in accordance with requirements of the savings formula to be mutually agreed upon which is attached hereto and made a part hereof as Exhibit C.

d. Provide available space for installation and operation of SYSTEM and protect SYSTEM in the same manner that USER protects its own property.

e. User will not alter, adjust or shut off the system without the written consent of MANAGER except in case of emergency. Any violation of this provision shall subject USER to a pro-rated fee equivalent to the rate of savings projected to be achieved as set forth in Exhibit D.

f. Inform MANAGER in writing of plans to install or eliminate energy consuming equipment on the premises and of any changes in operations which may affect energy consumption. Examples of such changes include changes in occupancy hours or days, changes in energy service or metering, and changes in use of the premises.

g. Adjust the amount of payment to the MANAGER as indicated by changes in the baseline data due to, but not necessarily limited to, extended operation hours or addition by USER of energy consuming equipment.

h. Pay to MANAGER (note #1) % of the "energy savings" realized following installation of the SYSTEM. Energy savings will be calculated and paid in the following manner:

1. During MANAGER'S study of USER'S energy use, a base figure will be determined, mutually agreed to and specifically identified in Exhibit C. The base use will be calculated on a monthly basis (or other basis consistent with the billing policies of USER'S energy suppliers). Energy use will be expressed in common units of energy measurement such as Therms of Gas, CCF of Gas, Kilowatts, Kilowatt Hours, Pounds of Steam, Gallons of Oil.

2. Following SYSTEM installation, the USER will send to the MANAGER copies of all energy bills within twenty (20) days of their receipt.

**EMC**

3. MANAGER, shall calculate and verify the savings achieved, by comparing energy use for the current period with use for the equivalent base billing period in accordance with Savings Formula set forth in Exhibit C. In determining the reduction in energy use, a factor, mutually agreed to in writing between the parties hereto, may be added to compensate for modifications to the USER'S facility and equipment, or for variances in occupancy or use of the premises. If there is no net reduction in energy use ofr the period, there will be no charge.

4. The reduction in use of each type of energy will be multiplied at the then current unit cost for the energy and further multiplied by (note #1) % to determine the amount due to MANAGER for its services.

5. Once it has been determined that there have been energy savings, MANAGER will notify USER of the amount due and USER will make payment within thirty (30) days after receiving the report of savings.

6. Any dispute regarding the energy savings calculation will be negotiated in good faith as between the parties hereto and, if unable to resolve the matter at issue, the parties shall resort to the arbitration in accordance with the disputes provision of this contract.

## 3. USER APPROVAL OF SYSTEM

THe USER will have the right to approve The System or any thereof to be installed before installation by MANAGER. The USER will not unreasonably withhold approval for installation of equipment necessary for the effective operation of the SYSTEM.

## 4. SUBCONTRACTING

MANAGER and USER agree that MANAGER shall have the right to subcontract any all of its obligations and rights and that such subcontract shall be effective upon the manager's securing the rights set forth on page one of this agreement.

**EMC**

## 5. ASSIGNMENT OF THIS AGREEMENT

This agreement may not be assigned without prior written consent having first been given by USER. Such prior consent will not be unreasonably withheld by USER. If the premises specified are sold, or a tenant other than USER occupies premises, USER undertakes and agrees to require any new owner or new tenant to assume all of the terms and conditions of this agreement as if such new owner or tenant had been original signators hereto.

## 6. CONDITIONS BEYOND THE CONTROL OF THE PARTIES

Should either party be prevented from performing its obligations, under this Agreement by causes beyond its control, this Agreement will remain in effect and obligations continued as soon as the disablement has been removed.

## 7. MUTUAL INDEMNIFACTION

Both USER and MANAGER agree to save the other party harmless from third party claims or actions resulting from operation and use of SYSTEMS and/or Premises to the extend that such claims or actions stem from any act be either USER or MANAGER, within the purview of scope of this Agreement.

## 8. TERMINATION OF THIS AGREEMENT

Either party may terminate this Agreement on thirty (30) days written notice to the other if the other party is indefault of the Agreement and this breach or default is not cured within this thirty (30) day period or receipt of such notice.

Should the Management Agreement between MANAGER and OWNER referred to on Page 2 above, be terminated or expire prior to the termination of the instant agreement, MANAGER agrees to use its best efforts to provide a substitute SYSTEM to USER which will provide the same services to USER on the same terms and conditions contained herein. Should such substitute SYSTEM be unacceptable to USER, USER shall have the right to terminate this Agreement.

If this Agreement is terminated, the System remains the property of OWNER and shall be removed from the premises by MANAGER or OWNER during normal hours after USER has been notified that this will be done.

**EMC**

### 9. TITLE AND TAXES

Materials and equipment which have become affixed and appurtenant to the premis_s, shall remain the property of the MANAGER or OWNER. Liability for any state   personal property, sales and use tax shall be determined in accordance with this clause.

### 10. INVALIDATION OF INDIVIDUAL AGREEMENT TERMS

If any term of this Agreement is invalidated by any legal means, the remaining terms shall remain in effect, provided the remaining terms are not materially affected by the invalidation and the terms remain valid and enforceable.

### 11. NOTICE

Any notice required to be given hereunder, whether oral or in writing as follows:

    a. In the case of MANAGER to:

        FLACK + KURTZ ENERGY MANAGEMENT CORP.
        475 5th Avenue
        New York, NY   10017

    b. In the case of USER to:

    c. In the case of the SUBMANAGER:

### 12. DISPUTES INVOLVING THIS AGREEMENT:

This Agreement shall be interpreted under the laws of the State of (note #3). Disputes concerning this Agreement shall be submitted to arbitration before the American Arbitration Association; however, either party may seek injuctive relief to maintain the status quo or prevent irreparable or continuing damages pending aribitration.

**EMC**

13. EXHIBITS

Exhibit A, "System" Exhibit B, "Specified Premises", Exhibit C, "Energy Cost Savings Formula", and Exhibit D, "Estimated Annual Savings", all of which are hereby made a part of this agreement as of the date and signature indicated on such Exhibit of mutual agreement thereon.

14. MODIFICATIONS

This Agreement, when signed, constitutes the full and final agreement between the parties and many not be amended or modified, except by a writing evidencing said change or changes signed by the parties hereto.

Accepted for:                              Accepted for:

FLACK + KURTZ ENERGY
MANAGEMENT CORP.


_____          _____
Jack W. Caloz
Vice President
Project Development


_____          _____
Date                                     Date

## NOTES

**EMC**

1. Percent (%) savings due will be determined by economics of system and mutually agreed to by Manager and User prior to implementation of System.

2. Term of Shared-Savings agreement will be determined by economics of system and mutually agreed to by Manager and User prior to implementation of system.

3. The state under which this agreement shall be interpreted under shall be mutually agreed upon by Manager and User prior to implementation of system.

## EXHIBIT A

## SYSTEMS

**EMC**

The system, systems, or energy conservant projects shall be defined and quantified in a report prepared by the Manager and submitted to the user. The projects to be implemented under this contract will be mutually agreed upon by Manager and User prior to commencement of construction.

## EXHIBIT C

## ENERGY COST SAVINGS FORMULA

**EMC**

Energy Cost Savings Formula and baseline energy consumption will be determined by Manager and mutually agreed upon by Owner prior to implementation of system.

## EXHIBIT B

## PREMISES

**EMC**

The Premises and/or specific projects covered by this agreement will be defined and specified by owner prior to performance of an energy audit and subsequent report.

## EXHIBIT D

## ESTIMATED ANNUAL SAVINGS

**EMC**

Estimated annual savings will be determined by Manager and detailed in the report prepared for owner.

# Index